BLOCKADE

The longest economic siege in history

Andrés Zaldívar Diéguez

Capitán San Luis Publishing House
Havana, 2007

Translation: **Ana V. Portela**
Overhaul: **Adrian M. Replanski**
Design: **Eugenio Sagués**
Desktop publishing: **Norma Ramírez Vega**

© Andrés Zaldívar Diéguez, 2007
© About the present edition: Editorial Capitán San Luis, 2007

ISBN: 978-959-211-305-3

Editorial Capitán San Luis, Ave. 25 No. 3406, entre 34 y 36, Playa, Ciudad de
La Habana, Cuba.
Impreso en Colombia - Printed in Colombia
Impreso por Gráficas de la Sabana Ltda.

To Gerardo Hernández Nordelo, Fernando
González Llort, Ramón Labañino Salazar,
Antonio Guerrero Rodríguez and René González
Sehwerert, five heroes who endure
unjust imprisonment in the United States
for combating terrorist actions against Cuba,
some of which are described in this book.

To my sons Aram and Abraham.
To the memory of my parents.

Rarely is a book the work of one individual. Those who help conceive it, contribute in different ways to its development, afford us an idea or little-known fact, who encourage and motivate us in the obsessive and at times painstaking process of conducting research work, reviewing and writing, or who create the innumerable conditions needed to undertake these efforts, are co-responsible for its creation. For one or more than one of these reasons, I will like to express my gratitude to Over Companioni, Manuel Hevia, Félix Batista, José M. Pérez, Manuel Fernández Crespo, Israel Behar, María Antonia Pantaleón, Mariano García, José Buajasán, Miguel Roque, Reycelda Rodríguez, Juana Fundora, Laraine Aguilar and Teté Ortega. To my colleagues Jacinto Valdés-Dapena, José Luis Méndez, María Antonia Román and Pedro Etcheverry, for giving me the opportunity of using many of the results of their own research work. For their help in all areas, including the search of more than one bibliographical rarity (an undertaking in which Isabel Jaramillo, Nuria Gregori and Daniel Salas also met with success), the translation of texts and the manuscript's final revision, I wish to thank the fraternal Ricardo Sánchez Villaverde. For their patience, understanding and support, I want to express my gratitude to Gabriela Báez, Aracelis Blanzaco, Dania Sao, Vania Silvera and Iris Calzadilla. In Chambas, to Rolando Fundora. For their logistical support, to Lorenzo Timitol, Lucía Palacios, Silvia Prieto, Mauro Villar, Reynold Álvarez, Gonzalo Artidó, Jorge Castillo and Ana Elda Pérez, not to mention Xiomara Quevedo, Celia Sánchez, Antonio Benítez and all who contributed, in one way or another, to the book's elaboration.

Special thanks go out to Pablo Berti and Yaíra Jiménez Roig for his important contribution. For their generosity and understanding, to Dr. Olga Miranda and the eminent economist Osvaldo Martínez. To my editor, Ana María Caballero, designer Eugenio Sagués, Viviana Fernández, Norma Ramírez and all my friends at the Capitán San Luis Publishing House, who have made this book possible.

Contents

Prologue / 13

Preface / 17

CHAPTER I The first actions / 35

> The background. The evolution of an economic warfare "doctrine" / 41

> The economic situation inherited by the Revolution. U.S. actions to prevent the triumph of the Revolution / 56

> The plots which culminated in the Bay of Pigs invasion. Acts of economic aggression as a means to undermine popular support for the Revolution / 61

> The meeting of the National Security Council of 17 March 1960. The *Program of Economic Pressures against the Castro regime* / 67

CHAPTER II Operation Mongoose and advances in the planning of economic warfare actions against Cuba / 74

> A new assessment of the operational situation: *Facts, Estimates and Projections* / 76

> *Cuba and Communism in the Hemisphere* / 77

The CIA's first subversive plan against the Cuban economy after the Bay of Pigs: the *Program of Covert Actions to Weaken the Castro Regime,* a foretaste of what, in the field of direct subversion, would assume the form of Operation Mongoose / 79

Legislative basis of the most important public economic action developed / 82

Operation Mongoose begins/ 83

The economic warfare measures of Operation Mongoose / 84

The official establishment of the blockade as part of Operation Mongoose / 88

A description of Mongoose Measures / 89

The Missile Crisis / 96

Chapter III Range of state terrorist actions against the Cuban economy / 98

Future Policy towards Cuba / 98

The prioritization of espionage in the design of new subversive policies / 100

CIA actions to lower world sugar prices / 101

Post-Mongoose reorganization of Cuba-related decision-making mechanisms. Impact on economic warfare / 102

A higher level in plans: the United States Policy towards Cuba / 103

The continued application of measures to eliminate maritime shipping to Cuba / 105

Design of new subversive measures against the economy by the Cottrell Committee / 108

Proposed New Covert Policy and Program Towards Cuba / 114

Approval of the *Proposal for Covert Policy and Integrated Program of Action towards Cuba* / 118

Establishing the fundamental elements of the blockade. Close of the initial cycle in the systematization of economic warfare actions against Cuba / 123

The most important blockade measures since 1963 / 124

Torricelli Act / 129

Helms-Burton Act / 130

CHAPTER IV Espionage and its use in the planning and execution of sabotage actions against the Cuban economy / 133

Background / 135

Public Information / 139

Espionage on the Cuban economy through subversive means and methods / 142

Oil Case / 143

The sugar agro-industry / 149

Milkman case / 149

Actions against maritime transportation and fishing / 152

Public exposure of CIA espionage and subversion in 1987 / 155

Interests in maritime, air and fishing sectors / 157

Agro-industrial sectors. Biological warfare / 159

Trade, financial and economic cooperation relations / 163

Finances / 166

Communications / 168

CHAPTER V Other components of economic warfare / 171

Terrorism as an economic weapon / 171

Propaganda as part of economic war / 183

Propaganda by radio means / 183

Studies on the Cuban economy in U.S. academic circles Ideological U.S. "support" for the "transition" to capitalism in Cuba. / 189

The picture in the mainstream press / 193

Embargo or Blockade? / 196

CHAPTER VI The battle at the United Nations and the economic war against Cuba in light of Cuban laws / 202

The international community is opposed to the economic war that Cuba is subjected to: the battle at the UN / 202

Food / 219

Finances / 222

Energy Sector / 225

Sugar sector / 226

Maritime transportation / 228

Tourism, travel by U.S. citizens to Cuba / 229

Air transportation / 232

New legislation / 235

The civil liability suit brought against the United States government for economic damages caused to the people of Cuba / 237

What are the measures the Government of the United States must adopt to put an end to economic war against Cuba? / 241

References / 243

Prologue

The ideas expounded on in the prologue to Spanish edition of this book have lost none of their validity. I began that preface affirming that when the economic blockade imposed on Cuba is mentioned at academic seminars, parliamentary debates or in the course of simple, casual conversations, it is often accompanied by a cynical rationalization —as abound in these circles—which would call it an embargo and reduce it to a sovereign U.S. government decision not to have trade relations with Cuba. According to this version of events, advanced on more than one occasion by U.S. ambassadors before the United Nations, the blockade is a strictly bilateral measure which in no way impedes Cuba's economic relations with other countries.

Even friends of the Cuban revolution are relatively uninformed about the history and scope of actions which the U.S. government has been conducting since 1959 to asphyxiate the country's economy and push its people to the brink of despair. Some think the "embargo" only deprives Cuba of access to the U.S. market and tourism and that, beyond this, Cuba can operate in the world market like any other country in the world.

For the several generations of Cubans who were born after and have grown up under the blockade, the latter sometimes disappears into the background and becomes just one more aspect of the country's reality, devoid of a clear explanation.

It would therefore be a mistake not to do everything in our power to explain to our friends abroad, to the many who are curious about these prohibitions which have been in effect for over 45 years and to our younger generations that part of the history of the Cuban revolution in power is the history of an intense and extensive economic war, a meticulously conducted and cruel war, waged against a small and poor country by the most formidable economic and military superpower that has ever existed.

In the course of nearly ffty years, the government of the United States has resorted to everything —save a military blockade and invading Cuba with its Armed Forces—and has failed in all undertakings, in a multifaceted process whose inner workings and shameful details are yet not fully understood. Cuban analysts like colleagues such as the recently deceased Olga Miranda, Nicanor León Cotayo and Alejandro Aguilar shed light on different aspects of this ongoing process, but they have far from exhausted the issue, because some documents, probably too brutal to be made public, have not been declassified and because the spectrum of anti-Cuban actions is so broad and wide-encompassing that it cannot be wholly captured by any one specialty, be it journalism, juridical science or financial analysis.

A total economic and genocidal war, today more intense than ever, a war in which the complex structures of the U.S. government and Congress have been deployed to weave a dense and elaborate cobweb of prohibitions, sanctions and aggressions, has been unleashed against Cuba.

The book English readers have before them, written by Dr. Andrés Zaldívar Diéguez, is a valuable contribution to the much-needed effort of offering Cubans and non-Cubans an account of a vile, four-decade-old war aimed at breaking the will of our people.

The concept of state terrorism deployed by the book does not stem from a poetic license disguised as political denunciation; rather, it captures a proven historical truth confirmed by Andrés Zaldívar through the effective use of documents declassified by different U.S. government agencies and by documented accounts of anti-Cuban actions, actions which at times have been successful and frustrated by our spirit of resistance at others, and which have always failed in their strategic aim to exterminate the Cuban revolution.

An analysis of the 17 March 1960 meeting of the U.S. National Security Council is crucial to understanding the meaning of the U.S. economic war against Cuba and its role as part of a series of actions which, one year later, would culminate in the catastrophic Bay of

14

Pigs invasion, an invasion which, in the works of U.S. authors, has earned the category of "the Bay of Pigs fiasco".

At this meeting, the Program of Covert Action against the Castro Regime, which would lead to the disastrous Bay of Pigs invasion, and the document entitled Program of Economic Pressures against Castro —still to be declassified, but whose content is partially betrayed by the minutes of the meeting and subsequent actions—were approved.

There, part of the same terrorist and subversive package, the suspension of oil supplies, the ending of trade relations, the withdrawal of investments, prohibitions on tourism to Cuba, manoeuvres to be undertaken at the docile OAS and the elimination of the sugar quota were all analyzed.

After tasting defeat at the Bay of Pigs, the United States began to plan and organize its economic warfare actions more meticulously. It undertook a huge foreign policy manoeuvre, resorting to all options save a direct military action, to subjugate its small neighbour.

The plan to liquidate the Cuban revolution in a few months' time was presented to U.S. government departments and agencies on 18 January 1962. Thirteen of the 32 tasks comprising Operation Mongoose were economic warfare actions which revealed a higher level of organization and which set a standard which has survived to this day.

The Operation already refers to actions aimed at making maritime transportation to Cuba more expensive and difficult, to induce bad harvests of food-producing crops, to prevent the sale of nickel and other products. Sabotage actions against the country, and the economy in particular, are also described.

Under Operation Mongoose, in the course of 14 months, 5,780 terrorist actions were reported; 716 of them were large-scale acts of sabotage against economic targets.

The blockade, economic war and acts of state terrorism against Cuba's economy have been part of a policy package which has spelled much blood and suffering, impossible to measure in financial terms, or to discern in the soft "embargo" sold by anti-Cuban propaganda. The financial damage they have meant for Cuba already exceeds 89 billion dollars.

Andrés Zaldívar offers an account of what could be described as the process through which U.S. economic warfare strategy was perfected up to 1963, when the initial cycle in the systematization

15

of this strategy ends, and, beyond 1963, of the most important decisions which have extended this war, including the Torricelli and Helms-Burton acts.

Especially interesting are chapters IV and V, which take up the subject of espionage and its use in the planning and execution of sabotage actions against Cuba's economy and which refer to interesting cases in the oil, sugar agro-industry and maritime transportation sectors, not to mention the use of terrorism in these actions.

I am pleased to see that this edition of the book, aimed at an English-speaking readership, has included the most recent manifestations of the economic war against Cuba in its preface, particularly those which appear in the "Bush Plan", approved by the U.S. president in May 2004 and ratified in July 2006, such that those who are least informed on these matters, because of their place of residence or the curtain of silence with which the mass media seek to conceal this policy of genocide towards Cuba may receive the most up-to-date information in the first pages of the book.

Reading Andrés Zaldívar's book, condensing a plethora of information so skilfully that it never overwhelms the reader, invariably proves a pleasant experience. There, we are faced with a good part of the history of a genocidal war against a people and become more conscious of the latter's spirit of resistance, which has never been dampened by a blockade whose duration and the overwhelming imbalance of forces that it entails are historically unparalleled.

This spirit of resistance is an ode to life, clashing against the cries of war and terror of the economic war.

Forty eight years of State terrorism have not been able subjugate our small country, just as they cannot subjugate our five anti-terrorist activists, imprisoned in U.S. jails. Our people, and they, as part of our people, are equipped with a weapon whose technology is inscrutable for the terrorists: the moral values created by the revolution.

Osvaldo Martínez
October 2007

Preface

The book that English readers now hold in their hands, on the US Government's economic war against the Cuban Revolution, was first published in Spanish in October of 2003. That edition covered the history of the blockade up to the first years of the George W. Bush administration. As chance would have it, the book was published two weeks before the US government adopted measures —the creation of a special advisory body to advance proposals aimed at intensifying hostile policies towards the largest of the Antilles—to destroy the Cuban Revolution once and for all. Developments since have had immense repercussions in the area that is the subject of this book and we must, at least briefly, address these developments in this new edition.

The abovementioned special advisory body was created on 10 October 2003 and was called the "Commission for Assistance to a Free Cuba", a curious name used to conceal precisely the opposite intention, that is, to overthrow Cuba's legitimately established government, fruit of a Revolution that secured freedom for its people —an endeavor in which the recommended economic measures would play a decisive role—, and to set up, once again and as occurred following the Spanish-Cuban-American War at the close of the 19th century, an interventionist government on the island. The Commission was co-chaired by Secretary of State Collin Powell and the Cuban-born Secretary of Housing and Urban Development Melquíades "Mel" Martínez, one of the standard-bearers of the administration's harshest measures against the Revolution. The fact that the executive secretary of that Commission was Roger Noriega, one of the architects of the anti-Cuban Helms-Burton Act and proponent of the most vehemently anti-Cuban actions, was an unmistakable sign that no constructive results could be expected from the Commission's recommendations. President George W. Bush mandated the Commission to "identify additional means (...) to bring about an expeditious end to the Castro dictatorship"[1].

For someone who is not familiar with US foreign policy towards Cuba over the last 50 years or so, who also believes —if there is anyone in the world who can still believe this—that the great and powerful nations respect international law, such flagrant meddling, on behalf of the United States, in the internal affairs of its small neighbor —meddling which goes as far as proposing the overthrow of its government and, to top things off, in a public document—may be surprising. At a different level, they may also think it odd that an action program be created to identify *additional* and not the *most important* or *basic* means to bring this about. These two facts have a simple explanation: a few months after the triumph of the Cuban Revolution in January 1959, in contradiction with all legal norms or principles, the essential means to destroy the revolution had been identified by the White House and each of the nine administrations which preceded that of George W. Bush, starting with that of Dwight D. Eisenhower, had devised new plans and measures which were added to the existing ones. The Helms-Burton Act, approved by President William Clinton in March 1996, is among the measures undertaken in the last ten years that have had the greatest impact on Cuba.

These actions —a brutal tightening of the screws in the economic sphere coupled with a redoubling of the United States' aggressive policy towards Cuba, aimed at hastening the collapse of the revolutionary government and impelling the country's return ("transition") to the Cuba that was left behind on 31 December 1958 when dictator Fulgencio Batista fled the island—not only meticulously describe the measures that would be implemented as part of a process to privatize the properties which began to be "confiscated"

---

[1] Department of State: *Report of the Commission for Assistance to a Free Cuba*, Chapter 1, 6 May 2004.

on 1 January 1959 and to dismantle the social justice programs undertaken by the Revolution. They also explain each and every one of the measures proposed by the Commission in the 450-page-long document submitted by Collin Powell to President Bush on 6 May 2004, measures which the President immediately made his own. A well-documented study of this text published in Cuba summarizes the document thus: "As strategic actions aimed at the overthrow of the Cuban government, the document proposes increased support for the recruitment, organization and financing of internal counterrevolutionary actors; the promotion of anti-Cuban political and diplomatic campaigns at different international fora; a redoubling of the war of disinformation against our country; securing financing and the commitment of international actors (…) in support of the US policy of hostility towards Cuba; *the adoption of new measures to step up blockade measures and the economic war against Cuba;* and what they have come to call "undermining the regime's succession plans", to include a template outlining the kind of changes to be brought about, in stages, and a meticulous description of the requisites that the puppet regime imposed on the island must meet."[2] (The italics are ours).

Thus, while the Eisenhower administration dreamt with the rapid destruction of the Revolution through subversive actions which culminated with the Bay of Pigs Invasion (1961), the Kennedy administration pursued this end through Operation Mongoose (1962) and the so called "multiple track" program (1963). In the 1980s, the Reagan administration brought the reemergence of the counterrevolutionary opposition, the intensification of the economic war on Cuba and the international isolation of the revolution through deceitful propaganda campaigns related to supposed human rights violations perpetrated in Cuba. In 1992, through the Torricelli Act, George Bush Sr. sought to give Cuba a coup de grace following the collapse of the socialist block in Europe. During the Clinton administration, the Helms-Burton Act, approved in 1996, sought to prevent foreign investment in Cuba and asphyxiate the country

---

[2] Ministry of Foreign Affairs: *Cuba and Human Rights. The intensification of the policy of hostility and aggression against the Cuban people implemented by the George W. Bush administration: a serious threat to the human rights of the Cuban people.* Special Newspaper Supplement. Havana, 2005, pp. 17-18.

economically. By May 2003, the George W. Bush administration already had a similar plan whose highly urgent aim was to rapidly do away with the Revolution through a combination of the harshest measures undertaken in the past.

It would be impossible, in these introductory lines, to even comment on all the measures that were made public on 6 May 2004; we must limit ourselves to an overview of those directly related to the economic war on Cuba[3]. In their brutality, these measures were in line with those that the Bush administration had implemented till then, giving continued expression to the virulent hostility of the anti-Cuban measures approved by Congress in the last years of the Clinton administration. While in 2000 the Treasury Department's Office of Foreign Assets Control (OFAC) gave 178 US tourists fines for merely having visited Cuba, in the first year of the Bush administration (2001), the figure had gone up to 698[4]. In 2003, the same year in which the "Commission for Assistance to a Free Cuba" was created, around 1, 230 US citizens received warning letters, the first measure taken as part of legal proceedings which ended with the fining and even the imprisonment of the violators. This year witnessed the intensification of the administration's measures against attempts by Congress to relax US policy towards Cuba. The most significant expression of these efforts was the threat of a veto which the US government faced in connection with a bill, which had bipartisan backing, to make restrictions on travel to Cuba more flexible. On 12 November, the Congressional bicameral Conference Committee reviewing the Departments of Transportation and Treasury and

---

[3] To successfully respond to this plan, the aggressive measures announced were given due consideration in Cuba. In the 1st session of July 2004, during the Third Period of Sessions of the 4th Legislative Assembly, the National Assembly of the People's Power of Cuba extensively analyzed the text during a discussion that saw the participation of numerous deputies and issued a declaration condemning the report. See: National Assembly of the People's Power: *Declaration of the National Assembly of the People's Power of the Republic of Cuba, Havana, 1 July 2004.* In: National Assembly of the People's Power: *Un documento nada serio que hay que tomar muy en serio (A laughable report which is no laughing matter),* Editora Politica, Havana, 2004, pp. 75-80. See also: Granma Newspaper, 2 July 2004.

[4] On 28 October 2000, the prohibition to travel to Cuba imposed on US citizens became a law. Because of questionable proceedings in Congress, the Dorgan-Gorton amendment, which would have given US citizens the right to travel freely to Cuba, was ignored. The result was a tightening of anti-Cuban economic measures.

Independent Agencies Appropriations Bill decided to eliminate the amendment calling for these policy changes, through a process that is considered to be antidemocratic and in violation of the very norms and regulations of Congress. That same year, US producers were forbidden to hold a fair to exhibit their food and agricultural products in the Cuban market.

This was the context within which new economic measures against Cuba came into effect. In addition to renewing the validity of given aspects of the Helms-Burton Act —possibly one of the most aberrant pieces of legislation that any country has ever adopted— these measures spelled a new turn of the screws in US policy whose negative impact on Cuba's economy was significant indeed.

Readers will fully grasp the scope of these measures when, upon finishing this book, they have a deeper understanding of the US government's obsession —spelled out in official documents dating all the way back to April 1960—with using hunger and shortages of every kind, produced by US economic measures, to push Cuba's population into actively opposing the Revolution, a revolution which was needed to eliminate the poverty, injustice and inequalities that had characterized all earlier periods in which the country was nothing but a US protectorate. The essence of the measures which began to be adopted in May 2004 is the sense of urgency that surrounds this objective, pursued through whatever measure that can be implemented to prevent the flow of hard currency into Cuba and ultimately strangle the country economically.

The approved measures, an exact measure of how extremely desperate US government officials are to paralyze Cuba's economic activity as soon as possible and at all costs—even at the risk of exterminating the island's population—razing all of the country's hard-currency-earning mechanisms to the ground, and the specific objectives pursued in each case, were:

> Limiting the flow of hard currency into the country as much as possible by making Cuba's commercial dealings with other nations as difficult as possible, through the use of blackmail and pressures against foreign counterparts and by preventing Cuba from making use of the hard currency obtained.

A clear precursor of this policy line can be caught sight of in US foreign policy from 1986 onward, at a time when the economic war against Cuba waged by Ronald Reagan's Republican administration

21

had reached a peak and lists of "Cuban designates" were being drawn up: these lists included individuals and entities in third countries considered representatives of Cuba's commercial interests, with whom all people or entities under the jurisdiction of the United States were forbidden to have dealings of any kind. But the sense of urgency which the George W. Bush administration sought to give its plan to destroy the Cuban Revolution also takes us back to an even more remote precursor: to the "global detectives" created by the Treasury Department in 1963, a kind of police force tasked with patrolling the world and detecting Cuba's commercial counterparts, so that all conceivable pressures could then be used to curtail such relations as much as possible.

This old objective was resurrected by the plan and given the following new form: "Neutralize Cuban government front companies by establishing a Cuban Asset Targeting Group comprised of appropriate law enforcement authorities, to investigate and identify new ways in which hard currency is moved in and out of Cuba". As can be seen, what is truly unprecedented in this is the misuse of the US taxpayer's money, inherent to the request for strengthening mechanisms to monitor and persecute Cuba's commercial activities around the world and to calling for the involvement of the Departments of State, Treasury and Commerce – though it is obvious that the CIA will also be given important tasks in the pursuit of these truly genocidal aims.

It is by no means a flight of the imagination to link the above text with the fine, for millions of dollars, imposed by the US Federal Reserve on the UBS (Union of Swiss Banks), slightly less than a week after the Report of the Commission for Assistance to a Free Cuba was submitted to the President, on the grounds that, by accepting or sending US dollars to Libya, Iran, Yugoslavia and Cuba, this institution was violating US economic sanctions against those countries. The propaganda campaign against Cuba unleashed during the scandal stirred up by this measure was quick to surface, and, through newspapers controlled by Miami's anti-Cuban lobby —in Cuba, this lobby is known as the South Florida Cuban-American mob—such as the New Herald, published in that city, the Bush administration and Congress were called on to step up measures in this direction. We shall return to this important issue later.

Measures aimed at limiting the entry of hard currency into the country resulting from trips to Cuba by Cuban-Americans who visit their families in the island, or the entry of parcels and packages with gifts for relatives. These series of measures met with considerable opposition, as they seriously undermine family links and also establish a restrictive definition of the concept of "family", thus limiting possibilities in this connection.

The measures include the following:

- "Limit family visits to Cuba to one (1) trip every three years under a specific license; individuals would be eligible to apply for a specific license three years after their last visit to Cuba; new arrivals from Cuba would be eligible to apply for a specific license three years after leaving Cuba";
- "Limit the definition of "family" for the purposes of family visits to immediate family (including grandparents, grandchildren, parents, siblings, spouses, and children);
- Reduce the current authorized per diem amount (the authorized amount allowed for food and lodging expenses for travel in Cuba) from $164 per day to $50 per day...(and)... limit the length of stay in Cuba for family visitation to 14 days.
- Direct U.S. law enforcement authorities to conduct "sting" operations against "mule" networks and others who illegally carry money to Cuba as a means to disrupt and discourage the sending of illegal remittances.
- Measures aimed at limiting the number of existing exceptions to prohibitions on travel to Cuba by US citizens as much as possible.

These new restrictions reveal nothing other than the failure of the aims described in Track II of the Torricelli Act of 1992, according to which so-called "people to people contacts" or US influence over Cuban civil society would lead to the collapse of the Revolution. The real course of events went in a direction opposite what US leaders hoped, and, if educational exchange programs yielded any influential results, they were those of Cuban society which, facing the extreme austerity measures of the Special Period, resulting from the loss of Cuba's main trade partners following the collapse of the Soviet Union and the European socialist block, showed its unshakable determination to defend the economic independence and social justice it had attained —unthinkable in other societies— and to continue moving forward. It became obvious that, all in all, what occurred with respect to trips of this nature between 1992 and 2004 did not favour the subversive designs of the US government, when one of the measures recommended by the report was to "Eliminate abuses of educational travel by limiting it to undergraduate or graduate degree granting institutions and for full-semester study programs, or shorter duration only when the program directly supports U.S. policy goals".

As mentioned before, the measures adopted also breathe new life into two of the most odious Titles of the Helms-Burton Act. The first is Title III, referring to claims for US properties nationalized in Cuba. The US government does not recognize the validity of the *processes of nationalization* (falsely referred to as a *confiscation processes*) of the properties of foreigners and Cuban citizens carried out in the 1960s and, in addition to this, would have people who at the time of these nationalizations were *Cuban citizens* be recognized as *US nationals*. The magic tricks of far-right conservative ideologues and politicians can make a Cuban whose property was nationalized in 1960, who ten years later became a US citizen, an "American" whose property was "confiscated" under Cuban law in 1960. According to the most respected experts on the subject, "the nationalizations carried out by the revolutionary government (...) became the Cuban people's heritage through a process of nationalization undertaken via a forced expropriation procedure which responded to public utility needs, under a constitutional mandate"[5]. They were nothing other than an act of self-defence which reclaimed the wealth and resources of the Cuban people, which, in the conditions inherited from the past following the triumph of the revolution in 1959, was indispensable to the development of the country.

This Title violates internationally recognized principles and concepts and as vital a principle of international law as the Act of State Doctrine. The nationalizations in Cuba were undertaken as "an act of self-defence and of reclaiming the wealth and resources of the Cuban people which were indispensable to the country's

---

[5] Olga Miranda Bravo: *Cuba/USA. Nacionalizaciones y bloqueo. Editorial de Ciencias sociales. La Habana, 2003, Second Edition, p. 2.*

development"[6]. With the Helms-Burton Act, the US government ignores several resolutions approved by the UN General Assembly, such as Special Resolution 626 (VII) of 21 December 1952, which states that "the right of people freely to use and exploit their natural wealth and resources is inherent in their sovereignty and is in accordance with the Purposes and Principles of the Charter of the United Nations". This Resolution was ratified by General Assembly Resolution 1803 (XVII) of 14 December 1962, titled "Permanent sovereignty over natural resources" and by the Charter of Economic Rights and Duties of States approved by the UN General Assembly through Resolution 3281 on 12 December 1974[7].

The anti-Cuban measures contained in the May 2004 plan, in a circuitous language aimed at maintaining the sword of Damocles dangling over the heads of foreigners investing in properties that were nationalized in Cuba (again: even though, at the time, they belonged to Cuban citizens who later became US citizens), express: "The process for implementation of Title III of the Cuban Liberty and Democratic Solidarity (LIBERTAD) Act should ensure that the full range of policy options are made available to the President, and that a detailed, rigorous and complete country-by-country analysis of policies and actions with respect to Cuba is provided to the President..."[8]

The other Title of the Helms-Burton Act whose validity is renewed is Title IV, which empowers the US government to deny businesspeople (and even their relatives), accused of "trafficking" —that is, having any kind of relation with—"US" properties nationalized in Cuba, entry into the United States.

The May 2004 report states, verbatim: "To deter foreign investment in Cuba in *confiscated properties*, claims to which are owned *by U.S. nationals*, aggressively pursue Title IV visa sanctions

---

[6] Olga Miranda Bravo: *Juridical aspects of the blockade and aggressions.* Expert testimony provided at the trial to review the law suit brought by the Cuban people against the United States for economic damages to Cuba. March 2000, p. 11.

[7] Quoted in Olga Miranda Bravo's *Cuba/USA. Nacionalizaciones y bloqueo,* pp. 14-15

[8] Department of State:*Commission for Assistance to a Free Cuba Report, Chapter I.* Quoted in *Un documento nada serio que hay que tomar muy en serio.* National Assembly of the People's Power.

against those foreign nationals *trafficking in (e.g., using or benefiting from) such property*, including devoting additional personnel and resources to application and enforcement". (The italics are ours). In the clearest of languages, the end of the above paragraph tells us that the US government shall spend more taxpayer's money to step up its acts of espionage and more closely monitor businesspeople from around the world, driven by the just intention of establishing business dealings with Cuba and of entering into mutually advantageous agreements with Cuban authorities. Using this information, in addition to other measures, US authorities shall deny these businesspeople entry into the United States.

There is no need for comments.

The economic measures included among the recommendations of the ill-named "Commission for Assistance to a Free Cuba" began to be officially implemented on 30 June 2004. We already saw how a number of them, including some of the most dangerous ones, such as the brutal pressures that were brought to bear upon the UBS, were already underway well before these were announced.

Among the newly-strengthened measures, those aimed at discouraging and monitoring trips by US citizens to Cuba occupy an important place. These measures call for the more rigorous application of fines and the institution of judicial proceedings against organizations and people who had travelled to Cuba. A foretaste of these punitive actions was afforded by the measures which began to be taken that month against Peter Goldsmith and Michele Geslin, residents of Cayo Hueso who organized a Key West – Cuba maritime competition with participants from around the world. Legal proceedings were instituted against them for promoting and organizing the Conch Republic Cup in 1997, 2000, 2002 and 2003[9]. In 1999, three Methodists from Milwaukee were fined 25 thousand dollars each for travelling to Cuba[10]. On 8 July 2004, the Coastguard Service stepped up measures to prevent vessels from sailing to Cuba.

[9] Quoted in Ministry of Foreign Affairs, p. 7. Original source: "Mano dura con los violadores del embargo a Cuba" *("No mercy for violators of Cuban embargo laws"),* by Gerardo Reyes, published in El Nuevo Herald on 11 June 2004.

[10] Quoted in Ministry of Foreign Affairs, p. 7. Original source: "Como en los mejores tiempos del maccarthismo" *("As in the good old times of McCarthyism"),* by Ángel Rodríguez Alvarez, Agencia Cubana de Noticias (Cuban News Agency, ACN).

Until then, vessels whose length did not exceed 100 meters did not require special permits for such trips. From that moment on, the Coastguard Service required that vessels produce permits, issued by other US federal agencies, which demonstrated that blockade regulations were not being violated.

According to State Department data, at the close of 2004, as a result of the implemented measures, the number of US citizens who had travelled to Cuba between July and December was only 50, 588, as compared to 119, 938 who did so in the course of those months in 2003. In 14 October that year, Deputy Assistant Secretary of State for Western Hemisphere Affairs Daniel W. Fisk stated that, as of 10 October, the new restrictions on trips and remittances had deprived Cuba of over 100 million of dollars in hard currency. It was estimated that, in the course of the year, that figure would go up to 375 million, which in turn would increase to 500 million, taking all other sources of revenue into account.

The economic measures adopted by the administration in June 2004 intensified the harassment of Cuba's tourist, commercial and financial operations in third countries. In 2004 alone, blockade regulations were applied to 13 companies with links to Cuba and their branches abroad, specializing in trips and the sending of packages and remittances. Access to the web-sites of these companies was even prohibited. In May 2004, Title IV of the Helms-Burton Act was rigorously applied, for the first time in over five years, against the Jamaican hotel branch Super Club. High executives of this firm, and their relatives, were informed that they would be denied entry into the United States, on the grounds that the hotel that this Jamaican firm was operating in Cuba had been constructed on lands which had been expropriated by the Revolution from a former Cuban national who now had US citizenship. Commenting on this measure, Assistant Secretary of State for Western Hemisphere Affairs Dan Fisk stated that, at the time, more than two dozen cases of visa-related sanctions applied because of similar reasons were under active investigation[11].

As we saw earlier, the most dangerous of all measures aimed at asphyxiating Cuba's economy were those designed to prevent Cuba

[11] Quoted in Ministry of Foreign Affairs, p. 11. Mention is made of Dan W. Fisk's declarations at the Cuban American Veterans Association in Miami, on 9 October 2004, published by the US Department of State's Bureau of International Information Programs and taken from: http://usinfo.state.gov/español.

from depositing, in foreign banks, the revenue in dollars it had made through tourism, sales in hard currency shops and other commercial services. Following the fine applied by the US Federal Reserve to the Union of Swiss Banks at the beginning of May 2004 and the onslaught of the propaganda campaign led by the Cuban-American mob, the Cuban government published a press note which read: "...the government of the United States brings pressures to bear on banks so that they will not accept Cuban funds gotten in entirely legal and honest ways (...) One cannot conceive of a more cynical and perverse formula: With its criminal blockade, the United States obliges those who send remittances and foreign visitors to Cuba to make all payments in cash and now, through crude pressures, it attempts to prevent Cuba from using that cash to pay for its imports"[12]

In line with the aims of the Cuban Asset Targeting Group created by the administration to study, as we saw before, the "ways in which hard currency is moved in and out of Cuba", the anti-Cuban propaganda campaign which began on June 2004 was aimed at revealing Cuba's commercial and financial counterparts and driven by the clear intention of eliminating these. No different were the sinister motives behind the article published by the Nuevo Herald on 9 June 2004, which falsely stated that the Cuban funds deposited in the UBS were destined to "unknown persons or entities in banks which had not been revealed", adding that *Those are the names that must be known. Florida congresspersons Ileana Ros-Lehtinen and Lincoln Díaz-Balart must put the pressure on to reveal where the money ended up and where it was coming from*" (the inverted commas in the quotation are ours).With an expediency that would be inexplicable were it not motivated by the same anti-Cuban sentiment, these congresspersons immediately wrote the Federal Reserve and the House's Finance Committee to request that the federal government determine "the origin and destination of some $3.9 billion that the Cuban government "laundered" through an international program of the Federal Reserve". These congresspersons reiterated this issue in press notes, dated 22 and 30 June, published when all of the anti-Cuban measures presented to President Bush on 6 May came into effect.

[12] "Cuba condemns new and cowardly measure by the government of the United States". Informational note issued by the Cuban government, published in Granma, 8 June 2004, p.1.

By then, the beginning of 2004, these severe measures were beginning to be felt in Cuba, which began to take the appropriate measures in response. A note sent by Fidel Castro to the round table program devoted to an analysis of this topic, televised on 25 October 2004, stated: "At this point, we began to see clearly that many banks were being pressured by US authorities who were attempting to block these transactions and create an extremely critical situation in our country"[13]. The far-right's propaganda campaign was of such magnitude that by the close of July, the UBS saw itself obliged to make declarations to discredit its claims. These declarations were reported on by the press agency France Press as follows: "The Union of Swiss Banks (USB), Switzerland's largest bank, denied yesterday having laundered money for Cuba, as was denounced by three members of the US House of Representatives who demand an investigation into this matter. A USB spokesperson in Zurich stated he had no knowledge of new investigations on the bank's activities and denied all accusations of laundering (...) According to the USB spokesperson, the US Federal Reserve and the Swiss Federal Banking Commission already examined the case"[14].

The situation was nearing the boiling point. Following new threatening declarations against Cuba made by the Cuban-American congresswoman Ileana Ros-Lehtinen on 16 September 2004, who, among other things, stated that "(...) other banks are being looked at" —a threat which was not to be taken lightly—Cuban authorities stepped up measures aimed at replacing the dollar in all Cuban transactions. Referring to the day in question, in his message to the round table program televised on 25 October 2004, Fidel Castro expressed: "That day, I asked the Central Bank of Cuba to speed up efforts in this matter and suggested that attention be focused on the possibility of replacing the US dollar with the Cuban convertible peso,

[13] See "Response to a real threat posed by a criminal US government measure", Granma, 26 October 2000, p. 4.
[14] France Press dispatch, Zurich, 25 July 2004. Quoted in "Response to a real threat posed by a Criminal US government measure". In 2007, the USB and BANISTMO, a Lloyds Bank of London subsidiary based in Bogota, Colombia, yielded to the United States' brutal pressures and have refused to accept quota payments from the National Assembly of the People's Power of Cuba to the Interparlamentary Union (UIP) and the Latin American Parliament (PAR-LATINO), whose accounts they handle.

such that the country were no longer vulnerable to new pressures from the Miami mob and the US government".

The catalyst in the implementation of this measure were the declarations of the Assistant Secretary of State for Western Hemisphere Affairs Daniel W. Fisk, made on 9 October 2004 and quoted above. After boasting of the heavy losses in hard currency revenue endured by Cuba, resulting from the measures proposed by the "Commission for Assistance to a Free Cuba", Dan Fisk stated that one of the most important results of that Commission had been the Cuban Asset Targeting Group, "staffed by law enforcement officials from several agencies to investigate and identify new ways hard currency moves in and out of Cuba, and to stop it"[15].

The obvious relationship between Miami's sustained propaganda campaign, claiming that Cuba had laundered money in its transactions with foreign banking institutions, and the work of US leaders, through the Cuban Asset Targeting Group, in this direction, prompted Cuba's vigorous response in defense of the country's interests: the replacement of the US dollar with the Cuban convertible peso, which was put into circulation through a measure which began to be implemented on 8 November that year and which, additionally, established a 10 percent tax applicable to the exchange of US cash for the convertible peso. This last measure was designed to offer "compensation for the risks and costs arising from the manipulation of US dollars in Cuba's economy, resulting from the abovementioned measures undertaken by the US government, which seek to prevent our country from using cash in US dollars for normal commercial ends"[16].

On 10 July 2006, the Bush administration presented a new version of the plan drawn up by the "Commission for Assistance to a Free Cuba" which ratified and extended the 2004 version. The new measures included the creation of an Inter-Agency Task Force devoted exclusively to hindering the sale of Cuban nickel around the world; the strengthening of the Cuban Asset Targeting Group; a

[15] Declarations by Dan W. Fisk before the Cuban-American Veterans Association, Miami, 9 October 2004, published by the US Department of State's Bureau of International Information Programs (http://usinfo.state.gov). Quoted in "Response to a real threat posed by a criminal US government measure".
[16] Quoted in "Response to a real threat posed by a criminal US government measure".

30

prohibition on the sale to Cuba of medical equipment to be used in large-scale programs offering medical services to foreigners — emphasizing international cooperation efforts in ophthalmologic surgery under Operation Miracle—, the training of doctors or aiding nations that have suffered natural disasters; sanctions for companies that enter into agreements with Cuba to prospect and extract oil; and the application of Title III of the Helms Burton Act on countries that undertake cooperative efforts with Cuba. The most irrational aspect of the new measures of July 2006 is the accompanying reference to a secret clause which contains recommendations which were not made public because of "national security reasons" and to ensure their "effective execution"[17].

The economic war measures against Cuba we have described so far, in all of their brutality, and the measures that Cuba had to implement in its own defense, are but a pale reflection of what Cuba has faced, with resolution, since the triumph of its liberating revolution in 1959. We cannot conclude this introduction without mentioning another aspect of this war, which, for nearly half a century, has gone hand-in-hand with the declared and public measures: the terrorist actions, acts of economic sabotage and the threat of violent reprisals against businesspeople in third countries interested in investing in Cuba, perpetrated by terrorist organizations created and protected by the US government or by its special services.

When, at the close of June 2004, the measures we have described began to be implemented, the leader of the terrorist organization Commandos F-4, Rodolfo Frómeta, appeared on Miami TV Channel 41 and, clearly seeking to complement these measures, stated that his organization had "(...) people inside and outside Cuba ready to carry out armed acts against the Cuban government" – in reference to terrorist actions against foreign investments in Cuba. A communiqué issued by this organization stated that "people who invest in Cuba are equally responsible for our hardships and, as such, their investments shall be considered military targets"[18]. The complicity of the two types of actions—the public ones undertaken

---

[17] See UN National Assembly, 61st period of sessions: Report of the Secretary General (A/61/132), United Nations Web Site, 8 August 2006. Response of the Cuban government, paragraphs 7 – 10.

[18] Quoted in Ministry of Foreign Affaire, p. 9. Source: "A television channel in Miami invites a terrorist group to talk about its actions against Cuba and Vene

by the administration and the terrorist ones perpetrated by its disciples and protégées—can be more firmly grasped if we look at how, on 9 May 2004, when the administration's new measures were made public at the beginning of May that year, Rodolfo Frómeta and other leaders of the terrorist organization Commandos F-4 made an open letter to President Bush public, including a proposal to carry out armed actions against Cuba. The letter affirmed that "(…) many are the exiles or leaders of organizations in exile making petitions for harsh sanctions and even for an invasion. We offer our support to both but, we reiterate, Commandos F-4 once again requests the we be allowed to have an active, physical role, with no restrictions". For the less informed reader, suffice it to mention that this request was not made by a group which rigorously adheres to the United States' Neutrality Act and formally requests that the administration authorize it to act against Cuba, but one of the five terrorist organizations based in south Florida —which includes the Cuban American National Foundation (CANF), Alpha 66, Commandos L and the National Democratic Unity Party (NDUP)— which, since 1990, has carried out actions of these nature against Cuba, including armed incursions aimed at sabotaging economic targets and encouraging the activities of rebel bands in mountainous regions.

We invite the readers to gain in more detailed knowledge of these issues we have briefly touched on —the administration's public measures and the terrorist actions against Cuba's economy— in the pages that follow. It is a rigorously true and verifiable story. We are positive readers will find it nothing short of a treaty on atrocities.

---

zuela with complete impunity" ("Un canal de televisión de Miami invita con total impunidad a un grupo terrorista a hablar sobre sus ataques a Cuba y Venezuela"), 18 June 2004, www.rebelión.org.

"When we got back from the airport, she threw up what she had for breakfast. Not much later, she yelled out: "Oh, I'm falling!" At ten at night that same day, she became dizzy again and we went back to the hospital. They decided to admit her. At midnight, I told her to go to sleep and she said she didn't want to, because she was going to die. Before closing her eyes, she gave me a very cold kiss and asked me not to let go of her hand. At around 2 in the morning, her hand started losing strength inside of mine. When I looked at her, she was light purple. Not much after this, she died. Six months later, because of this, her father died. It broke his heart".

Silvia Torres,
mother of 12-year-old Ernestina Oñate

"I was by her side on the 13th when she died, I have been carrying the pain inside of me for very long, all the time by her side, until 10 at night on the 13th, when she died. We fought till the end, the director of the hospital, the people of therapy, the doctors, until the end. **In the end, the cursed Interpheron medicine finally arrived".**

Félix Mesa Deantes,
father of Cintia Mesa Marrero,
3 years and 4 months old.

During the hemorrhagic dengue epidemic which in 1981 caused the deaths of 158 Cuban citizens —101 of them children— and affected 344,203 people, the U.S. Treasury Department, under blockade precepts, delayed authorization for the sale and transportation to Cuba of the insecticides and fumigation sprayers needed to combat the plague. Cuba was forced to purchase these in third countries, at an extra cost of millions of dollars. The delayed arrival in the country of these products was, no doubt, largely responsible for many of the deaths which occurred.

CHAPTER I The first actions

On hearing the sound of the approaching airplane, Walter Sosillo raised his eyes towards the North, trying to guess the exact place where it would appear. Until December 31, 1958, that peculiar purring noise inspired concern and, at times, less than subtle indignation in those who heard it, as it was a sure indication that the areas occupied by the rebel forces fighting Batista's dictatorship were about to be bombed. These forces were frequently offered food in the humble homes of peasants who lived in the combat zones. One of the most famous letters written by the young bearded commander, Fidel Castro to his close collaborator, Celia Sánchez, was, in fact, motivated by the bombing of the homes of defenseless peasants with wea-pons supplied by the U.S. government.

But it was January 1960, and little more than a year had already passed since the collapse of the tyranny. Now, when the sound of an airplane was heard, it was associated to a new word, related to positive changes occurring in the Cuban countryside. It was short and simple: INRA.[1] The most knowledgeable would say that it was not even a word, but an acronym; but there, things began to get complicated for many, and it was best to treat it as a word. Increasingly,

[1] Acronym for Instituto Nacional de Reforma Agraria (National Institute of Agrarian Reform), created by the homonymous law of May 17, 1959, which eliminated the division of land into large estates in Cuba.

what crisscrossed the skies and even landed in remote regions that were rapidly changing were INRA planes and, for the most pious who, out of habit, no longer expected anything from earthly powers, the new word, or the new acronym, evoked the good news announced by another bearded man that had something similar written on a legendarily redeeming cross.

But, although that noise was no longer a harbinger of bad things, even before seeing the plane young worker Walter Sosillo could not suppress a look of concern on his face. Walter and all his friends and acquaintances, like their parents and grandparents, for whom sugar-cane plantations were an extension of their very being, were pro-foundly troubled by the growing rumors that unidentified airplanes, big and small, were mercilessly bombing sugar mills and setting on fire the plantations they all depended on. For the first time ever, not long before this, before the end of the year, he had heard someone use the word **pirate** to refer to an airplane and, recalling the word then, relating it to the bombs that were dropped and the devastated fields, caused him the same concern that had assailed more than one of his predecessors almost exactly three centuries before, when Henry Morgan had razed the village of Puerto Príncipe to the ground. A new thought assaulted him, and he could not help smiling. As a boy, on the coast of La Herradura, he often imagined himself facing an attack of Morgan's pirates and forcing them to retreat. A grown man, long before hearing the word again, he had decided that now he would certainly put up a fight.

The initial purr that had announced the airplane was practically a deafening noise when he suddenly noticed a new sound, like that of a whistle, caused by something which rapidly cut the air as it fell, and ended with a muffled thump upon landing on the soft earth. Barely able to control the fear that gripped him on seeing that the bomb, miraculously, had not exploded, as the airplane left towards Lake La Güira and, heading North, was lost from sight over the high seas, Walter realized that he should not leave it where it had fallen. If it exploded there, the best fields in the area would be irreparably damaged. He had heard that a Rebel Army combatant had done something similar some months before in the Punta Alegre sugar mill area, near Chambas. It was then that he thought that even if it was crazy, Cabrera Estupiñán —he still remembered his surnames *from hearing them again and again—had acted like a true man, and, without thinking it over, but not without considerable effort, he removed the bomb from the hole it made on impact and placed it on his shoulders. Forgetting himself, he started to move away from the most hazardous area. Nothing, for him, happened after that.*

While new names had lengthened the list of the Homeland's dead in the little over twelve months since the rebel victory, none had, until then, been directly related to a new form of warfare that would later be identified as **economic warfare**. *And it was that simple, though maybe historians still need to come to an agreement on whether, with the death of 24-year-old worker Walter Sosillo on January 29, 1960, when a pirate airplane from the CIA's secret fleet bombed the Chaparra sugar mill area in the north of today's province of Las Tunas, the United States' economic war on the Cuban Revolution was indeed claiming its first human victim.*

There were many things the young worker Walter Sosillo did not even have the chance to find out. Although he was one of the protagonists of that day's action, he could not have known that, since October of 1959, the U.S. government, through the Central Intelligence Agency, had began to target sugar mills and sugarcane plantations for major acts of sabotage that sent out a clear message of intolerance to those who had dared promulgate, that May 17 which marked the beginning of a new stage in Cuba – U.S. relations, an Agrarian Reform Law that affected, by no means exclusively, a certain number of U.S. companies that were the owners of the country's best lands. Probably buying into the old fatalist slogan of "no sugar, no country", between October of 1959 and April of 1961, on the eve of the Bay of Pigs invasion, over fifty sugar industries and sugarcane fields were bombed in actions similar to that in which Walter Sosillo lost his life.

Another thing Walter Sosillo, a simple and humble young man, could not even have imagined was that, among those acting in the play in which his fate was sealed, was the very president of the United States, who went as far as saying that the bombings that had been carried out until late December 1959 did not yet meet his expectations. That is what the director of the Central Intelligence Agency answered Allen Dulles, when the latter went to see him in early January 1960 to tell

37

him about the CIA actions against Cuban sugar mills, like the one in which our main character died. That is what he told him: that he was not satisfied with what had been done so far, and he told Dulles to return "with a broader program".[2]

Another thing Walter Sosillo never even had opportunity to suppose was that actions like those in which he played a critical role and lost his life were not, by a long shot, the first of the kind described as "economic warfare", but that they had begun less than 24 hours after the tyrant Batista had fled the country, on the midnight of December 31, 1958, one week before the young and bearded guerilla leader Fidel Castro made his entrance into the capital. Indeed, what, if not an example of economic warfare, was the open-armed welcome, on Miami's piers, given Batista's cronies, murderers and embezzlers who fled with as much as 424 million dollars from the Republic's treasury,[3] sums which were quickly deposited in U.S. banks?[4]

The Proclamation of Cuba's National Assembly quoted above states: "The sums taken in this colossal theft ended up in US banks. Not one cent was returned to Cuba. All of the perpetrators, without exception, enjoyed impunity and had safe access to the stolen funds." As early as January 7, 1959, Cuban authorities requested the retention and return of the 17 million dollars stolen by the murderer Rolando Masferrer Rojas, adding, in later communiqués dated January 9, 12, 20 and 26, the names of 18 other fugitives and the sums stolen by them. Turning a deaf ear to these requests was the only answer U.S. authorities offered, even though an extradition treaty between the two countries was then in effect. According to

[2] Testimony of Gordon Gray, President Eisenhower's special assistant for National Security Affairs. See Gray to Don Wilson —Assistant Director, Dwight D. Eisenhower Library—, Dec. 3, 1974, p. 1. Gray Paper, box 2, DDL. Taken from Tomás Diez Acosta: *La guerra encubierta contra Cuba*. (*The covert war against Cuba*). Editora Política, Havana, 1997, p. 9

[3] National Bank of Cuba: 6 February 1959 report. In: "Proclama de la Asamblea Nacional del Poder Popular de la República de Cuba" ("Proclamation of the National Assembly of the People's Power of the Republic of Cuba"), 13 September 1999, *Granma* newspaper, Tuesday 14 September 1999, third edition, p. 4.

[4] *The New York Times*, April 19 1959. It appears in "Proclama de la Asamblea Nacional del Poder Popular de la República de Cuba", *op. cit.*

the chairman of the National Assembly, "that brutal plundering was one of the most severe blows dealt the national economy, absolutely unjustifiable, occurring before the government that replaced the tyranny had installed itself in Havana, and it occurred with the connivance or collaboration of U.S. authorities, who helped the thieves escape and welcomed them in their territory." [5]

Faced with the country's precarious financial situation, exacerbated by the colossal plundering of its public treasury, a delegation of the National Bank of Cuba was forced to request a modest credit from U.S. authorities to stabilize the Cuban currency. This gave the U.S. president the opportunity to undertake another key action, by rebuffing the request at a National Security Council meeting on February 12, 1959, where he commented that he found it "difficult to comprehend how he could do anything to stabilize the Cuban currency until the government of Cuba itself had become stabilized" (that is, until it followed the usual governmental course, ignoring the people's needs).[6] Ricardo Alarcón refers to this topic in the November 2000 speech quoted above. In this regard, he said: "In February of 1959, the United States National Security Council examined the matter. The verdict was very simple: 'to listen to the Cubans, but to neither give nor promise them anything at all'." [7]

What Walter Sosillo *had* heard long before dying, from the very first days following the revolutionary victory, were the threats that the United States directed at the Revolution for the mere crime of confronting the powerful and helping the poor, the very same poor who, according to the pious who no longer expected anything from earthly powers, were blessed because the kingdom of heavens would be theirs. In fact, many of those threats were what gave Walter Sosillo

---

[5] Ricardo Alarcón de Quesada: ("Deceit: a weapon inseparable from imperialist aggression") "El embuste: arma inseparable de la agresión imperialista." Presentation made at the 2nd World Friendship and Solidarity with Cuba Meeting, 10 November 2000. It appears in Ricardo Alarcón de Quesada and Miguel Álvarez Sánchez: *Guerra Económica de Estados Unidos contra Cuba.* Editora Política, 2001, p. 46.

[6] Department of State: *Foreign Relations of United States,* Volume VI, Document 250, 1991, pp. 397-398.

[7] Quoted in Ricardo Alarcón de Quesada and Miguel Álvarez Sánchez, p. 47.

the conviction he would do anything that was needed –something he proved when he sacrificed his life— to confront those he always imagined were much like the pirates of his childhood games. But he never imagined that some of those menacing declarations by authorized representatives of that country, about the use of economic weapons to confront the victorious Revolution, were part of the same economic warfare in which he would be the first to die. On January 21, 1959, in response to the execution of war criminals from Batista's dictatorship—a measure of elementary justice— legislator Wayne Hays made the first reference to the possibility of the U.S. administration cutting the sugar quota and applying other economic measures against Cuba. This gesture would be repeated thereafter, as a litany, by many others, who threatened to use a club they would soon deliberately brandish.

At this point, before continuing our narration, we should highlight some elements, ask ourselves some questions and try to answer them. The main topic of the book that readers have in front of them is, in effect, the United States' economic war against the Cuban Revolution. This economic war has numerous points in common with other manifestations of U.S. hostility toward the regime established in Cuba after the defeat of the Batista tyranny. At the same time, it has many unique features which justify a separate study. It does not have a life of its own, but is, rather, an inseparable part of a broader political project: to destroy the Revolution. Another point that we want to highlight is that we will not make any groundless statements and this will force us, in many cases, to rely extensively on bibliographical references. For this we apologize, though we know many interested readers will appreciate these, which can prove useful for future research work.

Many are the questions we can ask ourselves. For the many readers who frequently hear of economic warfare and its deployment against Cuba, who do not know how a doctrine of economic warfare was gradually elaborated in the powerful nations, a question in this connection may prove very useful. For others, it may be extremely important to know how open economic measures were intertwined with measures that are subversive in nature, the kind that characterizes the work of the United States' Central Intelligence

Agency. Another group of readers will no doubt be interested in knowing the initial process –following the victory of the Revolution and, more precisely, the passing of the Agrarian Reform Law in Cuba—in which the system of measures against the Cuban economy was designed.

We will answer all these questions below. In the chapters that follow, we will look at the evolution of this process to the present day.

The background. The evolution of an economic warfare "doctrine"

The actions that make up what is today known as economic warfare, those that powerful States undertake to damage the internal economies of adversarial States in order to reach a future social, political and—as part of the latter— frequently military aim, have a very long history behind them.

Though resorted to since classical times,[8] what gave shape to a doctrine of economic warfare as such were events which took place in Europe over the last few centuries, when wars were extremely frequent in those territories and naval powers, with England at the head, sought to limit their opponents' trade with neutral countries during wartime. In the 17th century and, most significantly, from the Napoleonic wars onwards, the concept of neutrality and its use by countries interested in avoiding war gradually gained in strength, a process which culminated in the establishment of the rights and duties of countries with a status of permanent neutrality by The Hague's Institute of International Law in 1875. The instrument mainly refers to the legal status of States that, of their own free will, choose not to take part in wars emerging and waged among other States.

---

[8] With the creation of the Italic Confederation in 272 B.C., Rome prohibited its allies from trading directly with each other, to secure a monopoly on intermediary trade for Roman merchants. After defeating Macedonia in 167 B.C., Rome prohibited it from exploiting its gold and silver mines, to prevent the resurgence of its former might. (V. Diakov and S. Kovalov: *Historia de la antigüedad. Roma (History of antiquity. Rome)*. Instituto Cubano del Libro, La Habana, 1966, pp. 97-124.)

The evolution of the basic features of this economic warfare doctrine went through the following stages:

1. Three to four centuries ago, in times of war, a naval blockade would be set up around the adversary's ports and coast and used, as a basic weapon, to prevent it from obtaining the supplies needed for the war effort and to impede its exports. These measures affected both the State that endured the measure and the neutral countries that traded with it.[9]

The essential nature and purpose of the blockade as a weapon of war, to prevent trade by the enemy and bring pressures to bear on neutral countries that trade with it, has not changed in the course of centuries. In 1601, Queen Elizabeth I of England issued a proclamation in which, after referring to King Philip II of Spain's acts of "treachery" and noting Spain's dependence on supplies received from overseas, she ordered "the stopping, hindrance and impeaching of all commerce and *traffic* with him in his territories of Spain and Portugal [...] (in order to achieve) peace and quiet of all these parts of Christendome"[10] (the italics are the author's).

2. The movement against blockade excesses began by neutral countries in the late 18th century, with the creation of the League of Armed Neutrality by Russian rulers Catherine II (1780) and Paul I (1800), to protect the trade operations of member countries from frequent English attacks, which led to the creation of International Law rules designed to safeguard their interests.

Among these were two noteworthy rules. One, established following the Crimean war, in the Declaration of Paris of 1856, stated that, in

---

9 David L. Gordon and Royden Dangerfield: *The Hidden Weapon. The Story of Economic Warfare.* Harper & Brothers Publishers, New York, 1947, pp. 16-17. The authors, officials of the Board of Economic Warfare attached to the U.S. Department of State during the Second World War, and, as such, protagonists in the economic war waged against the Nazi-Fascist Axis, have produced, in our opinion, a classic work on the subject which we will frequently use as reference.

10 We place emphasis on the word *traffic* because it strikes us as highly significant that one of the key words used in the aberrant Helms-Burton Act, with which they would qualify any action involving or affecting a U.S. property nationalized with the passing of revolutionary laws in Cuba, should have such a remote and questionable precursor.

order to be considered legal, a blockade must be effective;[11] The rules set down by the Declaration of London of 1909, whereby a blockade must be formally declared and appropriately notified to the opponents and neutral countries, established that *it could not extend beyond the coastal ports and seas owned or occupied by the enemy* and, repeating a concept of the Declaration of Paris, that it should be effective.[12]

3. The importance accorded to and evolution of the concept of *contraband*, which comes to be considered a violation of the blockade and gives the blockading power the right to stop and search vessels in transit to the blockaded area ("visit and reach") and to confiscate articles falling under the categories of "absolute contraband" (military supplies) or "conditional contraband" (ordinary articles whose destination would be the blockaded country's armed forces). Until the beginning of World War I, neither food, consumer goods, raw materials nor industrial products that were not sent to the armed forces were considered contraband, nor could conditional contraband be confiscated in the open sea.[13]

World War I had a major impact on the evolution of the above precepts and on the blockade-contraband relationship.

In a narrow sense, at the time a blockade was understood to be a "close siege of enemy ports and seacoasts, -the picketing of a string of warships at intervals close enough to prevent blockade runners from slipping through".[14]

But, in 1914, the English navy was powerful enough the be able to mine enemy ports and coasts and, in order to avoid enemy

[11] The deterrents to be applied should be aimed at enemy vessels or those in violation of the blockade and not against neutral ships transporting authorized goods and quantities. See David L. Gordon and Royden Dangerfield: p. 17. The extraterritoriality of the U.S. blockade measures against Cuba are similarly questioned in third countries.

[12] Idem

[13] Ibid., p. 18. In writing the history of economic warfare, the concept of contraband is important, and the evolution of the content that was conferred to it shaped the blockade in new ways, until reaching the stage achieved in World War II, principal benchmark used by the United States for its blockade on Cuba in time of peace, starting 1959.

[14] Ibid., pp. 18-19

submarine attacks in the high seas, it could use **control ports** in England or loading points in other countries to conduct searches on suspicious vessels, and the concept of a **long-distance blockade**, objected to by the London Declaration, gained force. Another new reality faced by England at the time was the need —made official by the Royal Ordinance of August 20, 1914— to totally prevent the entry into Germany, directly or through European neutrals, of what was previously considered **conditional contraband** in iron ore and coal, justified by the argument that modern war machines were made of iron and used coal as fuel.

Opposition to this ordinance by the United States — a neutral country until 1917 and hypocritical champion of "freedom of the seas" while it worked to its advantage— forced England to change it and to issue a new one on October 29, 1914, under which **conditional contraband** could only be confiscated if it was bound for an enemy nation, but the list of goods considered absolute contraband was broadened.

The situation changed dramatically in the first quarter of 1915, when the actions of German submarines against merchant, and even passenger, ships had such an impact on U.S. public opinion that, without much opposition, it accepted the Reprisals Order in Council of 11 March 1915, according to which Great Britain would block any goods originating in, going or belonging to the countries with which it was at war, regardless of whether it was "contraband" in the sense given this term until then. Thus, the transition was complete: the restricted-blockade regulations were extended to long-distance blockade and were no longer founded on the unstable grounds of contraband laws.

The extension of the concept of contraband and long-distance blockade effected by England worked to prevent the direct entry of overseas goods into Germany, and their indirect traffic through neutral European countries was controlled by preventing trade in these articles that was in excess of the normal pre-war commercial level, through an *agreement-based rationing* system that established the approved quotas and the issuing of a **(navicert)** permit, at the loading port, to the ships carrying them. Those who attempted to evade the **navicert** permit system were "blacklisted" and the ship owners and builders were unable to maintain normal trade with English ports and interests.

44

As a result of this, in two short years (1914-1916), the old English blockade became a new and more complex economic warfare phenomenon which involved such practices as totally prohibiting the blockaded country from having trade with other countries; rationing based on agreements with the neutrals in order to halt the re-export of goods; control at ports of origin; the extension of permits for the transportation of loads, or navicerts, and, finally, the creation and application of "black lists".

When the United States joined World War I in 1917, the theory and practice of blockade and the newly emerged concept of economic warfare experienced significant changes: the most important of the until then neutral countries and, also, an obstinate champion of "freedom of the seas", began to adopt, as its own, the restrictions unilaterally imposed by England and, because of the superiority of its naval might, began to displace the latter as the main blockading power. In 1917, to adapt itself to the prevailing circumstances, the United States issued the *Trading with the Enemy Act*, implemented during the First and Second World Wars and upon which, a mere 15 years after the conclusion of the latter, it based its economic warfare actions against the Cuban Revolution and continues to do so today.

In the period between the world wars, economic pressures were used as a weapon against the new government of ex-czarist Russia. International documents of the time suggest nothing to the contrary. A draft protocol against economic aggression, submitted to the League of Nations' European Commission by the Soviet delegation in May of 1931 stated: *"Minimizing the crisis suffered by the national economies of most countries requires, in addition to renouncing war as a means of solving international conflicts, the complete ceasing of all forms of economic aggression, both open and covert, by some countries or groups of countries against other countries or groups of countries."*[15] This is also caught sight of in the text of the November 1932 Nonaggression Pact between the USSR and France, whose Article 4 stated that "[...] each of the high contracting parties commits [...] to not enter into any international agreement that results in the *prohibition to buy goods from the other party, or to sell them thereto, or to grant it credit, and to not adopting any measure that results in*

---

[15] *Documentos de política exterior de la URSS 1917-1967* (*USSR Foreign Policy Documents. 1917-1967*). Editorial Progreso, Moscow, s/f, pp. 79-80.

the exclusion of the other party from any participation in foreign trade thereof"[16] (the italics in both quotations are ours).

Between 1939 and 1941, before the United States' entry into World War II, Great Britain, on its own, set up a blockade on the Nazi-fascist Axis. With the creation of the Ministry of Economic Warfare (MEW) on the basis of the experiences of 1914, it forbade the entry into German ports of a nearly exhaustive list of goods which almost made no distinction between absolute contraband and conditional contraband, announcing that ships caught carrying any of these products would be confiscated, at control ports in England, Gibraltar, the Shetland Islands in northern Scotland and other strategic points.

To prevent any evasions of the blockade through neutral European countries (Switzerland, Sweden, Spain, Portugal and Turkey) which could act as potential intermediaries, the policy of rationing their imports was reinstated, on the basis of a case-by-case analysis of their needs according to the pre-war levels, with no additional quotas for re-exporting. Those shipments were granted the **navicerts** or transportation permits and the ships carrying these were issued special certificates, without which they would not receive English – and later U.S.—marine facilities nor could the shipments be insured, since the insurance companies were mainly of those nationalities. The unwanted ships, ship owners and companies swelled those "black lists" and were treated as enemies. Direct German exports were prohibited, and to prevent them from being made through European neutrals, the latter's trade was carefully controlled. None could export a product with more than a certain level of "enemy content" in raw materials for manufacturing, usually 5%.

The difference with the old blockade of enemy ports and coasts is obvious: no wonder the new form of economic warfare –which relied more on a specialized bureaucracy scattered across the world than on warships—is described in the literature with the name of "paper blockade",[17] predecessor of that imposed on Cuba after the 1959 Revolution. It is obvious that that blockade was much tighter than previous ones.

[16] Ibidem, p. 81.
[17] Ibid., p. 28.

The English Ministry of Economic Warfare not only set up trade controls but also supplemented them by evaluating the economic foundations of the enemy's military potential, helped in the planning of military operations and identified the industries to be targeted for strategic bombings: when an industry was damaged by the bombings, the economic warfare experts geared their efforts towards preventing the country from obtaining abroad the means to get it running again. This procedure was immediately incorporated into U.S. economic warfare theory and practice and, as we will see later on, was thus applied to Cuba as from 1959, *with the difference that major economic facilities were targeted and have often been destroyed through terrorist actions without there being a declared state of war*. The reconstruction or restoration of these targets was then impeded or hindered through blockade measures. We will later look at some examples.

Several months before the United States' entry into World War II, an Economic Defense Committee that took the initial steps in coordinating the work of the Departments of State, Treasury, Commerce, War and Navy in this direction was created. After Pearl Harbor, this advisory body became the Economic Warfare Committee, later renamed the Foreign Economic Administration, which started to work in coordination with the British Ministry of Economic Warfare. Its branch in the U.S. embassy to London was the Economic Warfare Division, which was incorporated into the British Blockade Committee, composed of all relevant agencies, and similar cooperation agencies were set up in Washington and other cities.

According to experts, in this period the United States quickly acquired the English know-how which had already been applied in the last two years. Parallel this, *an extended concept of economic warfare goals, strategy and tactics that went beyond the English conception was gradually developed in Washington*.

Particularly significant was the combined Anglo-American effort to detect blockade leaks, which established intelligence operations within "smuggling operations" (i.e. blockade breaches) and the black market, a practice which was based on the notion that any efforts to eliminate these activities basically depended on a sound intelligence program. To this end, the United States used FBI agents in Latin America and agents from the Office of Strategic Services (OSS, predecessor of the CIA) in the Iberian Peninsula, as well as reports from the Office of Naval Intelligence, from the army's G-2 and from consular officials.

Financial warfare, as an integral part of economic warfare, was another practice where the relationship between the United States and Great Britain proved particularly fruitful, as these two countries had two unparalleled weapons: the dollar and the pound sterling, with all the financial resources and institutions they symbolize. Its goals were:

1. To prevent the use of financial funds by adversaries in third countries.
2. To dismantle their enemies' external trade, severing the links of their companies' main offices with their branches abroad and ensuring these were not restored through front companies or indirectly, and that no new funds were obtained to fuel their economies.
3. To raise the cost of economic collaboration with the Nazi-fascist Axis for people in third countries, forcing them to break those ties and attacking those who sought them, in search of profits, where it hurt them most: making them lose their monetary resources.
4. At the end of the war, to prevent capital flight which could favor the Fascist forces.

The Anglo-American financial warfare measures went from the control of Axis funds and properties abroad and of its attempts at commercial transactions under a neutral veil, to "blacklisting" and the application of economic pressures against those interested in supporting them.

After the Nazi invasion of Norway and Denmark in April 1940, the United States froze the funds of those countries in U.S. banks to prevent their use by the invaders, an action that was later repeated with those of the Netherlands, France, the Baltic States and the Balkans and, as from July 1941, with the Axis countries, so that U.S. financial institutions were not used for their military purposes.

Simultaneously, a census of all the enemy properties in U.S. territory was taken and the analysis and control of firms from neutral countries was started, in an attempt to separate the legitimate ones from those that covered up Axis interests through fronts, facilitated by European financial practices which included: the preference of bearer shares and the laws of certain countries, especially Switzerland, that offered themselves as safe ports for international capital.

Among the transactions tracked down by the U.S. Treasury Department in the United States were: the transfer of nominal control over German agencies in that country to neutral citizens, keeping those links secret; the transfer of ownership, with a clause enabling a future repurchase, a seemingly legitimate sale which concealed the retention of certain rights by the owner; the use of bearer securities through which true ownership could not be identified; or the exchange of common shares for other interests, which involved a change in the nominal holder but preserved the German financial interests and their influence.

When the war ended, the discovery of enemy fronts and the distinction of "legitimate" transactions from those that were not were described as "prominently successful" by the Treasury Department's Office for the Control of Foreign Funds. This agency had delegated the task of managing and overseeing the above activities to banks and other financial institutions, taking advantage of their experience and knowledge of their clients' business. It established general licenses for innocuous transactions and maintained close interaction with other federal agencies, the Economic Warfare Committee and the Federal Bureau of Investigation (FBI) among them.

Two years before Pearl Harbor, the United States had begun opening files on firms and people represented there and in Latin American countries, suspected of collaborating with Axis economic and subversive efforts. The Proclaimed List of Certain Blocked Nationals, similar to the British Statutory List of 1939, which prohibited trade with foreigners who were considered enemies, was established on July 17, 1941, and, under newly-established prohibitions, banks could not offer clients on the list any service, refused to accept any new deposits, liquidated their old funds as soon as possible and did not allow them to make transactions in dollars or pounds if they did not have a license. No U.S. or British interest could be transferred to people appearing on those lists, and they could not make purchases, move their property, use their deposits, shipments or insurance facilities, advertise in their newspapers, or rent space in buildings whose owners were nationals of those countries.

Prior to the attack on Pearl Harbor, the United States, Canada and Great Britain cooperated closely in the use of "blacklist" sanctions. There were regular consultations between their representatives; they exchanged information on actions aimed at evading blockade restrictions; and the firms or people included in a country's list were automatically added to the other's, although the United States was in charge of managing the list for Latin America, backyard of its interests, and Great Britain managed the Eastern Hemisphere's, where it had developed coherent actions and policies long before the United States entered the war.

A poorly known technique of economic warfare, nonexistent in World War I but applied widely by Great Britain and the United States in World War II, consisted in so-called "previous purchases", geared towards preventing access, by the enemy, to raw materials or finished, scarce or very valuable goods, produced by third countries, through previous acquisition of the goods or of the firms or companies that produced them.

In Spain, Portugal and Turkey, this practice found its highest expression in the so-called *wolfram campaign*. This mineral, of a high tungsten content, was vital in the production of extremely hard steel alloys used in the manufacture of high-speed cutting machines, armored vehicles and especially penetrating projectiles. After the means of communication with the Far East were cut, German needs could only be met through the extraction of this ore in the Iberian Peninsula, all of which —or the mines from which it was extracted— was gradually acquired by the British and the Americans, in quantities exceeding their own needs, as part of a commercial war that even today is worthy of analysis. [18]

But the economic warfare actions undertaken by the United States during World War II were not only aimed against the Nazi-fascist Axis, but also against their then Soviet allies.

The English-language version of the work *Strategy of Containment*, by the U.S. political scientist J. L. Gaddis,[19] states that the Strategic Affairs Office experts in charge of analyzing the

[18] Ibid., p. 105.

[19] John Lewis Gaddis: *Strategy of Containment*. New York, 1982. Quoted by Nikolai Yaklovev: *La CIA contra la URSS (The CIA against the Soviet Union)*. Editorial Progreso, Moscú, 1983. There is a Spanish version: John Lewis Gaddis: *Estra tegias de Contención*. Grupo Editor Latinoamericano, Colección Estudios

state of Soviet-American relations during the war, focused less on actions against Hitler than on measures to influence Soviet leaders to act according to the strategic interests of the United States[20]. In those moments of war against Nazism, in which most of the weight fell on the Eastern Front, the U.S. secret services did not prioritize collaborating more efficiently with the common antifascist cause, but rather, according to Gaddis, "what was being studied was the "coordination" problem; "how to correlate the carrots and the sticks to get concessions from the USSR in exchange for assistance received."[21]

The U.S. and English economic warfare experience, acquired in World War I and applied to the greatest extent possible during World War II, is summarized in a few words by its major experts: "The weapons used in this struggle were chiefly nonmilitary [...]. It involved secret negotiations, trade concessions, economic pressure and financial skulduggery."[22] It is clear that these authors refer only to the more open manifestations of this war, failing to mention the destruction of economic targets in which the economic warfare strategists actively participated –and still participate—through military operations, sabotage or other terrorist actions involving secret means and methods.

When World War II ended, the systematization of the experience acquired by the United States enabled its political, military and intelligence strategists to theorize about the particularities of the different forms of struggle applied during the war, and it allowed them to devise a doctrinal corpus that served as the foundation of U.S. postwar actions. Gordon and Dangerfield, extensively quoted so far, obviously fulfilled this task with respect to economic warfare.

Another major strategist who emerged during World War II was Sherman Kent, one of the architects of the Intelligence community in the United States and one of its most important theorists. For many years, Kent was at the head of the CIA's Office of National Estimates[23].

Internacionales, Buenos Aires, 1989. Its text does not fully coincide with the English original.

[20] John Lewis Gaddis: *Strategy of Containment*, p. 18.

[21] Ibid., pp. 19-20

[22] David L. Gordon and Royden Dangerfield: ob. cit., p. 1.

[23] Donald P. Steury: *Sherman Kent*. Center for the Study of Intelligence. http://www.cia.gov/csi/books/shermankent/intro-html.

In his book *Strategic Intelligence for American World Policy*, published in 1949 but still studied in U.S. universities and described by Donald P. Steury as "the most lucid of its kind",[24] Sherman Kent expressed: "War is not always conventional: indeed, a large part of war–of the remotest and most recent wars—has always been carried out with non conventional [...] weapons: [...] political and economic weapons. The kinds of war in which they are used [...] (are) political warfare and economic warfare." [25]

The purposes of these kinds of war were described by this author as follows: "In these non-conventional wars you try to do two things: *to weaken the enemy's will and capacity for resistance* and to strengthen your own will and capacity to prevail."[26] Further on, he adds that the instruments of economic warfare "are the carrot and the stick": "blockade, freezing of funds, boycott, embargo and blacklisting on the one hand; subsidies, loans, bilateral treaties, exchange and the trade agreements on the other"[27] (the italics in the quotation are ours).

Two instances of the use of "carrots" as instruments of economic warfare following the end of World War II, clarifies Kent's quote: the subordination of U.S. economic assistance –for the reconstruction of the devastated Soviet Union—to political concessions to be made by the USSR,[28] as well as the Marshall Plan's multi-million-dollar

---

[24] Idem.

[25] Sherman Kent: *Inteligencia Estratégica para la Política Mundial Norteamericana*. Segunda edición. Princenton University Press, Ciencias Políticas y Sociales, 1950, p. 38.

[26] Idem.

[27] Ibid., p. 40

[28] The war having come to an end, "the new administration believed that it had power over the Russians in several ways. Harriman himself stressed the importance of postwar reconstruction assistance that the United States would be in a position to control, whether through rehabilitation loans or through repair shipments from its occupation zone in Germany [...]. Truman quickly confirmed that unconditional assistance would not extend beyond the end of the war. Loans would cease to be made, and postwar repair shipments would be conditioned, at least implicitly, to future political cooperation." See John Lewis Gaddis: *Estrategias de Contención*, p. 31. In a footnote to these points, Gaddis remarked that the Postdam Protocol, on U.S. insistence, specified that the Soviet Union would receive 10% of the industrial equipment that was "not needed" for the operation of the postwar German economy, but it was the western powers who would determine what was necessary.

investments in Europe to contain the growing influence of the communists and other left-wing forces, within the framework of confrontation against Soviet "expansionism,"[29] all of it described by U.S. theoreticians as "the economic instruments of containment."[30]

A "carrot," too, was the differential economic treatment accorded by the United States to some of the Eastern European socialist countries that had emerged from World War II, designed to weaken their ties to the Soviet Union, begun in 1948 in U.S.-Yugoslavian relations when Belgrade's severance of relations with Moscow was confirmed,[31] and continued thereafter in relations with other allies of the USSR.[32]. According to National Security Council (NSC) document 58/2 of December 1949, such economic assistance or differential treatment to promote "schisms in communist regimes" should not entail any feelings of guilt if the final objective was "to bring about the elimination of Soviet power in the satellite countries."[33]

[29] The U.S. containment strategy ideologist, George F. Kennan, considered that to face the post-war "Soviet challenge", the United States should restore "the balance of power by encouraging the self-assurance of threatened nations," and that, for this purpose, the best means were "the strengthening of the natural forces of resistance within the countries that the communists are attacking." So, to this end, right since the political announcement of the economic assistance program, a lot was being done to restore that self-assurance. Quoted in John Lewis Gaddis, p. 51. Further on, he adds: "What the United States was in a position to do was to ensure the economic recovery of Western Europe was a success. This would have the advantage not only of restoring the balance of power but also of eliminating or at least mitigating the conditions that had, in the first place, made local communism popular. What's more, it would put severe stress on Moscow's control of Eastern Europe, because the Soviet Union was much less equipped to emulate the United States". (p. 59).

[30] Ibid., p. 77.

[31] In view of the schism, the U.S. Administration supported the Policy Planning Staff's proposal that the internal nature of the Tito régime should not affect the economic assistance it could receive, so that "Titoism should continue to exist as an erosive and disintegrating force within the Soviet sphere." Quoted in John Lewis Gaddis., pp. 80-82.

[32] "In spite of the signs that the Russians were strengthening their control there, the Administration devoted a lot of time and thought, during 1949, to ways of promoting greater dissidence among the satellites, by means that ranged from The Voice of America broadcasts and human rights campaigns at the United Nations to economic pressure and covert actions." Ibid., p. 83.

[33] Idem.

Before the first half of the 20th century had ended, another event occurred that decisively contributed to give a criminal and dark shade to economic warfare actions, which had been described somewhat aseptically, in a narrow sense, in Gordon and Dangerfield's work: the establishment of the Central Intelligence Agency (CIA) in 1947.

If in 1941-1945, the United States displaced Great Britain in the use of public instruments of economic warfare, the creation of the CIA represented increased opportunities to put into effect other actions geared towards secretly damaging the economy of its opponents. Emerging as a result of the National Security Act enacted that year, its duties included obtaining and processing information, counseling and coordinating; and a fifth duty elliptically captured the wide and indefinite field of "covert actions" in which it could intervene: "to perform such other functions and duties related to intelligence affecting the national security as the National Security Council may from time to time direct"[34] (the italics in the quote are ours).

Specific measures implemented by that agency in 1948 specified *the execution of economic warfare actions* by the CIA as part of its secret operations,[35] explicitly adding it to a list of other actions, like "subversion against hostile States, helping the secret resistance movement, supporting anticommunist groups in the threatened countries of the free world," and others.[36] On that occasion, a new concept –which had not been neglected—was incorporated into intelligence doctrine: that of *plausible denial*, according to which criminal actions that the CIA was authorized to undertake against foreign states not to the liking of Washington, *should be carried out in such way that the U.S. Government could not be accused of ordering them*, a practice designed to conceal and protect the high-risk decisions made by the president and other senior officials. In the documents that govern the activity of U.S. secret services, revised and updated thirty-five years later during the

---

[34] National security Act of 1947, Public Law 253, July 26, 1947. Appears in D. Scott Breckinridge: *The CIA and the U.S. Intelligence System*. Westview Press/ Boulder and London, 1986, p. 328

[35] In 1954, the United States National Security Council defined "secret operations" as "all activities [...] planned and executed so that any responsibility that the U.S. Government could have for them should not be evident for unauthorized people and that, if discovered, should allow the U.S. Government to allege not to have any responsibility for them." See John Lewis Gaddis. Quoted in p. 176.

[36] Guideline 10/2 of the United States National Security Council, June 18, 1948.

Reagan Administration, as recorded in Executive Order 12333 of December 4, 1981 and subsequent documents, this concept remains unchanged.[37]

In his book-accusation *Inside the Company: CIA Diary*, former CIA officer Philip Agee makes reference to the body set up within that institution for economic actions. According to his own words, when reviewing the internal structure of the CIA during the time he was in the agency; "the Economic Warfare Section of the PP staff is a subsection under Paramilitary Operations, because its mission includes the sabotage of key economic activities in a target country and the denial of critical imports, e. g. Petroleum".[38]

The decade before the victory of the Revolution, characterized by expectations in Cuba of an electoral solution to the serious evils of the late 1940's and early 1950's; by the March 10th take-over; by the heroic deeds of the Centennial Generation in the Moncada barracks, the *Granma* and the Sierra Maestra, was also witness to the CIA's most significant "secret operations" which, amid the anticommunist hysteria of the time, typified the sharpest confrontations of the Cold War, in turn the successor of that last war.

The coup against Premier Mohammed Mossadegh and the maintenance of Mohammed Reza Pahlevi on the throne as Sha of Iran in 1953, and the overthrow of Jacobo Arbenz in Guatemala in 1954, are significant actions among numerous others executed at the time. No wonder the Bay of Pigs invasion was inspired both by CIA actions against Jacobo Árbenz in 1954 Guatemala[39] and by a battle on a

---

[37] In the glossary of terms used in that order we find: "Special Activities means activities conducted in support of national foreign policy objectives abroad which are planned and executed so that the role of the United States Government is not apparent or acknowledged publicly [...]." Executive order 12333, December 4, 1981. Appears in Scott D. Breckinridge: ob. cit., p. 347.

[38] Philip Agee: *Inside the Company: CIA Diary*. Penguin Books, 1975, p. 84.

[39] The CIA *task force* that organized the overthrow of Arbenz in Guatemala in 1954 was practically the same one that participated in the planning and execution of the actions that culminated in the Bay of Pigs invasion. In addition to Richard Bissell, CIA plans assistant director, there was Tracy Barnes and other figures who, according to Fabián Escalante *La guerra secreta (The secret war)* Editorial de Ciencias Sociales, La Habana, 2002, p. 10) "would make history" in the Bay of Pigs, including: David Atlee Phillips, Howard Hunt, David Morales and Frank Bender. Once again, a certain expression by Karl Marx (*The 18th Brumaire of Louis Bonaparte*) was confirmed, that certain historical events first manifest themselves as tragedies and the second time as comedies.

beach head in the Pacific during World War II, in which one of the heroes was the U.S. army officer who later, on a CIA contract, led the training of the members of the brigade that invaded Cuba in 1961[40].

It was also a time when, in the place of the political-military doctrine of "massive reprisal" and others similar, the "flexible reaction" doctrine gained momentum. This doctrine was better suited to national liberation movements and usually inclusive of psychological warfare and political-ideological subversion actions. This period saw the revival of "area studies" —in the context of which studies on Cuba are later developed— in with those on the Cuban economy contributed to the supply of information used in the elaboration of subversive economic warfare strategies.

This entire aberrant arsenal, inherited from the Cold War and developed to the greatest possible extent through CIA "special actions" during the 50's, were the weapons used by the Empire against the victorious Cuban Revolution of January 1959.

The economic situation inherited by the Revolution. U.S. actions to prevent the triumph of the Revolution

For a more complete understanding of what the economic war unleashed by the U.S. government against Cuba has meant and means for the Cuban people, it is convenient to understand the situation inherited by the Revolution following its victory in January 1, 1959, as it is that impoverished nation which felt the irrational fury of the actions aimed at preventing the changes for which the Sierra Maestra struggle had been waged.

According to the most qualified experts, the features that characterized the then existing situation were three: a poor, underdeveloped and highly dependent economy.[41]

---

[40] Juan Carlos Rodríguez: *La batalla inevitable (The inevitable battle)*. Editorial Capitán San Luis, La Habana, 1996, pp. 16-17.

[41] Osvaldo Martínez: Special Newspaper Supplement N° 18. Informational Round Table Program televised on Cuban television on 5 July 2000.

The existing economic structure was essentially agricultural, based on extensive farming, with much of the land divided into large estates and a large rural population living under conditions of poverty and destitution.

With no industrial development to produce other strong sectors, the country's sugar industry was the only truly important one. Dependence on the United States showed in several essential aspects: the United States controlled exports and the different sugar trade channels; U.S. companies owned about 1.2 million hectares of the best lands in the country, and they directly controlled the electricity and telephone services, fuel supplies, bank credits, and a large part of the few small industries that existed, the dairy, rubber and nickel industries among them.

Cuban trade was controlled by the United States, whereby its market received 60% of exports, and whence 75 - 80% of the imports of the time originated, with a marked trade imbalance.

Unemployment and underemployment were scourges which characterized the internal economic situation, together affecting a population estimated at one-fourth to one-third of the existing work force.

In the social sphere, there was an illiteracy rate of about 23%, almost twice as high in the country's rural areas –the most neglected and forsaken— with overall figures of about a million illiterates and a similar figure of semi-illiterates, in a population which was then of about 6 million people. There were 600,000 children with no schools to go to and, paradoxically, 10,000 teachers who were unemployed, and only 55% of school-age children were registered. The average educational level of the population as a whole was the second grade.

There was only one doctor for every 1,076 inhabitants, although this figure is misleading: the distribution of doctors in the big cities deprived vast layers of the population of access to medical services. The country's capital, with only 22% of the population, accounted for 61% of the hospital beds available, rural medicine being nonexistent. According to surveys of the time,[42] in those areas, 14%

---

[42] The most significant of which was carried out by the Agrupación Católica Universitaria (The University Catholic Association).

of workers suffered or had suffered tuberculosis; 13 % had typhoid fever, 36% intestinal parasitism and 31% malaria. Infant mortality was over 60 for every 1,000 live births, and life expectancy was under 65 years.

At the time, only one-third of the dwellings were made of masonry, and in the rural areas, 78% were palm-board huts with earthen floors. Thirty percent of the lowest-income population earned only 4% of the country's total revenue. Social security only covered 53% of the workers.

In his television presentation, Osvaldo Martínez concluded: "It was against this poor, underdeveloped and dependent economy that the U.S. Government's aggressive policy, in the economic field, would be implemented right from the very beginning." [43]

The struggle in the Sierra Maestra encountered opposition in the U.S. government, while the Batista tyranny was bolstered and supported economically and militarily.

Carlos Alzugaray's well-documented book *Crónica de un fraca-so imperial (Chronicle of an imperial failure)*[44] exhaustively details the efforts made in both directions and –when the victory of the revolution was imminent—the steps that were taken to ensure the tyranny was succeeded by a government that defended U.S. interests and could thwart the revolutionary triumph. The author explains that "during the Batista period, the Pentagon supplied over $16 million in military materiel and sophisticated weapons for the Cuban Armed Forces and organized hands-on training for more than 500 Cuban officers in its Panama Canal Zone facilities and in military bases in the United States."[45]

By early 1958, the intentions of the United States were to abort the triumph of the Revolution through the holding of elections, to ensure a transition to a new government that would undermine the armed struggle's legitimacy,[46] but it did not succeed given

[43] Quoted in Osvaldo Martínez.

[44] Carlos Alzugaray: *Crónica de un fracaso imperial (Chronicle of an imperial failure).* Editorial de Ciencias Sociales, La Habana, 2000.

[45] Ibid., p. 99. This author takes it from Morris H. Morley: Imperial State and Revolution. *The United States and Cuba, 1952-1986,* Cambridge University Press, Great Britain, Cambridge, 1987, who, in turn, had taken it from Michael T. Klare: *War Without End: U.S. Planning for the Next Vietnams.* Vintage Books, New York, 1972, p. 278.

[46] Ibid., pp. 94-119.

Batista's obstinacy and began toying with the possibility of a military coup.[47]

By the end of the year, the situation became more and more favorable for the rebel forces. According to Alzugaray:

Many of the documents reflect the frustration and bewilderment of U.S. officials in view of the failure of the United States government's Cuba policy in its attempt to prevent the victory of the Revolution. On the first days following the electoral farce[48] there was an attempt to trace a strategy similar to the one pursued during the year [...]. This alternative soon proved unworkable. Next, there was a futile attempt to speed up Batista's departure from office and his replacement by a Civil-Military Junta, which was also a failure, within an even shorter period of time. Thereafter, the U.S. Government tried to identify a "third force" or "strong man" that would prevent the 26 of July Movement, led by Fidel Castro, from acceding to power. Again, this effort was unsuccessful.[49]

It was then, in late 1958, that, at a National Security Council meeting where the CIA director once again commented on the critical situation in Cuba, President Eisenhower repeatedly "suggested that perhaps Batista should be induced to turn power over to his successor". The CIA director said that "such a move should be made to look like a coup against Batista. The President agreed"[50].

Some days later, on December 23, at a time when the successful struggle in the mountains and plains heralded the tyranny's nearing debacle and the National Security Council analyzed the Cuban situation in greater depth, the CIA director commented: "We ought to prevent a Castro victory."[51] On December 26, a very upset President Eisenhower "expressed a feeling that for one reason or another the main elements of the Cuban situation had not been presented to him" and that "better coordination" was required[52] to prevent the rebels' victory. At a later date the

[47] Ibid., p. 120.
[48] In early November 1958.
[49] Quoted in Carlos Alzugaray, p. 164.
[50] Department of State. Quoted in volume VI, 1991, doc. 186, p. 300. Also in Carlos Alzugaray: Quoted in pp. 182-183.
[51] Department of State: Quoted in pp. 302-303.
[52] Ibid., p. 311.

president told CIA director Allen Dulles that "he did not wish the specifics of covert operations to be presented to the NSC."[53]

There is no doubt about the macabre nature of such an instruction, for the purposes of concealing the most reprehensible actions, the earliest attempts to murder Fidel Castro among them. No wonder the most renowned experts on the two Eisenhower administrations, when referring to his way of steering foreign policy, said: "Covert actions were that policy's essential element [...]. The most covert aspect of Eisenhower's covert actions was his own involvement in them. Although he discussed these privately with the Dulles brothers, he was, for the most part, very cautious in ensuring that, if something came out badly, no incriminating document turned up in the Oval Office." [54]

This crucial moment in Cuba-U.S. relations has also been described by other authors. Jacinto Valdés-Dapena highlights the comments of the then chief of the Central Intelligence Agency's Western Hemisphere Division, Colonel King, in the analysis of the causes behind the Bay of Pigs fiasco:

Colonel King [...] explained that, in late 1958, the CIA made two attempts to prevent the revolutionary forces headed by Fidel Castro from seizing political power in Cuba. The first attempt was in November of 1958, when it contacted Justo Carrillo, of the Montecristi Group, to draw up a plan to prevent the victory of the Rebel Army and remove Fidel Castro as the main leader of the revolutionary movement fighting against the tyranny. The second attempt would take place that same year, in December, when the former U.S. ambassador to Brazil and Peru, William Pawley, with the support of the chief of the CIA Station in Havana, addressed Batista to propose the creation of a junta, to which Batista would hand power over.[55]

This was the foul atmosphere that prevailed in the powerful Northern neighbor, loaded with hostility towards the young Revolution, when victory was attained on January 1st, 1959. This explains the welcome given the murderers and embezzlers, who, as

[53] Idem.
[54] Christopher Andrew: *For the President´s Eyes Only: Secret Intelligence and the American Presidency from Wahington to Bush.* Herper Collins Publishers, New York, 1995. Quoted by Carlos Alzugaray, p. 55.
[55] Jacinto Valdés-Dapena: *Operación Mangosta: preludio de la invasión directa a Cuba (Operation Mongoose: prelude a to direct invasion of Cuba).* Editorial Capitán San Luis, La Habana, 2002, pp. 10-11.

it were, carried the stolen booty on their backs, upon their arrival on U.S. coasts, as it does the threatening statements and denying the country loans that were indispensable for it.

The plots which culminated in the Bay of Pigs invasion. Acts of economic aggression as a means to undermine popular support for the Revolution

Cuba's Agrarian Reform Law, urgently needed to bring about the economic and social development of the nation that could no longer be delayed, prompted the U.S. government's decision to put an end to the Revolution. U.S. official documents confirm this. This can be gathered from the statements by the State Department Assistant Secretary of State for Inter-American Affairs Roy Rubboton, at a meeting of the National Security Council held on January 14, 1960: "[...] the period from January to March might be characterized as the honeymoon period of the Castro government. In April a downward trend in U.S.-Cuban relations had been evident [...] In June we had reached the decision that it was not possible to achieve our objectives with Castro in power and had agreed to undertake the program referred to by Mr. Merchant"[56] to eliminate the Revolution through subversive measures. This was the first step in what would become the first great fiasco in Latin America for the United States: the Bay of Pigs invasion.

The Agrarian Reform Law mainly affected "[...] large national and foreign owners of large land estates of up to 150 000 hectares, extensively exploited or not cultivated at all. The law provided for differed forms of compensation under reasonable terms and plausible time periods. There were simply no funds to do it otherwise. Cuban law, in a non-industrialized country, was much less radical and more generous than the law imposed on Japan by U.S. General Douglas MacArthur at the end of World War II. In the case of Cuba, the United States made an impossible demand: immediate, complete and effective payment."[57]

[56] Department of State. Quoted in volume VI, p. 742.
[57] Proclamation of the National Assembly of the People's Power of the Republic of Cuba, 13 September 1999, Granma newspaper, Tuesday, 14 September 1999, third edition, p. 4.

Referring to this demand, the chairman of the National Assembly of the People's Power explained: "The elimination of large landed estates and the giving of the lands to the peasants was the cause behind Washington's economic aggression and, also, the decision to attack the country militarily." [58]

On June 11, 1959, a U.S. government diplomatic note signed by Secretary of State Christian Herter stated: "The text of Cuba's Agrarian Law causes grave concerns in the U.S. Government with respect to the adequacy of the provisions on compensations to citizens whose properties could be expropriated [...]." Further on, the same note adds: "The United States recognizes that, according to Inter-national Law, a State is empowered, within it jurisdiction, for public purposes and in the absence of contractual provisions or any other agreement to the contrary, to carry out expropriations; however, this right must be accompanied by the corresponding obligation of a State to offer prompt, appropriate and effective compensation." [59]

As assessed in *Law suit brought against the government of the United States by the Cuban people for economic damages to Cuba*: "The compensation conditions summarized in the words 'prompt, appropriate and effective' were clearly an unfair demand which was impossible to meet by a poor country, historically exploited and plundered –precisely by those now demanding it—and that had just been through an intense war of liberation, and expressed the arrogant refusal to accept the rational compensation formula contained in the Agrarian Reform Law." [60]

A curious meeting held on June 24, 1959 between U.S. Secretary of State Christian Herter and Robert Klieberg —who owned the Texas cattle emporium King Ranch— accompanied by the manager of his property in the Cuban province of Camagüey (estimated at three million dollars) threatened with expropriation by the Agrarian Reform Law, is deeply illustrative of how the U.S. government's reaction

---

[58] Ricardo Alarcón and Miguel Álvarez: Quoted in p. 47.

[59] Nicanor León Cotayo: *El Bloqueo a Cuba (The blockade on Cuba)*. Editorial de Ciencias Sociales, La Habana, 1983, pp. 41-42.

[60] Council of State Publishing House: *Demanda del pueblo cubano al Gobierno de Estados Unidos por los daños económicos ocasionados a Cuba (Law suit brought against the government of the United States by the Cuban people for economic damages to Cuba)*, brought before the Provincial Court of the People's Power of Havana on 3 January 2000, La Habana, 2000, pp. 17-18.

to the Cuban Law was little else than support for big business, and that its policy has, ever since, been driven by those economic interests rather than considerations based on International Law and on respect for a nation's independence and sovereignty to decide how to employ its own resources.

Mr. Klieberg told Secretary Herter of his conviction that the U.S. government should adopt a firm position against the Law (described as "communist-inspired"), and that "the best way to achieve the necessary result was by economic pressure", which would not be difficult given Cuba's strong dependence on sugar exports and its privileged place in the U.S. market quota system. According to Klieberg, through the elimination of the Cuban quota "the sugar industry would promptly suffer an abrupt decline, causing widespread further unemployment. The large number of people thus forced out of work would begin to go hungry." According to this representative of big capital, it would bear witness to "the catastrophic nature of Castro's program," ignoring the fact that it would actually bear witness to the genocidal nature of U.S. policy.

The importance that we attach to this meeting –which we describe as methodologically insightful—has to do with the fact that, even though Secretary Herter described the proposed measures as ones "of economic war" and commented that it was one thing to implement them in times of war and quite a different thing to do so in peacetime, this was the line the U.S. government would follow, from a few days following the meeting on, against Cuba.[61]

Those were crucial moments. A thorough analysis of what happened in the following months shows that the U.S. government had, since early in the second half of 1959, been planning and executing actions that would lead to the Bay of Pigs invasion in April of 1961. Among those actions were open economic measures; acts of terrorism and sabotage against the sugar industry designed to frighten the people and, in addition to this, damage their economy, as well as the creation of a *task* force inside the CIA that would repeat the coup against the Jacobo Arbenz government in Guatemala and put an end to the Revolution once and for all.

[61] Department of State: Quoted in volume VI, 1991, PP. 539-541. Quoted in the Proclamation of the National Assembly of the People's Power of the Republic of Cuba, 13 September 1999, *Granma* newspaper, Tuesday, 14 September 1999, third edition, pp. 4-5, from where we take part of the translation into English.

With respect to open economic war measures, a document dated July 1, 1959 already reveals an incipient trend. It was a memorandum from the director of the Department of State's Office for Regional Economic Affairs to the Assistant Secretary of State for Inter-American Affairs, obviously in response to the request that plans to overthrow the Revolution should be prepared. That memorandum described public economic warfare measures inherited from World War II as weapons that could be used. Its recommendations were:

— No loans to stabilize the Cuban balance of payments. If in the first six months following Fidel Castro's victory in Cuba, the U.S. sought to "[...] strengthen the moderates around him in the hope that the extreme leftists would be discredited or shoved aside [...]", "with the signature of the Agrarian Reform Law, it seems clear that our original hope was a vain one; Castro's Government is not the kind worth saving".
— It recalled that there were "many other weapons in the arsenal of economic warfare: prohibition against public and private loans, discriminatory trade treatment, discouragement of investment and impeding of financial transactions."
— The reduction or suspension of the sugar quota would "rally nearly all Cubans behind Castro", and such a decision could make Cuba "[...] more communist influenced or intolerably anti-American", such that "Cuban relations with the U.S. (would) deteriorate further". For this author, "cutting the sugar quota is the ultimate weapon in relation with Cuba." [62]

The fact that this proposal was approved by the State Department's Assistant Secretary of State for Inter-American Affairs Roy Rubbotom[63] lends weight to the official's above-quoted words of January 14, 1960 and confirms that plans to overthrow the Revolution started in mid-1959, after the approval of the Agrarian Reform Law.

---

[62] See *Cuban Economic Prospects, 1959 and Proposed U.S. Action*, memorandum from the director of the Office for Regional Economic Affairs of the Department of State, dated 1 July 1959, sent for the consideration of the Assistant Secretary of State for Inter-American Affairs. Department of State: Quoted in volume VI, pp. 546-551.

[63] On the memorandum's margin, Rubbotom stamped this laconic answer: "Yes." Proclamation of the National Assembly of the People's Power of the Republic of Cuba, p. 5.

There was another measure of this sort which was of great significance. On July 8, 1959 the congressional response to the Cuban Agrarian Reform Law was made public: to grant the President greater powers to suspend assistance to any country that "confiscated U.S. property without fair compensation," a measure that, without directly mentioning Cuba's Agrarian Reform Law, was devised to put pressure on and blackmail Cuba. The club was thus being raised to announce its imminent use.

At the time, both executive and congressional bodies heatedly debated –as attested to by declassified documents of the time— whether a more appropriate measure of reprisal would be to suspend the Cuban sugar quota in the U.S. market, and they decided to hold out for the time being because of such a measure's irreversibility. Another public economic warfare measure implemented was the cancellation (27 August 1959) by the American Foreign Power Company, a subsidiary of Electric Bond and Share, of $15 million in financing for its branch in Cuba, the Compañía Cubana de Electricidad, whose bonds it had signed the previous week.[64]

On September 9, 1959, the director for the Caribbean area of the Office of Foreign Trade of the U.S. Department of Commerce, Al Powell, reaffirmed that anti-Cuban measures were being prepared and taking shape in the U.S."[...] for the purposes of hitting Castro in the head."[65]

During the last week of October of 1959, plans for the reduction of the Cuban sugar quota were specified at the meeting of representatives of beet and cane sugar producers from the United States, Puerto Rico and Hawaii with Assistant Secretaries of State Thomas Mann and Roy Rubottom. According to a news agency cable that gathered impressions from the participants "[...] The criticisms leveled at the United States by the revolutionary leader have increased support for the idea of reducing sugar imports from Cuba."[66]

The Cuban government clearly perceived the U.S. government's economic warfare measures as a reprisal for Cuban actions aimed at political and economic independence and social justice.

[64] Nicanor León Cotayo: *El Bloqueo a Cuba (The Blockade on Cuba)*, p. 58
[65] Ibid., p. 59. Also by the same author: *Sitiada la esperanza (Hope besieged)*, pp. 32-33.
[66] Nicanor León Cotayo: *Sitiada la esperanza (Hope besieged)*, p. 34.

In his speech of October 21st, 1959, Fidel Castro expressed: "[...] we are practically being told that if the Agrarian Reform is carried through, we will strangle you economically [...]. In other words, that on top of having 600,000 unemployed, on top of having a production per capita of 300 pesos, on top of having one fifth of the hospitals we need, of the schools we need and of the most basic things we need, on top of all that, if we do something to get rid of all that, they threaten to starve us."

Acts of terrorism and sabotage against the sugar industry, the backbone of Cuba's economy, constituted a second dimension of measures aimed at overthrowing the Revolution.

The purpose of these acts of aggression and the relationship between the public measures and subversive actions were exposed by the leader of the Revolution in his October 26th speech, after two U.S. airplanes bombed the country's capital, killing 2 and wounding 45 people: "That is, they are threatening the people of Cuba, on one hand, with economic strangulation, with taking away their sugar quota; and, on the other hand, subjecting them to terror, so that scourged, on one hand, by economic problems and on the other by terror, the Cuban people will abandon their great revolutionary process, abandon the aspiration of establishing justice on our soil."[67] An outstanding role, in this connection, was played by the bombing of sugar mills and sugarcane plantations that we talked about at the beginning, in which the young worker Walter Sosillo was killed. To carry out these aggressions, an open economic warfare measure was simultaneously implemented: the United Kingdom was pressurized into canceling the sale of 15 combat airplanes to Cuba which was being negotiated at the time.

Though we have not described them here so as not to stray from our topic, it is necessary to understand the internal dynamics of the subversive actions that were carried out by the U.S. Embassy-based local CIA station at the time, aimed at encouraging and leading counterrevolutionary opposition and other terrorist actions. All of these actions, including those aimed at assassinating the leader of the Revolution, were within the framework of powers granted the CIA from the time of its creation in 1947 and were part of the ordinary work of the local CIA station based in the U.S. embassy in the Cuban capital and of those who coordinated them from headquarters.

[67] Ibid., pp. 34-36.

Therefore, it was not necessary to wait for the creation of a special *task force* to execute many of them.

Witnessing a significant increase during the first months of 1960 (10 in January, 12 in February, 15 in March), the terrorist actions by air against Cuban sugarcane plantations and industries characterized this early stage of actions from abroad, and doubtlessly posed a serious threat to the economy's decisive sector, and they were complemented by other numerous actions carried out from overseas for the same purpose. Those actions had surely already been incorporated into the general plan, devised by the *task force,* to overthrow the Revolution, which, as we will see shortly, took shape in March of 1960.

A third line of action was the creation of that *task force* which – using the schemes applied in Guatemala—would be responsible for devising and executing plans to destroy the Revolution. The information that indicates that part of CIA and State Department plans were approved by President Eisenhower in late October may refer to some of its initial measures. The truth is that, by year-end, this *task force* was already organized, though officially it was created in January. In 1959, Jack Esterline, Chief of the CIA station in Venezuela, had been summoned from Caracas to assume its direction.

The meeting of the National Security Council of 17 March 1960. The *Program of Economic Pressures against the Castro regime*

A decisive moment in the implementation of economic warfare measures against Cuba was the meeting in which the U.S. government agreed to eliminate the Revolution through the plans that culminated in the Bay of Pigs invasion. The same officials that had led the coup against Arbenz in Guatemala a few years before had worked intensely in their preparation. To supplement the military plans, the first subversive plan against the Cuban economy, combining open pressures with covert measures, was approved the same day.

According to the minutes of the United States National Security Council meeting of March 17th, 1960, both the *Covert Action Program against Castro* –which included military and propaganda measures as well as the creation of a counterrevolutionary opposition in Cuba—and another document titled *Program of Economic Pressures against the Castro Regime* –encompassing economic warfare measures designed to create such a state of dissatisfaction among the Cuban people with respect to their basic needs that they would have no other choice than to support the forces that immediately started to train abroad to overthrow to the Revolution—were approved on that date. Although it has not been declassified, according to the adopted minutes for the meeting, the following aspects were included in it:[68]

1. Convenience of cutting off oil supplies to Cuba. When arguing for this measure, the then Secretary of Treasury Robert Anderson explained that, with respect to Cuba's economy, "the effect would be devastating on them within a month or six weeks".
2. Steps to suspend any relationship between the two countries, rendering the 1903 and 1934 trade agreements ineffective.
3. Ability to persuade the U.S. businesspeople established in the country to withdraw and to contribute to economic chaos, as well as the suspension of new investments.
4. Reduction of U.S. tourism in order to diminish the entry of foreign currency into Cuba.

So far, little emphasis has been placed on the common origin of long-term anti-Cuban economic measures and the preparation of the plans to put an end to the Revolution by force, which add to the criminal and subversive essence of economic warfare on Cuba. Little emphasis has been made, too, on a methodologically important aspect regarding that common origin: economic warfare was systematized as a consubstantial part of the Bay of Pigs invasion. From the outset, the economic war on Cuba has had this sharply subversive character, which has remained unchanged, though in different contexts, for more than forty years.

This means that the economic war against Cuba has always been part of a wider system of actions designed to destroy the Revolution. The role assigned economic warfare measures has been that of creating internal conditions of hunger and disease, so that the people

[68] Department of State: in volume VI, 1991, document 486, pp. 861-863. Appears translated in Tomás Diez Acosta: *La guerra encubierta (The covert war)*. Editora Política, La Habana, 1997, document 3, pp. 21-23.

have no other choice but to surrender to their enemies. It has no other name but genocide, and it is thus recognized in international juridical documents.

A report by State Department Official I. D. Mallory dated April 6, 1960, declassified in 1991, seems to reflect a certain debate on how to achieve greater internal support, in Cuba, for subversive operations that were being organized at the time, and it highlighted the purpose of the economic pressures that were being applied: "If the above are accepted or cannot be successfully countered, it follows that every possible means should be undertaken promptly to weaken the economic life of Cuba. If such a policy is adopted, it should be the result of a positive decision which would call forth a line of action which, while as adroit and inconspicuous as possible, makes the greatest inroads in denying money and supplies to Cuba, to decrease monetary and real wages, to bring about hunger, desperation and *overthrow the government*" (the italics in the quote are ours).[69]

On June 27, 1960, the U.S. State Department made one of the most significant assessments to launch the public economic warfare measures, with the participation of the State, Treasury and Defense secretaries and senior representatives of the White House, CIA, Department of Agriculture and Department of State staffs. Based on a long list of points to be clarified prepared by the White House representatives, there was debate about:

1. The procedures to implement economic measures against Cuba, in particular the need or not to invoke the 1917 *Trading with the Enemy Act* or the legal scope of the president's approval, on March 17, of the *Program of Economic Pressures against the Castro Regime*.
2. The scope of the economic measures being debated on. In this regard, the question was how far to go with those measures. There was consensus that severe economic measures should be adopted against Cuba, the U.S. having the will and ability to carry the economic measures against Cuba to their logical

---

[69] Department of State: in volume VI, 1991, p. 885. Quoted in the Proclamation of the National Assembly of the People's Power of the Republic of Cuba, 13 September 1999, *Granma* newspaper, Tuesday, 14 September 1999, third edition, p. 5.

conclusion. The secretary of State: "[...] expressed agreement with Secretary Anderson that nibbling was no good, that we should either take actions which will hurt or leave well enough alone"; according to the secretary of the Treasury, the application of some measures "would be a great mistake unless the U.S. Government is prepared to go all the way", and "[...] he expressed the opinion that the group seemed to be in general agreement that we should take all or none. He urged that, time-wise, the faster the better. The Cubans are now in trouble over their petroleum situation and we should not delay in following up on the situation"

3. The amount of the sugar quota reduction. The same day of this meeting, Congress passed the sugar legislation giving the president authority to reduce the Cuban quota in the U.S. market in the amount he deemed convenient.

4. Critical situation regarding oil in Cuba. Possibility that the government would intervene the oil companies.

5. The government's policy on U.S. companies trading with Cuba until that moment.

6. On the potential support or rejection in Latin America and Europe of the economic measures devised. Measures to attract OAS member countries to the U.S. position. European, mainly English, support of that position. "Our European allies are pretty well convinced of the correctness of the U.S. position, vis-á-vis Castro" and "our arms policy" and "[...] the British have been cooperating very well in the current oil situation."

7. Similarities with the measures applied against Mossadegh in Iran in 1953.

8. Role of economic pressures within the context of the wider subversive program approved.

There is no question that this meeting set the basic guidelines for the launching of the economic warfare actions carried out thereafter and geared towards creating a tense internal situation. It most important components were:

1. Reduction of Cuba's 1960 sugar quota by 700 000 tons, a decision made by the president on July 3 of that year, making use of the prerogative granted by Congress seven days before.

70

Cuba's dependence on the U.S. sugar market during the whole republican period had been such that we cannot accuse the head of the executive or his advisers of having been naïve to assume that this measure would totally destabilize the economy and cause confusion and chaos and, thereby, lead to major opposition towards the Revolution.

2. Suspension, on September 29, of the operations of the Nicaro nickel concentrate plant, in Oriente.[70]

It should be noted that the day before this measure became official, the first air supply to the "insurgent forces" that already operated in the Escambray mountains had been carried out, as well as the first introduction of weapons by sea,[71] all as part of the parallel *Covert Action Program against the Castro Regime*. That night, Havana was shaken by the explosion of several bombs; during a popular demonstration, the leader of the Revolution announced the creation of the Committees for the Defense of the Revolution.

3. On September 30, the Department of State announced having recommended to U.S. citizens "to refrain" from traveling to Cuba unless for "urgent reasons".

4. That same month the government started to apply pressures to cut credits previously granted by private banks.

5. On October 19, the Department of State took what has later been described as the second definitive step towards the establishment of the blockade, with the announcement of "general control measures to ban U.S. exports to Cuba"; a ban on the sale, transfer or contract of any U.S. ship to the Government of Cuba or Cuban citizens; it also announced it was applying pressures on the Canadian government to convince it to back the economic measures against Cuba.

When the undersecretaries of State and Trade submitted this measure to the president in the October 13 meeting, it was predicted that "it will have a very good effect in making the United States position clear, *including an encouraging effect on the*

---

[70] Group of Authors: *Agresiones de Estados Unidos a Cuba revolucionaria (Aggressions by the United Status against revolutionary Cuba)*. Sociedad Cubana de Derecho Internacional, Editorial de Ciencias Sociales, La Habana, 1989, p. 240.

[71] *CIA Inspector General Report on the Bay of Pigs Operation*, paragraph 4, item 41.

dissident groups now becoming active in Cuba" (the italics in the quotation are ours). The related note from the Assistant Secretary of State for Inter-American Affairs to Secretary Christian Herter, dated October 19, said that those measures *"will contribute to the growing dissatisfaction and unrest in the country. It will also bolster the morale of the opposition groups now active in Cuba and elsewhere".*[72] We should not overlook any of those assessments, since these are the first instances of recognition, on behalf of high U.S. officials, of the purpose of the economic measures.

6. U.S. Government decision declaring illegal the sale, transfer or leasing of any U.S. ship to the Government of Cuba or to a Cuban citizen, effective as from 12:00 p.m., October 20, 1960.[73]

7. In a press conference held on October 20, 1960, Canadian Prime Minister John Diefenbaker revealed the petition by the Eisenhower Administration to impose an embargo on Canada's trade with Cuba.[74]

8. In December, by presidential decision, the entirety of the sugar quota was cut in the U.S. market for the first three months of 1961. The gradual nature of this process reflects, first of all, the intention to imply that the decisions were temporary, valid only as long as the revolutionary government was not overthrown; and, also, the brevity of time in which the operation was expected to succeed.

9. On March 10, 1961, the Department of Commerce issues an exports bulletin adding 16 items to the list of food products and medicines that could not be shipped to Cuba without a special license. At the time, the Council of the Chambers of Commerce of the United States adopted a resolution requesting "an immediate and complete embargo on Cuban exports to the United States." In this environment, prior to the Bay of Pigs invasion, Republican representative from California, Craighoesmer, proposed an amendment according to which U.S. ships and airplanes could stop any ship approaching Cuba. Some, when commenting on this proposal, recalled the incident early that month, when the U.S. cargo carrier *Janet Quinn*

---

[72] Department of State: in volume VI, 1991, pp. 1084 and 1091
[73] Group of Authors: *Agresiones de Estados Unidos a Cuba revolucionaria*, p. 240.
[74] Idem.

collided, in the Strait of Gibraltar, against the Soviet tanker *Trud*, which was sailing towards Havana. The Soviets said that the cargo carrier had charged against the Soviet tanker deliberately to affect fuel shipments to Cuba.[75]

10. On March 13, 1961, one month before the Bay of Pigs invasion, a pirate gunboat attacked the Hermanos Díaz oil refinery in Santiago de Cuba, damaging equipment and several tanks and killing several people.

11. On March 31, practically on the eve of the invasion, President Kennedy completely eliminated the Cuban sugar quota in the U.S. market. This can be regarded –and it is no exaggeration— a kind of economic ultimatum to add followers to those who thought that only by eliminating the Revolution could the Cuban economy return to normality.

[75] Ibid., p. 242

CHAPTER II Operation Mongoose and advances in the planning of economic warfare actions against Cuba

On April 27, 1961, scarcely seven days after the debacle on Cuban soil, the recently created Department of State Operations Center forwarded a so-called *Cuba Plan* to the National Security Council, which included open and covert actions which were to be undertaken against the largest of the West Indies after the Bay of Pigs fiasco.

The reticence with respect to applying the *Trading with the Enemy Act* against Cuba shown a year before, at the meeting held on June 27, 1960, should not to be forgotten. Such a measure was considered exceptional and, in the mid 60's, its application was believed unnecessary. It was thought that the implementation of a plan similar to that used against Arbenz in Guatemala, without many changes, would solve the Cuban situation. In addition to this, the *Program of Economic Pressures against the Castro Regime*, approved by the president on March 17, 1960, largely replaced that Act, and, under its mantle, both the subversive measures already mentioned and the Department of State regulations of October 19, 1960, which virtually launched the economic blockade against the island, were carried out. Obviously, as a result of the impact of the Bay of Pigs fiasco some days before, that criterion dramatically changed.

In their book The Fish is Red[1], U.S. authors Warren Hinckle and William Turner masterfully describe President Kennedy's mood,

---

[1] Warren Hinkle and William Turner: *The Fish is Red. The Story of the Secret War Against Castro,* Harper & Row Publishers, New York, 1981.

who scarcely three months after arriving at the White House, had to confess before the world responsibility for the defeat suffered at the Bay of Pigs. The mood was shared by the Administration as a whole. This can be readily perceived in the economic measures proposed in the Cuba Plan, which some months later would be a reality: the application on Cuba of the Trading with the Enemy Act; the reduction, through amendments or regulations, of food and medicine exports to Cuba and intensified acts of economic sabotage, so that nothing but scorched-earth —what Rome achieved in Carthage once—was left of the small island that dared challenge the Empire.

Another idea which served as a pretext for the thorough execution of their new plans was present in these proposals: to bring pressures to bear on OAS member States so that they would apply individual economic measures and approve a collective "quarantine" that would completely isolate the young Revolution in the hemisphere.

The document openly promoted a line of action that has always accompanied economic warfare and, in general, all subversive actions: espionage. It called for the development of "the fullest and most accurate intelligence possible on the attitude of the Cuban people towards Castro. Such intelligence is essential before deciding upon possible courses of decisive action." It stated that if such espionage produced support of the Revolution, what needed to be done was "to change the views of the maximum number of Cubans" through "[...] slower methods 'such' as quarantine and [other] efforts [...]."[2] The policy expressed by the aforementioned State Department official, on April 6, 1960, continued —and has continued over forty years later—: "[...] the only possible way of alienating internal support is through dissatisfaction and discouragement based on discontent over economic difficulties [...]."[3]

At the National Security Council's April 27, 1961 meeting, the president did not yet make a decision with respect to suppressing trade with Cuba, an item that was postponed, "[...] pending developments in Cuba in the next few weeks." Thus began the sinister process of designing a top-secret scorched-earth policy, which would only emerge by year-end with Operation Mongoose.

All U.S. embassies in Latin America were immediately notified of a campaign approved on that date, which called on them to work

[2] Department of State: In volume X, 1997, pp. 391-396.
[3] See note 69 in previous chapter

towards continental measures against Cuba that were to include economic and political isolation. To carry this project through, the 8th OAS Meeting of Consultation was also held in January of 1962 within the framework of Operation Mongoose, and it served as pretext to set up an economic blockade on the island.

A new assessment of the operational situation: *Facts, Estimates and Projections*

On May 2, 1961, a report titled *Facts, Estimates and Projections* is jointly drawn up by the working group of the State Department Bureau of Intelligence and Investigations and the CIA Office of National Estimates. Identifying what were believed to be the Revolution's economic strengths, opportunities and weaknesses, it laid the foundation for the measures that would be applied to weaken the former and exacerbate the latter. The economic vulnerabilities included "[...] its foreign exchange position, spare parts and raw material shortages, lack of sufficient technical and managerial personnel, declining per capita income and consumer shortages and the growing black market," in response to which the proposal of deploying"[...] the Trading with the Enemy Act against Cuba [...] and a campaign of limited sabotage against Cuba's industries and the services" was again advanced. The report added that "[...] A program of extensive sabotage or a complete blockade would cause serious economic breakdown, especially in urban and industrial sectors."[4]

In this document, one can already sense the atmosphere that would characterize Operation Mongoose in the economic sphere and, from that point on, the economic war on Cuba.

Also on May 2, 1961, in the context of a reassessment of the plans against Cuba, the CIA sends White House staff member Richard Goodwin its new proposals for covert actions to damage the Cuban economy. The CIA reported it had covert agents in the six Cuban provinces that existed then, who could participate in these actions, plus "[...] some additional ones who might be infiltrated, who could "[...] carry out acts of sabotage". It stressed that "individual

---

[4] Department of State: ob. cit., volume X, 1997, pp. 417-422.

acts of sabotage are possible with relatively few men and small amounts of material [...]" and that they had capacity for maritime actions[5] in which weapons could be disembarked and buried to carry out "[...] under water sabotage of shipping and small raider operations [...]." It added that the CIA had an air division (B- 26 bombers and transport C-46 and C-54 airplanes) that could be used in attacks against "chosen targets," including "[...] refineries, power plants, tire plants [...]", which, if successful, could have the effect of "extensive sabotage."[6]

CIA involvement in covert actions against the Cuban economy through agents based in the country ("in every province," according to the declassified document) cannot be stressed enough. These actions served not only as a means to provide the U.S. government with information about the impact of its measures on Cuba's economic and social life, enabling it to adjust and enhance them, but also as instruments for acts of sabotage and terrorism, most of which were extremely harmful.

This subversive aspect of U.S. government actions is not usually mentioned in research papers and chronologies about the economic war on Cuba published in both the United States and our country, something which dims our understanding of that war as a complex system of measures in which open and covert actions are intimately related, and in which the covert measures reinforce and multiply the effects of the blockade and other public measures.

Cuba and Communism in the Hemisphere

On May 4, 1961, the National Security Council presented a document, entitled *Cuba and Communism in the Hemisphere*, prepared by an Inter-agency Working Group on Cuba headed by Undersecretary of State for Political Affairs Paul Nitze. After analyzing how U.S. interests were threatened by the survival of the Cuban Revolution and Cuba's internal situation, its trends and vulnerabilities, Nitze expressed his support for the proposals advanced some days before to put an end to the revolution.

[5] The remnants of the infiltration teams created in the preparatory phase of the *Program of Covert Actions Against the Castro Regime*, approved in March 1960.
[6] Department of State: In volume X, 1997, pp. 428-430.

Item 7 of the document proposed measures to quarantine the island and weaken its government and, in addition to increased continental isolation and an action plan to be implemented through the OAS, the application of the *Trading with the Enemy Act* to exacerbate "[...] foreign exchange difficulties [...]."[7]

On May 5, 1961, the National Security Council approved the document *Cuba and Communism in the Hemisphere*. The final decision to quarantine the island and to invoke the *Trading with the Enemy Act* had not yet been adopted: the imperative, then, was to create the needed conditions. President Kennedy's decision was recorded in the minutes thus: "Agreed not to impose an immediate trade embargo on Cuba."

The internal debate surrounding the adoption of the most appropriate measures against Cuba can be appreciated in the agreements. The Secretary of State had to analyze the effects of an "embargo" on U.S. trade with Cuba, and the consensus was that, when imposed, it should be as far-reaching as possible.

With respect to Latin America, the meeting stressed the need to step up pressures to sever diplomatic relations and, among other measures, of "limiting economic relations with Cuba."[8]

Prior to this meeting, President Kennedy's special adviser had recommended that he abstain from invoking the *Trading with the Enemy Act* or any other legislation. He had told him, verbatim: "Possible economic sanctions against Castro should be carefully reviewed; it's not clear what their effect would be or whether they should be applied by the Trading with the Enemy Act, the Battle Law, or a direct embargo."[9] We have no doubt whatsoever that describing the main economic measure against Cuba, adopted just a few months later, as an "embargo" was the result of this "careful review", which even altered the very meaning of the word.

The note made by another participant at the same National Security Council meeting of May 5, 1961 is very eloquent and clearly reflects the prevailing spirit at the time, which would gradually consolidate itself in later months until the establishment of the blockade in February of the following year and the deployment of an unprecedented secret war against the Cuban economy: "It was decided that if we do invoke trade restrictions we will go all the

---

[7] Ibid., pp. 459-475.
[8] Department of State: In document 205, pp. 481-483.
[9] Ibid., document 203, pp. 476-479.

way. We will invoke the restrictions the first time we link them to some situation. It may be necessary to induce a situation, although Castro will probably soon create the situation himself."[10]

The CIA's first subversive plan against the Cuban economy after the Bay of Pigs: the *Program of Covert Actions to Weaken the Castro Regime*, a foretaste of what, in the field of direct subversion, would assume the form of Operation Mongoose

Dated May 19, 1961, the CIA document entitled *Program of Covert Actions to Weaken the Castro Regime* was one of the annexes to *Cuba and Communism in the Hemisphere,* drafted by the Inter-agency Working Group headed by Undersecretary Nitze, and included CIA proposals sent to the White House early in the month. In addition to espionage, stronger counterrevolutionary bands in Cuba's mountains, propaganda and other subversive actions, it called for acts of sabotage against selected targets, prioritizing facilities such as refineries, electric power plants, short-wave stations, radio and TV installations, strategic freeway bridges and railroads, military and naval facilities and equipment and industrial plants and sugar refineries. The report mentioned that "[...] This will first require building up unprecedented capabilities through recruitment, training and infiltration of sabotage teams."[11]

These are the plans Jacinto Valdés-Dapena refers to when he says: "In July 1961, a U.S. Central Intelligence Agency plan aimed at stepping up subversive actions against Cuba became known." Emphasizing these subversive actions and economic warfare actions described above, he added: "This plan set up guidelines for the creation of a broad resistance organization that was subject to CIA control, [...] to support counterrevolutionary organizations in the country capable of executing underground operations; and to create bases for primary operations in the United States."[12]

[10] Ibid., document 206, pp. 484-488.
[11] Ibid., document 223, pp. 554-560
[12] Jacinto Valdés-Dapena Vivanco: *La CIA contra Cuba.* La actividad subversiva de la CIA y la contrarrevolución (1961-1968). (The CIA against Cuba. CIA suversive activity and counterrevolution). Editorial Capitán San Luis, Havana, 2002, p. 45.

Such measures were already being implemented, as functions inherent to the CIA and other branches of the intelligence community, and did not require express presidential approval. Later, they were included in Operation Mongoose, as part of a broader concept of anti-Cuban subversion and, following recommendations from the Taylor Commission, the Administration as a whole became the subject behind the actions that were carried out, exceeding, in its involvement, the role played by the CIA in actions prior to the *Covert Action Program Against the Castro Regime* that culminated with the Bay of Pigs invasion.

On June 13, 1961, President Kennedy was presented with the results of the analysis on the causes of the Bay of Pigs fiasco, made by the commission headed by General Maxwell Taylor. Its conclusion was that operations like those which led to the Bay of Pigs "[...] should be planned and executed by a governmental mechanism capable of bringing into play, in addition to military and covert techniques, all other forces, political, economic, ideological and intelligence, which can contribute to its success. No such mechanism presently exists but should be created [...]"[13]. It had a major impact on measures later implemented against Cuba, including economic warfare actions.

State terrorism against Cuba was taking shape, particularly state terrorism against the Cuban economy.

The report concluded with the recommendation that measures against Cuba should be reconsidered "[...] in the light of all presently known factors" and that "[...] new guidance (should) be provided for political, military, *economic* and propaganda actions against Castro"[14] (the italicized word is ours).

On August 22, 1961, upon returning from the sessions of the Inter-American Economic and Social Council held in Punta del Este,

[13] Department of State: In document 233, *"Memorandum No. 3 From the Cuba Study Group to President Kennedy. Conclusions of the Cuban Study Group"*, pp. 603-605.

[14] Taken from The Bay of Pigs: New Evidence from Documents and Testimony of the Kennedy Administration, the Anti-Castro Resistance, and Brigade 2506, Part 7: Post-mortem results, document 6, Memorandum for the President of the Research Group on Cuba, Immediate causes of the failure of Operation Zapata. The Taylor Report is in Department of State, vol X, pp. 576-606. It appears, translated, in *Playa Girón: la gran conjura (The Bay of Pigs:the great conspiracy)*. Editorial Capitán San Luis, La Habana, 1991, pp. 38-108.

Uruguay, where the Alliance for Progress was established, the appointed head of the White House Task Force on Cuba, Richard Goodwin, sent a memorandum to President Kennedy in which he suggested the need to "Quietly intensify [...] economic pressure. This means selectively discouraging those doing business with Castro, aiming sabotage activities at key sectors of the industrial plant, such as refineries, invoking the Trading with the Enemy Act upon the first apparent provocation and focusing some expert attention on the problem of economic warfare." Further on, he added: "Continue and step up covert activities aimed, in the first instance, at the destruction of economic units and diversion of resources into anti-underground activities. This should be done by Cuban members of Cuban groups with political aims and ideologies [...]."[15]

We leave it up to the reader to label such proposals, evaluated at the highest federal level. What blossoms out of these proposals is economic warfare as a system, with public and secret measures, a system which has continued to be used, uninterruptedly, ever since.

On August 30, 1961, at a White House meeting of the Cuba Task Force headed by Richard Goodwin, in addition to other measures against Cuba, it was proposed that: "Our covert actions would now be directed towards the destruction of targets important to the economy, e.g. refineries and plants using U.S. equipment, etc. This would be done within the general framework of covert operations which is based on the principle that para-military activities ought to be carried out through Cuban revolutionary groups[16] which have a potential for establishing an effective political opposition to Castro within Cuba. Within this principle we will do all we can to identify and suggest targets whose destruction will have the maximum economic impact." Another item addressed there and noted in a memorandum from Richard Goodwin to President Kennedy, was the statement that: "we will intensify our surveillance of Cuban trade with other countries and especially U.S. subsidiaries in third countries and then employ informal methods to attempt to divert this trade, depriving Cuba of markets and sources of supply." The impact of

---

[15] Department of State: In volume X, 1997, document 256, pp. 640-641.
[16] The U.S. government's manipulation of the issue of counterrevolutionary emigration in its dirty war against Cuba should be noted.

this facet of economic warfare had until then is revealed by the phrase with which the previous paragraph ended: "I understand that we have already had a few successes in this effort."[17]

What surveillance did they refer to? What informal methods were being used? Spying on each and every Cuban action to strengthen its economy and broaden its trade is the answer to the first of these questions, both then and now. All sorts of "informal methods," the use of pressures and blackmail against other countries. We can say it again and again: both then and now.

Legislative basis of the most important public economic action developed

On September 4, 1961, the U.S. Congress, discussing the Foreign Assistance Act of 1961, prohibited all forms of assistance to the Cuban government and, as a means to achieve this, authorized the president to establish and maintain a total "embargo" on the totality of trade between the United States and Cuba. This legislative act is the most significant precedent to the establishment of the blockade in early February 1962. It gave the latter a legal foundation and it was carried out as congressional measure, but it was entirely in line with the steps the president was hastily taking in the shadows as part of Operation Mongoose. To date, it has not been exposed as just another measure of that operation: it is not necessary.

The truth of the matter is that authorization was needed to apply it in its entirety, and its reach cannot be fully grasped if we ignore the framework of immensely subversive actions against the Cuban economy of which it was part. Here we have another result of the "careful review" which, with respect to invoking the Trading with the Enemy Act, was recommended to President Kennedy when, on May 5 of that year, he received the document *Cuba and Communism in the Hemisphere*.

Such authorization was needed, too, to take actions against Cuba "to their logical conclusion," as agreed upon at National Security Council meetings. It was the power then granted the President on all matters relating to the blockade on Cuba that he renounced in 1996,

---

[17] Department of State: In volume X, 1997, pp. 645-646.

by approving the Helms-Burton Act and codifying all blockade-related measures.

Operation Mongoose begins

On November 3, 1961, Operation Mongoose begins.

On this date President Kennedy authorized what was known only to a very small circle of officials involved in its execution: the development of a new subversive program against Cuba, under that name, which would include the various options for aggressive action that had been handled and integrated under the principles of the Taylor Commission.[18] At that meeting, Attorney-General Robert Kennedy said: "My idea is to stir things up on the island with espionage, sabotage, general disorder, run and operated by Cubans themselves with every group but Bastitaites and Communists. Do not know if we will be successful in overthrowing Castro but we have nothing to lose in my estimate."[19]

On November 6, 1961, the head of the White House Cuban Task Force Richard Goodwin, in a conversation with an undersecretary of State, mentions a major aspect of the newly-undertaken Operation Mongoose: it would include covert and non-covert economic measures. In order to understand the true reach of the Operation, this differentiation is of paramount importance, as both types of actions were combined in a single system which covertly destroyed economic targets or sectors that, thanks to the "legal" persecution to which these were subjected around the world, were difficult to replace.[20]

It is useful to look at the atmosphere of persecution which surrounds Cuba's foreign economic affairs in the last documents quoted, which describe the economic war against Cuba in the new period that was starting, and which not only existed on paper but was scrupulously and thoroughly materialized. It is no accident that the first of the five points presented by Cuba for the settlement of the Missile Crisis, one year later, was precisely that persecution of Cuban trade across the world must stop.

---

[18] An in-depth analysis of this process is made by Jacinto Valdés-Dapena: *Operación Mangosta*

[19] Department of State: ob. cit., volume X, 1997, document 270, pp. 666-667.

[20] Ibid., pp. 666-667.

On November 30, 1961, President Kennedy signed the memorandum approving Operation Mongoose. General Edward G. Lansdale is appointed to lead the operation team and the proposals for actions received from the governmental Departments and Agencies involved –the embryo of what would later be the Operation's measures, including economic ones—are circulated. The actions would be carried out under the supervision of the (Enlarged) Special Group headed by General Maxwell Taylor and Attorney-General Robert Kennedy.[21]

The economic warfare measures of Operation Mongoose

On January 18, 1962, General Lansdale presented the government Departments and Agencies involved with the document entitled *The Cuba Project* (*Operation Mongoose*), a plan which hoped to destroy the Revolution in a matter of months. It contained 13 economic measures, which supplemented and developed previous plans and actions of the kind, and laid the groundwork for what would become the United States economic war against the Cuban Revolution. It also contained 4 intelligence, 6 political, 4 psychological (propaganda) and 5 military tasks.[22]

The economic measures section included the following tasks:

"Task 11: State to prepare recommendations to the President on U.S. trade with Cuba, as a follow-up to OAS meeting. (If the minimum result of the meeting is to condemn Cuba as an accomplice of the Sino-Soviet bloc and adoption of a general statement that Cuba represents a threat to peace and security in the Hemisphere, State is prepared to recommend to the President that remaining trade between the United States and Cuba be barred).

"Task 12: State to plan, with Commerce and other U.S. agencies, on how to halt the *diversion* of *vital* items in the Cuban trade. Due date 15 February. Cooperation of other OAS nations, particularly Canada and Mexico, is to be explored by State" (italics in original).

---

[21] Ibid., document 278.

[22] Department of State: In volume X, document The Cuba Project, pp. 713 and ss. See also: Jacinto Valdés-Dapena: *Operación Mangosta (Operation Mongoose)*, pp. 34-54.

"Task 13: State with Commerce and others involved, to plan on how to make a 'positive list' of items to Latin America be subject to the same licensing procedures as applied to such shipments to other parts of the free world. Due 15 February".

"Task 14: State to obtain from Commerce proposal to amend present export control of technical data (petrochemical, communications equipment) so that Cuba is treated the same as the Sino-Soviet bloc. Due 15 February".

"Task 15: State by 15 February to submit recommendations on issuance of transportation order (T-3) under authority of the Defense Production Act of 1950 (enacted September 8 1950, 64 Stat. 798, et seq.) forbidding U.S.-owned vessels to engage in trade with Cuba".

"Task 16: State plan for 15 February on feasible extension of U.S. port treatment now given to Bloc and Cuban vessels to *charter* vessels of Bloc and Cuba (Treasure to advise on this)" (italics in original).

"Task 17: State to report by 15 February on feasibility of harassing Bloc shipping by refusing entry into U.S. ports (statedly for security reasons) if vessels have called or will call at Cuban ports".

"Task 18: *Two and a half lines of source text not declassified*". (italics in original).

"Task 19: State to report by 15 February on possibilities for obtaining the discreet cooperation of the National Foreign Trade Council to urge U.S. shippers to refuse to ship on vessels which call at Cuban ports (Commerce to assist on this)".

"Task 20: State to report by 15 February on possibilities of obtain the discreet cooperation of the U.S. Chamber of Commerce and the National Association of Manufacturers to influence the U.S. firms having subsidiaries abroad to adhere to the spirit of U.S. economic sanctions (Commerce to assist on this)".

"Task 21: CIA to submit plan by 15 February for inducing failures in food crops in Cuba (*1 line of source text not declassified*)". (italics in original).

"Task 22: State to report by February 15 on status of plan to gain cooperation of NATO allies (bilaterally and in the NATO forum, as appropriate). Objective is to persuade these nations to take steps to isolate Cuba from the West".

"Task 23: State to report by 15 February on status of actions undertaken with Japan, which has comparatively significant trade with Cuba, along lines similar to those with NATIO nations".

"Task 24: CIA to submit plan by February on disruption of the supply of Cuban nickel to the Soviet Union [*3 lines of source text not declassified*)". (italics in original).

But the measures against the Cuban economy which were part of Operation Mongoose not only included public measures of economic, commercial or financial policy, or biological warfare, as expressed in Task 21.

Task 30, the item regarding military actions, stated: "CIA to submit by February 15 its operational schedule for sabotage actions inside Cuba, including timing proposed and how to affect the generation and support of a popular movement, to achieve the Project goals".

In this connection, an authoritative study on the topic states that "during the Operation's official period of validity, that is to say, in the space of about fourteen months, there were 5 780 terrorists actions against our country registered; 716 were major acts of sabotage of economic targets".[23]

At the January 19, 1962 meeting with high government officials involved in Operation Mongoose, Attorney-General Robert Kennedy demanded the strict execution of the 32 tasks submitted by General Lansdale. Robert Kennedy explained that after Lansdale was entrusted with the task of examining "the Cuban issue," by late November 1961 he had already reached three conclusions: one, that it was possible to overthrow the Revolution; two, that the sugar harvest should be attacked immediately and three, that enough actions should be carried out "to keep Castro so busy with internal problems (economic, political and social) that he would have no time for meddling abroad, especially in Latin America".[24]

The great failure of the Empire's strategists analyzing the Cuban Revolution is clear in the first conclusions shown. What is really tragic is not that, at the time, Edward Lansdale believed in the feasibility of destroying the Cuban Revolution, but the fact that this idea has persisted for more than forty years.

At the same meeting, Robert Kennedy showed interest in the progress that was being made in the organization of a center for the interrogation of Cuban refugees arriving in Miami, designed to obtain

[23] Oficina de Publicaciones del Consejo de Estado: In Hecho Decimocuarto, pp. 76-77.
[24] Department of State: In document 292, p. 719

up-to-date information on Cuba's internal situation. Espionage at the service of economic warfare —and the other forms of anti-Cuban subversive activity—gained momentum thereafter.

As can be seen, the idea of striking the economy at its most sensitive point (the sugar harvest) was present from the very moment of Operation Mongoose's creation. At the same meeting, it was explained that it was much too late for the United States to destroy the sugar harvest already underway, in spite of the fact that terrorist actions "to keep the authorities busy" mainly targeted the harvest and other economic sectors. Economic considerations were highly important in espionage efforts undertaken to ensure the successful execution of Operation tasks.

On February 2, the Department of Defense representative to Operation Mongoose, Brigadier General William H. Craig, sends General Lansdale different proposals to prompt, harass or neutralize Cuban actions. While the proposed actions, by and large, were aimed at Cuban military targets, some were direct acts of aggression against economic sectors which included:

1. Operation "No Love Lost", to distract and confuse Cuban pilots by means of radio conversations between refugee pilots flying in areas near the national territory, controlling Cuban air-ground communication frequencies used for airport control.
2. Operation "Smasher", to disorganize or neutralize military and commercial communication facilities in Cuba, through the introduction of technically modified spare parts for communication equipment (vacuum tubes with silicon-carbide at their base that became conductors when hot) to cause undetectable short circuits. The facilities targeted included: the Compañía Cubana de Teléfonos, Radio Corporación de Cuba on Carlos III Avenue, the Cuban American Telephone and Telegraph Company, which operated 6 submarine cables connecting Cuba to the United States; commercial radio and television stations and, through them, military radio and land line communications receiving services from commercial lines. Recall that, from the time of the CIA's *Program of Covert Actions to Weaken the Castro Regime* –May 19, 1961—the destruction of these targets had been considered a top priority. To meet these purposes, they used several networks of CIA agents in the

communications sector that were promptly dismantled by State Security.

3. Operation "Break-Up," through which corrosive materials would be secretly introduced into Cuba to cause airplane, ground vehicle or ship accidents, actions which were scrupulously executed by agents specifically recruited for that purpose.

4. Operation "Full-Up," to destroy confidence in the fuel supplied by the socialist block by giving people the idea that it was contaminated. This was to be achieved by introducing a biological agent in the airplane fuel facilities, which would flourish and occupy the whole space inside the tank.

The official establishment of the blockade as part of Operation Mongoose

On February 3, 1962, under the legal authority of Section 620 (a) of the Foreign Assistance Act (September 4, 1961), President Kennedy signed Presidential Executive Order 3447, Federal Resolution No. 1085 of 6 February, effective as of the following day, establishing an economic, commercial and financial blockade on Cuba.

The guidelines set down in Operation Mongoose were adhered to, as such a measure was justified in its preamble as follows: "Considering: that the Eighth Meeting of the Ministers of Foreign Affairs, serving as Organs of Consultation in the application of the Inter-American Treaty for Reciprocal Assistance (IATRA), resolves, in its final declaration, that the current Government of Cuba is incompatible with the principles and objectives of the Inter-American System [...]."

The Cuban author Nicanor León Cotayo re-creates that moment masterfully, with the depth of someone who has all the available information on this process. [25]

U.S. press agencies profusely highlighted how, in the White House garden, President Kennedy welcomed then Secretary of State Dean Rusk as a hero. Rusk had returned from the Eighth OAS Meeting of Ministers of Foreign Affairs with the anti-Cuban declaration adopted there. What was not mentioned then was the relationship

[25] Nicanor León Cotayo: *El Bloqueo a Cuba,* pp. 1-2.

between Operation Mongoose and the OAS meeting and its anti-Cuban declaration, painstakingly lobbied for in the preceding few months, and the president's subsequent approval of Presidential Executive Order 3447, because this was, at the time, one of the U.S. government's most closely guarded secrets.

A description of Mongoose Measures

On February 20, 1962, a new version of the Operation was presented. It was drawn up using the responses offered by the government Departments and Agencies which had received the first version, from Chief of Operations General Lansdale, on January 18, in pursuit of "a realistic course of action."

The Basic Action Plan consisted of a basic plan inside Cuba (divided into 6 phases, between March and October, in which a popular uprising was supposed to take place) and 6 support plans in the political, economic, psychological, military, sabotage and intelligence spheres. [26]

The economic support plan contained the following tasks:

1. To persuade OAS and NATO member countries, as well as other "freedom loving" countries, to stop trading with Havana, for the purposes of creating an "anti-regime" feeling in the Cuban people *out of economic problems* (the italics are ours). It was said that the Revolution could be weakened if the flow of dollars towards the country was eliminated through the loss of credit lines, for which the complete cooperation of allied and friendly countries was needed. The Department of State would be responsible for this task, and the Department of Commerce and the CIA would participate in its execution, as they have continued to do for more than forty years.

    The document containing this task was secretly distributed among authorized officials precisely the day after two high government

---

[26] Taken from *The Bay of Pigs: New Evidence from Documents and Testimony of the Kennedy Administration, the Anti-Castro Resistance, and Brigade 2506*. Part 6: Operation Mongoose and the revival of the covert efforts, document 13. See also Jacinto Valdés-Dapena: *Operación Mangosta*.

officials (Walt W. Rostow and Richard Goodwin) left for Europe, with the same objective. The extraterritoriality of the anti-Cuban economic measures find an important precedent in that trip just as in other actions which have already been mentioned.

2. To paralyze transportation of U.S. products to Cuba through third countries, especially through Mexico and Canada, for the purposes of reducing the supply of critical items and components required for Cuban economic programs, especially sugar production, thermoelectric power plants, communications and transport. The Department of State was responsible for this task, in whose execution the CIA and the Departments of Commerce and Justice would participate.

3. To prepare a "positive list" ("black list") of Latin American products, subject to license procedures for other parts of the "free world," to reduce the supply of articles of special interest to Cuba. It would be a responsibility of the Department of State, with the participation of the Department of Commerce and the CIA.

4. To harass shipping operations to or from Cuba, so as to delay the arrival of and reduce supplies required for the economy. Oddly enough, the comment on this measure by the authors of this plan and the participating agencies remains classified.

5. To secure the cooperation of the National Council of Foreign Trade by mid-March to delay or impede the contracting of ships sailing toward Cuban ports, to reduce supplies to Cuba. The Department of State is responsible for this task and the Department of Commerce and the CIA would participate in its execution.

6. To secure, by mid-March, the cooperation of the Chamber of Commerce and the National Association of Manufacturers to influence U.S. firms with branches in other countries to adhere to the spirit of the United States' economic boycott on the Government of Cuba, to harass the Cuban economy. It would be the responsibility of the Department of State and the Departments of Commerce and the CIA would participate in its execution.

7. For the month of June, a campaign of rumors about Cuban products in "free world" markets had been designed to discourage their sales and to minimize the entry of foreign currencies into the country. The prioritized targets of such rumors would be fruits, sugar and tobacco, and the CIA would be

primarily in charge, with the participation of the Department of State and the United States Information Agency (USIA).

Other support plans also pursued economic warfare ends. These included:

In the military support plan:

1. Violations of Cuban air and maritime space, to divert the attention of the authorities and "to help prevent the transportation of supplies required by the regime," which would be a responsibility of the Department of Defense, with the support of the CIA.
2. Through the same agencies and participating bodies (Defense Department and CIA) to delay, disrupt or prevent Cuban transport and communications, to harass Cuban civil aviation and ships.
3. To jam Cuban communications in order to confuse and block them. This task would be a responsibility of the Department of Defense, aided by the CIA and the United States Information Agency.

In the sabotage support plan:

Obviously, the plan to support acts of sabotage —a mani-festation of economic warfare by covert means—would have a direct impact on the economic targets against which it was carried out. It included:

1. To sabotage Cuban nickel supplies to the Soviet Union, an action pursued both to prevent the supply of that strategic material to the USSR and to limit Cuba's ability to pay for imports from that country. Responsibility for such actions or any related comments have not been declassified.
2. To sabotage oil supplies to paralyze transport. Who would do it or how it was to be achieved was never declassified. We should remember that back in May-June of 1960 oil companies had been pressured into reducing and, later, suspending the import of crude oil into the country, and these companies served as cover for a boycott of supplies of this product to the country.

We cannot overemphasize the targeting of oil supplies in enemy sabotage actions from that point on. Does it strike anyone as mere chance that the first measure of the short-lived junta which staged a coup against President Chávez in Venezuela, in April 2002, was to suspend shipments of crude to Cuba?

3. Sabotage against communications, by commandos trained abroad, with the purported purpose of encouraging the "spirit of resistance to the regime." Television broadcasts ("CMQ TV") and other radio stations, as well as State Security transmission stations were considered priority targets, when these coincided with the "critical needs" of a popular uprising.

4. Sabotage against electric power plants "to increase tension in the authorities and halt activities in dramatic actions perceived by all." These actions were planned mainly for the months of July and August, for electric plants in Havana, Santiago de Cuba, Cienfuegos, Vicente, Santa Clara, Cuatro Caminos and Matanzas. Depending on the requirements, these acts of sabotage could be carried out by commandos brought into the country for that purpose.

At President Kennedy's March 16, 1962 meeting with the top government officials involved in Operation Mongoose, in which the president sought information on the results obtained, CIA Director John McCone said that the acts of sabotage planned were being carried out. General Lansdale stated that a number of actions were in store and that they were planning other, necessary actions, such as the targeting of Cuban coastal border defense patrol boats, whose sabotage had been ordered –both by the CIA and the Navy—to prevent these boats from interfering with the terrorist attacks on economic or other targets on the coastal area. When President Kennedy asked how they would be carried out, General Lansdale replied that fuel, lubricants, crews and boats as a whole were potential targets, as per the criterion that "a boat taken to be repaired was a boat that was not patrolling at a critical moment." [27] This criterion was also applied to marine transport ships.

In the August 7th CIA document, the CIA representative for Operation Mongoose William Harvey presented, under the title *Covert*

[27] Edward G. Landsdale: *Memorandum for the Record.* Meeting with President, 16 March 1962. Facsimile of the original document declassified by the United States National Security Archive.

Activities, the Agency's reply to the demand made by the Operation's chief of Operations –dated July 25, 1962—to put pressure on different spheres, into which the actions were divided, to bring about the overthrow of the Revolution.[28]

Paragraph B of the Economic Tasks consisted of four items:

1. To participate in the planning and execution of inter-agency economic tasks.
2. To carry out the maximum possible number of acts of sabotage against the main Cuban industries and public services, prioritizing public transport, communications, electric power plants and services.

It was said that no sabotage of food supplies, medical services or directly against the population would be carried out. The actions undertaken are what prove this assertion false. It was stated that at the time, and in the foreseeable future, those acts of sabotage would have a greater chance of success in the hands of commandos infiltrated into the country for that purpose. In view of the counterrevolutionary forces they still had inside the country, this was recognition that they did not have an internal operational foundation to guarantee the materialization of their expectations. By this date, it was already evident that the strength of the Revolution and the popular support it enjoyed would defeat Operation Mongoose.

3. Through active aggressive measures and other operations, to damage Cuban resources for productive purposes.
4. To induce the Cuban population (i.e., an internal fifth column) to continue carrying out minor acts of sabotage.

In the section devoted to the execution of the programmed tasks, in reference to paramilitary actions under paragraph C, sabotage against economic targets was addressed from different angles:

—   It was recognized that they had 10 to 15 commandos (infiltration *teams*) with about a dozen members each, to carry out the burial of weapons and major acts of sabotage *against selected targets*,

[28] Taken from *The Bay of Pigs [...]*. Part 6: Covert Activities, document 16.

and authorization for the recruitment of non-Cuban mercenaries to strengthen those groups was requested.
— In the case of spy networks in the cities, missions included the gathering and acquisition of information of interest, such as the selection of targets to be sabotaged by network members or other people.

On August 31st, in an official notification by General Lansdale to the Enlarged Special Group, the second phase of the Operation was presented. It was to begin September 6, and actions directly linked to economic aggressions were to be stepped up. The instructions were to "conduct selected major sabotage operations against key Cuban industries and public utilities, with priority attention being given to transportation, communication, power plants and utilities," so as "to reduce available economic supplies and services." The considerations which accompany this task include: "Depending upon circumstances, sabotage will be conducted either by specially trained, carefully selected commando/sabotage teams infiltrated especially for the operation and exfiltrated at the completion of the operation or by internal assets if such can be developed with the necessary access to the target". The selected targets were: Matahambre Mine – Santa Lucía; Texaco Refinery – Santiago; Shell/Esso Refineries – Havana; Regla Steam Electric plant – Havana; Steam Electric plant – Matanzas; Moa Bay nickel plant; Cárdenas paper factory and Micro Wave towers.[29]

In compliance with blockade provisions, on October 2nd, 1962, the Department of State sent a memorandum to President Kennedy specifying the measures he should approve to step up the war against Cuba-bound marine transportation. As one of the alternatives, it suggested he: "[...] should close all United States ports to any ship that on the same continuous voyage was used or is being used in Bloc-Cuba trade". It also recommended that he "[...] should instruct the Secretary of State to explore every avenue to obtain cooperation from other countries in restricting the use of their ships in Bloc-Cuba trade".[30]

[29] Department of State: In volume X, 1997, pp. 974-1000
[30] Department of State, *Foreign Relations of the States*, volume XI, 1996, document 2, pp. 3-4

Following this, the United States asked all Latin American and NATO countries to draw up new measures to strengthen the total blockade on Cuba; it informed them that its ports would be closed to all ships, from any country, if at least one of the ships under its flag were discovered carrying weapons to Cuba; about the non-eligibility of ships involved in trade with Cuba carrying foreign assistance from the United States; the order to refrain from trade with Cuba given all U.S.-owned or flagged ships, even if operating under foreign registration; and the exclusion from U.S. ports of any ship that, in the same journey, was used or was being used in trade with the "Sino-Soviet bloc."

The White House ordered the U.S. Maritime Commission to set up a "black list" of all ships actively involved in trade with Cuba based on CIA and Naval Intelligence data.

On October 4, 1962, at the Enlarged Special Group meeting to discuss the progress of Operation Mongoose, Attorney-General Robert Kennedy expressed President Kennedy's dissatisfaction with the Operation's progress and over the acts of sabotage, which were not producing the devastating effect expected,[31] and he demanded they receive a higher priority.

In view of the supporting comments made by the CIA director, the outcome of the discussion was the clear and reaffirmed conviction that headway had to be made in the planning and proposal of major sabotage actions against the Cuban economy, and General Lansdale was tasked with preparing a plan to mine Cuban ports.[32]

On October 8, 1962, in response to the appeal to step up sabotage actions, CIA representative for Operation Mongoose William Harvey presented a memorandum for the sabotage of Cuban ships. These actions would take advantage of the ships' stopovers at ports in capitalist countries. Requiring general approval, no prior consultations were needed for every separate action.[33]

---

[31] This is probably one of the sincerest recognitions of the effectiveness of Cuba's counter-measures to the endless brutality Cuba was being subjected to. The inexperienced State Security apparatus, in intimate coordination with the whole of the people, the true protagonist of that confrontation, aborted the plans devised against it.

[32] Department of State: In volume XI, 1996, pp. 11-13.

[33] Ibid., p. 16.

Thirteen paragraphs, with 40 lines of text, including different types of actions that could be executed, were not declassified.

On October 16, 1962, at a meeting with senior CIA and Department of Defense officials held in Attorney-General Robert Kennedy's office, Mr. Kennedy again expressed the President's "general dissatisfaction" with the Operation, which had already been underway for a year but had yielded disappointing results and had failed to carry out the major acts of sabotage that should have had a significant impact on Cuba's internal situation. Consequently, Robert Kennedy would assume the direction of the actions, which would thenceforth be discussed with him on a daily basis.

At the meeting, the Attorney General spoke in glowing terms about a sabotage plan he had received that morning from CIA Deputy Director General Carter. [34]

That same day, the United States Merchant Marine Institute requested an emergency meeting of the International Chamber of Shipping in London to consider an official trade embargo on Cuba.[35]

The Missile Crisis

On October 22, 1962, Cuba was suffering the onslaught of this undeclared war, designed to promote a widespread popular uprising in the month of October which would provide a pretext for direct U.S. military intervention. This was taking place at the time of the Missile Crisis, unleashed as a result of the intransigent position assumed by the United States in view of Cuba's decision to contribute to the defense of the socialist block and to secure its own defense against threats of U.S. intervention.

On the 28th of that month, the Cuban government signed a statement presenting five points for the solution of the crisis. The correct perception of the purpose behind economic warfare actions, geared towards an uprising that would prompt military intervention, is explicit in the first of Cuba's demands: an end to the economic

---

[34] Ibid., pp. 46-47.

[35] Chronology on the Ministry of Foreign Affairs's web site *Cuba vs. Bloqueo*, (Cuba vs. Blockade) which was in turn taken by Morris Morley: *Cuba vs. Bloqueo*. http://www.cubavsbloqueo.cu

blockade and the commercial and economic pressures exercised by the United States against Cuba throughout world.

The second point stated: "An end to all the subversive activities, to the dropping and disembarking of weapons and explosives by air and sea, to the organizing of mercenary invasions, spy infiltration and sabotage, all of which are carried out from United States territory and that of some conspiratorial countries." The third point called for an end to pirate attacks against our ships and coasts, actions with serious effects on the economy.

Imperial arrogance prevented the U.S. government from reaching the most appropriate conclusions and adopting the most realistic decisions. It has continued to apply an increasingly aggressive policy for over forty years.

Chapter III Range of state terrorist actions against the Cuban economy

Future Policy towards Cuba

On December 4, 1962 —although Operation Mongoose had not yet been officially terminated— the Executive Committee of the National Security Council discussed a document, titled *Future Policy towards Cuba*, which considered the new situation that had arisen following the Missile Crisis, and a consensus was reached on the need to re-engineer anti-Cuban actions. McGeorge Bundy's December 6th memorandum to the president, in which he submitted the discussed document, remarks that covert actions are treated in broad terms and expresses the idea that espionage activities should be immediately undertaken. These activities, we can infer, would serve as the basis for the planning of future actions.

It should be remembered that on the eve of the Missile Crisis, Operation Mongoose had taken sabotage actions to unprecedented levels. The appeal to common sense that the Crisis entailed —if we can use the word common sense in this case— forced the Empire to try to reformulate its policy in this respect. Regrettably, this did not occur and sabotage continued to be one of the pillars of economic warfare actions against Cuba, in acts of terrorism that deprive the U.S. government of the moral authority to be the judge on these matters it claims to be.

Future Policy towards Cuba stressed that the ultimate goal of U.S. policy was to overthrow the Revolution and replace it with a sympathetic government, and that the immediate goal was to weaken the regime, frustrate its "subversive intentions", reduce its influence in the Hemisphere and increase the costs that supporting Cuba represented for the socialist block. To achieve this, the U.S. was to implement a policy of containment, sapping, discrediting and isolation by means of economic, diplomatic, psychological and "other" pressures (a euphemistic allusion to the covert actions that were outlined further on, in Annex A of the document).

The open economic measures that were planned were:

1. Through the OAS, to extend the economic blockade to all items (excepting, it was falsely stated, food, medicine and medical supplies); a stricter restriction of air and marine communication with Cuba by the countries of the Hemisphere.
2. The implementation, against Cuba, of four points of marine restrictions, opening a new chapter in this sphere, as will be seen further on.
3. Cuba's inclusion in NATO's COCOM list, which included countries to which no items considered strategic could be shipped.
4. To hold exchanges with industrialized nations in order to limit the arrival of spare parts and equipment to Cuba, even if these were not included in the COCOM list of items considered strategic.
5. To persuade non-socialist countries to limit Cubana Airlines services and to deny Cuba-bound Soviet ships air traffic rights.
6. To persuade Latin American countries to limit trips to Cuba by their citizens.

The economic warfare measures that were included in Annex A of this document, which referred to covert actions, were the following:

1. Assistance to selected groups of Cuban exiles to encourage the Cuban population to carry out acts of sabotage.
2. To use selected groups of exiles to sabotage major facilities, such that these actions could be attributed to Cubans residing in the country.[1]

[1] Which opened a new chapter in the use of terrorist organizations in exile, with disastrous consequences.

3. To sabotage Cuban shipments and vessels, as well as Cuba-bound shipments and vessels from the socialist block.
4. To aid countries (which were not in the socialist block) that bought Cuban sugar to find other supply sources, even through subsidies.

The Future Policy towards Cuba program embodies a new stage of covert actions that entail a greater use of counterrevolutionary émigrés, trained and equipped to execute actions in such a way that they appeared to act independently of the U.S. government.[2]

The prioritization of espionage in the design of new subversive policies

On December 6th, 1962, National Security Action Memorandum Nº 208, dated December 4th, was forwarded by President Kennedy's Special Assistant for National Security Affairs McGeorge Bundy to the CIA director, with the information requirements the U.S. government wanted to obtain through low or high-flying spy-plane flights over Cuban territory. Although the chief priority was to acquire new evidence of the deployment of "offensive weapons" and, in general, the presence of Soviet troops in Cuba, these requirements included information on the economy that could be obtained as secondary data during those flights.[3]

On December 15, in reply to this memorandum, the CIA director stated that the CIA was redoubling its efforts in several directions. These efforts included an increased use of agents and legal travelers visiting the country, interrogating "refugees" arriving in the United States and other countries and work in coordination with the special services of other countries.[4]

An analysis of these cases of espionage undertaken by Cuban Security agencies at the time, as we will see in the following chapter, confirms that, in addition to information on Soviet military assistance to Cuba, economic information was always a high priority.

On January 18, 1963, President Kennedy, through McGeorge Bundy, urged the CIA director to broaden the collection of information

[2] Department of State: In volume XI, 1996, pp. 586-590.
[3] Ibid., pp. 590-591.
[4] Ibid., pp. 624-625.

100

on Cuba, in addition to that obtained through air reconnaissance. He was interested in knowing everything the CIA was doing to encourage visits by friendly experts and observers of other nationalities; the mechanisms to obtain information through Cuba's diplomatic missions to third countries, and additional measures that the CIA could adopt. The President expressed that if visits by high-ranking individuals with access to the country's top authorities were encouraged, their reports would be more valuable.[5]

Such an interest was directly linked to the growing number of espionage activities that sought information on the state and prospects of the Cuban economy, a critical element in the planning and execution of economic warfare policy against the Revolution.

CIA actions to lower world sugar prices

Consistent with the subversive actions incorporated into the so-called *Future Policy towards Cuba* program of December 4, 1962, designed to alienate customers from the Cuban sugar market and limit the country's financial revenues in foreign currencies, on December 17 President Kennedy expressed his concern over the high prices of sugar in the world market, about which he had read in a CIA report from the previous day, entitled *Rising World Sugar Prices and the Effect on Cuba*, and inquired into what measures could be adopted to change the situation.[6]

The agenda for the April 30th, 1963 meeting of the National Security Council Standing Group stated that the Department of State was examining the possibility of using the sugar market to complicate the life of the Cuban regime and that it hoped to submit that study the following week.

On May 3, 1963, a memorandum from Assistant Secretary of State Edwin Martin to Acting Secretary George Ball, prompted by the Standing Group's April 30th meeting, which called for an analysis of measures that could be adopted to minimize Cuban sugar revenues, expressed that high prices and adjusted markets were brining about a true sugar deficit on the world market which was not artificially caused by the USSR and would probably persist until 1965. The memorandum concluded that the United States could

[5] Ibid., p. 665.
[6] Ibid., p. 626.

101

not figure out a means to reduce Cuban sugar revenues, a situation which would likely not change until 1965.[7]

On May 15, 1963, in response to this disturbing fact, National Security Action Memorandum N° 244, forwarded by President Kennedy's Special Assistant McGeorge Bundy to the Secretary of Agriculture, entrusted the latter with a study on the existing situation and feasible alternatives to force down high international sugar prices and thereby —in addition to two other objectives— limit the positive effects had by such a rise on the Cuban economy. The proposals were to be discussed at the National Security Council Standing Group's meeting of May 28th. It stated that both the Department of State and the CIA were interested in that study and were willing to cooperate.[8]

At the meeting of the National Security Council Special Group held on July 16, 1963, Assistant Undersecretary of Agriculture Sundquist addressed a plan devised by his Department on July 5, entitled *A Contingent Plan for Increasing World Production of Sugar*, which was in line with President Kennedy's interest in reducing Cuba's intake of foreign currency through the rise of world sugar prices.[9]

Lastly, at the meeting of the National Security Council Special Group held on October 1[st][10], satisfaction was shown with the progress that the program to reduce world sugar prices was making. This prorgam would deprive Cuba of the financial benefits derived from the rise announced late in 1962.

This example, presented succinctly and bluntly, should suffice to portray how far the war against Cuba had gone.

Post-Mongoose reorganization of Cuba-related decision-making mechanisms. Impact on economic warfare

McGeorge Bundy's memorandum to President Kennedy, responding to his instructions to reorganize U.S. government structures responsible for Cuba-related affairs was dated January 4, 1963. It prompted the creation of an Office for Cuban Affairs within the Department of State —whose Coordinator would also preside over the Cuba inter-agency group, subordinate to the secretary of State

[7] Ibid., pp. 800-801.
[8] Ibid., pp. 817-818.
[9] Ibid., pp. 851-852.
[10] Ibid., pp. 871-872

as regards daily tasks and to the president in interdepartmental coordinating work—and the dismantling of Operation Mongoose structures. The text stated that transportation orders and the broader aspects of economic pressures on Cuba were yet to be defined (implying the new post-Missile Crisis context), and that it was necessary to discuss these issues with OAS member states and other allies.[11]

Upon presidential approval, on January 8 the Secretary of State was informed of this reorganization and of the existence of an Interdepartmental Coordination Committee on Cuban affairs, composed of the Coordinator and the representatives of the Department of Defense (Secretary Cyrus Vance) and the CIA (Deputy Director Richard Helms). It was stated that the Coordinator of Cuban affairs would assume the same responsibilities with respect to open and covert actions. [12]

On January 19, 1963, a CIA study on Cuba's economic performance in 1961 and 1962 was presented. It included forecasts for 1963-1965 that promised better business performance and increased investments in industry which would result in agricultural and industrial growth by the end of that period.[13] As we will see, actions against the Cuban economy were stepped up to prevent this.

Between January 22 and 25, 1963, government structures actively involved in the new Interdepartmental Coordination Committee on Cuban affairs, and the new actors called on stage, debate what the final goals of future policy towards Cuba, and the steps to reach them, should be, under the conditions derived from the Missile Crisis.

A higher level in plans: the United States Policy towards Cuba

The economic warfare-related items that were presented in the document titled *United States Policy towards Cuba*, discussed at the National Security Council Executive Committee meeting of January 25, were essentially the first alternative:

1. The four points of the "shipping orders," regarding the establishment of the "black lists," were: to close U.S. ports to all vessels

---

[11] Ibid., pp. 648-651.
[12] Ibid., pp. 656-657.
[13] Ibid., pp. 665-666.

from countries that carried weapons to Cuba; to prohibit ships that had carried goods to Cuba from entering U.S. ports for 120 days following their stop at a Cuban port; to prohibit all ships with the U.S. flag or owned by U.S. citizens or residents from entering Cuban ports or carrying goods to or from Cuban ports and to prohibit any load paid by U.S. government departments to be carried on vessels whose owners had vessels involved in trade between Cuba and the socialist bloc.

2. To bring pressures to bear on Mexico, Chile and Brazil to secure their support for the adoption of an OAS resolution that recommended a broadening of trade restrictions on Cuba, to include not only weapons but also any strategic items; to prohibit the use of vessels in the transportation of forbidden items to Cuba and to prohibit vessels that participated in trade between Cuba and socialist countries from accessing their countries' ports; to deny aircrafts en route to Cuba permits to fly over the territory transit rights and to call on other countries to apply similar measures.

3. Once support from the three countries mentioned above was secured, in contact with the remaining OAS countries, to achieve, within ten days, the adoption of the aforementioned resolution.

4. At the first NATO meeting following the OAS resolution, to require NATO to include Cuba in the list of countries to which the sending of strategic items is prohibited (COCOM list).

5. Thereafter, to reach an agreement with industrialized nations to prevent loads of critical components and equipment, whether included in the COCOM list or not, from arriving in Cuba.

6. In addition to what was mentioned above with respect to the "black lists," under Section 107 of the Foreign Assistance Act, to continue pressuring "free world" countries into preventing their vessels from taking part in Cuba's trade with socialist countries.

Covert actions in support of this alternative, in the United States Policy towards Cuba, included:

— to intensify acts of espionage in Cuba to a maximum, in pursuit of a source of intelligence needed for the successful execution of their plans;

— "to support" (i.e. to encourage, lead and control) actions by certain factions of the counterrevolutionary exile community in the United States that were acting to overthrow the revolutionary government and sought to strengthen an internal fifth column, and to rely on them in obtaining intelligence;

— to encourage the propaganda actions of the counterrevolutionary exile community. As we will discuss at length later, this point referred to actions by people of Cuban origin, on the CIA's payroll, who, through their propaganda activities, would encourage acts of sabotage against the Cuban economy.

The general goals of the second alternative of actions set out in the new *United States Policy towards Cuba* included the destruction of the Revolution and, among other categories of actions to that end, economic "pressures".

1. As part of its immediate objectives, among other numerous actions, it included weakening the Cuban economy and eroding internal support for the Revolution. Let us not forget that, within the existing political-subversive framework, this was achieved through economic warfare.
2. It also included the adoption of economic and other covert measures, to isolate, undermine and discredit the Revolution, creating the conditions for its destruction.
3. Intensification of espionage activities.
4. To secure the support of Latin American countries in these anti-Cuban actions.
5. Annexes with the open and covert measures that would be executed to achieve the pursued ends were to be prepared.

The continued application of measures to eliminate maritime shipping to Cuba

The National Security Council Executive Committee meeting that debated the new *United States Policy towards Cuba* heatedly discussed the implications that the application of the four points of the "shipping orders" would have for broad U.S. interests, mainly as regards the reactions of the USSR and other allied countries. The meeting recognized that the latter were supporting U.S. policy, which was obvious during the first nineteen days of January that year, as Cuban trade with U.S. allies had practically ceased. It was recognized that even if the "black lists" of "shipping orders" were not approved, the remaining "pressures" would suffice to isolate Cuba economically; thus, President Kennedy decided to postpone a decision on the approval of the four points of the "shipping orders," although the Department of Agriculture and other agencies would immediately be instructed not to transport loads on vessels involved in trade with Cuba.

President Kennedy called into question the actual value of the measure involving the Latin American countries; the Secretary of State explained that its result would be limited given the little trade existing between these countries and Cuba, but that it would help in the inclusion of Cuba in NATO's COCOM list of strategic products and, thus, to pressure industrialized countries into eliminating all exports of spare parts and machinery to the island, all of which was approved by the president. The Secretary of State and the CIA director recognized that the lack of spare parts and equipment was already affecting the Cuban economy seriously.

At that meeting, expressing an idea which would contribute to the subsequent increase of terrorist actions by groups of counterrevolutionary exiles, Attorney-General Robert Kennedy insisted U.S. policy should rely on these actors for the anti-Cuban actions that had been discussed.[14]

Soon after, National Security Action Memorandum N° 220 was issued, prohibiting shipments of loads paid by the U.S. government (Departments of State, Defense, Agriculture; General Services Administration and Agency for International Development) on foreign ships that had called at Cuban ports as of January 1st, 1963. For this purpose, a "black list" of ships was drawn up. This measure had a severe impact on Cuba, an island that depended entirely on marine transport to maintain its foreign trade.[15]

The severity of this measure is vividly expressed by Krinsky and Golove, when they say: "In early 1963 the United States acted to intensify pressure on third countries to isolate Cuba economically. National Security Action Memorandum 220 of February 5, 1963 [...] constituted a blacklist of all foreign vessels which engaged in trade with Cuba, and it was vigorously enforced through periodic publication in the Federal Register of the names of all ships that had

---

[14] Ibid., pp. 681-687.
[15] Ibid. p. 693.

called at a Cuban port".[16] A later measure, of December 16, increased this isolation even more.

In the first quarter of 1963 only 59 ships called at Cuban ports, compared to 352 in the same period in 1962. Between June 1962 and June 1963, there was a 60% decrease in the number of ships from capitalist countries involved in trade with Cuba, from 932 in 1962 to 359 in 1963. Between 1962 and 1963, the number dropped from 22 to 14.

At the February 5 meeting where National Action Memorandum N° 220 was approved, it was expressed that actions directed at the International Longshoremen's Association were being carried out to secure the support of the affiliated unions and from the union movement, as a whole, for these anti-Cuban measures.[17]

The National Security Council evaluation of Cuba's situation conducted on February 14, 1963 affirmed that the island was "substantially isolated from the 'Free World'", as expressed, at the economic level, by the precipitous decrease in shipments from those countries in previous months. Shipments had dropped to half their level before the Missile Crisis and a significant decline in trade was witnessed in the preceding few years. Airline services were also very limited and only Mexico and Spain allowed their airlines to fly to Cuba. It was pointed out that this isolation was not accidental, but, rather, had been actively achieved by means of U.S. unilateral (restrictions on shipments), bilateral (on the representations of "certain countries" that traded with Cuba) and multilateral measures (as exemplified by the OAS measures).

In spite of this — and taking into account the fact that import levels (imports from socialist countries) remained similar to those of other periods, it was concluded that the true challenge faced by the United States was isolating Cuba from the socialist bloc.[18]

At the National Security Council meeting where U.S. measures in Latin America were analyzed, President Kennedy expressed an interest in the state of the measures to isolate Cuba, mentioning, in connection to economic warfare, the measures to prevent trade with allied countries and those that had been adopted for vessels that

[16] Michael Krinsky and David Golove: *United States Economic Measures Against Cuba Proceedings in the United Nations and International Law Issues.* Aletheia Press, Northamptom, Massachusets, 1993, pp. 112-113.

[17] Department of State: In volume XI, 1996, p. 692.

[18] Ibid., pp. 699-700.

carried shipments to Cuba. It was evident that arrangements with Great Britain were needed in this connection and that pressures had been brought to bear on NATO countries recently. Similarly, the OAS would also be involved in future actions against Cuba. To conclude, the president demanded that pressures on Cuba, including economic measures aimed at its foreign trade and shipping, continue in order to increase the country's isolation.[19]

In response to this, in March 1963, the Department of Commerce worked closely with the Department of State, the CIA and other agencies to perfect measures designed to harass Cuba's trade with third countries.

Referring to this, Fabián Escalante expressed:

> The idea was not to abandon all the different kinds of pressures but, on the contrary, to combine them. The economic, information, cultural and political blockade would be stepped up. To this end, in the first months of 1963 the Treasury Department created a special police force, the "global detectives", whose mission was to visit the capitals of all countries that traded with Cuba, to pressure governments, business people and, even, to inform CIA operatives of Cuba-bound loads warehoused in ports, so that they could be sabotaged.[20]

Design of new subversive measures against the economy by the Cottrell Committee

On April 1, 1963, a meeting of the Coordinating Committee for Cuban Affairs (Cottrell Committee) —where the highest Department of Defense and CIA officials (Richard Helms and Desmond FitzGerald) and Department of State representatives participated— was held to discuss the subversive actions that were being planned against Cuba. These were discussed and submitted to President Kennedy through a memorandum addressed to Special Assistant for National Security Affairs McGeorge Bundy. In subsequent documents, it is clarified that those proposals had to be evaluated and approved or discarded at the April 4 meeting of the Special Group (5412).

[19] Ibid., pp. 713-718.
[20] Fabián Escalante Font: p. 117.

108

The proposals for the economic warfare actions were:

1. "Operation Aerostat", which was to drop about half a million leaflets — containing, among other pieces of propaganda material, cartoons showing sabotage techniques—over Havana.
2. The sabotage of 19 Cuban vessels, to include three types of sabotage: the placing of mines in the vessels' hulls, the incineration of shipments and the introduction of abrasive substances into the machinery.
3. Although it was believed that the use of mines could "dramatically" raise the anti-Castroites' morale, the Committee did not support this option because such actions could be attributed to submarines. The sinking of ships through these means was therefore discarded as an option. Proof of the seriousness of the matters discussed is that part of the reasoning behind this decision was not declassified. Thus, it was agreed that the acts of sabotage to be proposed to the Special Group would consist in the use of incendiary and abrasive substances that could be controlled to produce their effects in international waters and the vessel's machinery. The meeting pointed out that these actions could be carried out through Cubans recruited by the CIA, or by means of contacts with the anti-Cuban terrorist organization *Directorio Revolucionario Estudiantil* (DRE), which proved how closely the activities of this organization were monitored by the U.S. government.
4. To readjust terrorist actions by counterrevolutionary exile groups and maintain control over their actions. This brought about the new concept of so-called "autonomous operations."

Commenting on these proposals, the Committee considered the convenience of continuing to extend the use of covert measures and a careful cost-effect evaluation of actions against Soviet targets, expressing the feeling that the risks were not as great as they seemed.

The Committee advocated the use of covert measures and considered that a good sabotage program was one of the best tools that could be used to damage the Cuban economy.[21]

On April 3, 1963, at a new Cottrell Committee meeting held to analyze covert actions against Cuba, CIA Plans Director Desmond

---

[21] Department of State: In volume XI, 1996, pp. 748-750.

FitzGerald advocated that the convenience of using mines to sabotage Cuban ships, discarded at the previous day's meeting, be reconsidered. He pointed out that, at a meeting with Kennedy that morning, the president had opined that the sabotage program's "noise level" had to be raised for "moral purposes" and had underestimated the mines' ability to sink vessels. It was agreed not to include that point in the proposal that would be discussed at the Special Group meeting the following day, but within another proposal of important acts of sabotage that would be made available to the president the following week.[22]

On April 9, 1963, Special Aide Joe Califano sent a memorandum to Secretary Vance, conveying the president's decision on the items submitted to the Special Group by the Cottrell Committee:

— President Kennedy approved the sabotage of cargos on Cuban ships (the proposed act of sabotage, which was obviously approved, was the use of incendiary mechanisms) and the destruction of their engines through the use of abrasive substances.
— He turned down the proposal to use an aerostat for propaganda purposes.

This Special Group meeting approved the use of Department of Defense facilities and personnel for the training of CIA agents that were to operate inside Cuba.[23]

On April 10, 1963, the Interdepartmental Coordinating Committee on Cuban Affairs meeting, held to discuss the anti-Cuban covert action proposals that would be evaluated at the Special Group meeting the following day, reviewed a proposal for intelligence operations and acts of sabotage against three major economic targets: a rail bridge, the means of transportation of an oil reserve and a molasses transportation vessel. With respect to these, it was said that President Kennedy wanted to raise the noise level and actions were to be executed quickly, even if they were not as significant as desired and the more harmful ones would take longer to plan and execute. None were to be carried out before April 22, so as not to affect negotiations between James Donovan and the Cuban government .

[22] Ibid., pp. 750-751.
[23] Ibid., pp. 754-755.

The convenience of mining Cuban vessels, or not, was discussed in depth, and to avoid problems with third countries, it was pointed out that those actions should take into account the country in question. FitzGerald spoke of existing limitations facing such actions in the Havana harbor and, in general, with respect to acts of sabotage in Cuba involving Cuban agents. What he described as *the most significant target that could be sabotaged*, in an action which would hurt Cuba severely, was not declassified in this document. But, owing to its complexity, it could take eight months to carry out, and plans in this connection had to be urgently undertaken.

Desmond FitzGerald's statement may refer to the CIA-planned sabotage of Ñico López, the most important refinery in the country, where the Company had an agent. He had been recruited in the United States in the second half of 1961 as he completed his engineering studies at the University of Louisiana and, after returning to Cuba as a repatriate in 1962, had been placed in that industry as head of the maintenance department. In the following chapter, we will look at the instructions sent to this agent to destroy the refinery in greater detail.

With respect to attacks from abroad, it was stressed that each of them had to be approved individually. This was surely due to the great impact that recent attacks against Soviet vessels had had.

At the end of the meeting, the chief of the CIA Plans Division commented that he perceived that President Kennedy wanted more actions and that, though they were working on a plan in that connection, they should begin with less complex acts of sabotage because these required less preparation, and that later on they could focus on more important targets.[24]

On April 11, 1963, at the Special Group meeting tasked with the approval of secret operations, in which the president's Special Adviser McGeorge Bundy, CIA Director McCone, CIA Plans Division Chief Desmond FitzGerald and other senior officials participated, the Interdepartmental Coordinating Committee on Cuban Affairs presented three documents, containing anti-Cuban actions, which had been discussed the previous day at the meeting of the Cottrell Coordinating Committee on Cuban affairs.

One of those documents proposed three acts of sabotage against economic targets which would be carried out between April 15 and May 15. The other, more general document was entitled *A Covert*

24 Ibid., pp. 761-762

Harassment/Sabotage Program against Cuba. Owing to its highly sensitive nature, instructions to destroy and leave no evidence of the third document were given at this very meeting.

At the meeting, Desmond FitzGerald presented a report on the most recent results of the program for the infiltration of agents in Cuba and its performance in the following months which was approved by the Group.

According to the declassified minutes, this meeting extensively evaluated the clarity with which proposals for acts of sabotage were to be made to that group, which was to point out the general and specific objectives pursued by the CIA in their execution; existing capacity to execute them; likelihood of success; prospective benefits; the dangers stemming from their execution and probable response measures by the Cuban government.

The meeting acknowledged that the actions entrusted to counterrevolutionary groups in exile posed a dilemma, since, given the position they had openly assumed after the attacks on the Soviet ships, they would have many difficulties in maintaining plausible denial of government involvement in those acts, or would be showing signs of inefficiency in their control.

Drawing from the points raised at this Special Group meeting, the CIA and Department of State would draw up a document which would be submitted to President Kennedy for approval on April 19. The document was to include an extensive sabotage program and examples of specific operations; the actions to be carried out and their prospective benefits; the results that could be obtained with the available internal resources; their possible impact; and the way those acts of sabotage conformed to the general Cuba policy.[25]

Different aspects of sabotage actions in Cuba were addressed at CIA Director John McCone's meeting with President Kennedy on April 15, 1963. Kennedy and McCone spoke about the difficulties faced by exile organizations involved in sabotage actions. They discussed whether these, initially conceived as maritime actions from without the island, could be presented as actions that had been executed from within the country. The CIA director said that he was considering these matters as part of a comprehensive program to destroy the Revolution.[26]

[25] Ibid., pp. 757-758.
[26] Ibid., pp. 763-764.

On April 17, 1963, in a memorandum to President Kennedy, Secretary of State Dean Rusk offered a thorough evaluation of the results that pressures brought to bear on third countries, to limit maritime shipping to Cuba, had yielded. The most interesting points presented were:

— Liberia, Turkey, Honduras and Panama had established ordinances barring their ships from all trade with Cuba. West Germany prohibited the ships under its registry from participating in trade between socialist countries and Cuba. Greece also adopted measures. Lebanon had offered its cooperation and would reformulate its marine laws in three months. Repeated meetings with British authorities had not yet produced any results, as the latter had not yet found a legal basis for barring their vessels from trading with Cuba, although they were holding informal meetings with the ship owners for that purpose.

— Section 107(b) of the 1963 Foreign Assistance Act (Public Law 87-874; 76 Stat 1163-1170), which prohibited U.S. economic assistance to any country that allowed vessels under its flag to carry economic assistance items to Cuba, had proven very useful in this connection. It was also said that ship owners and shipping agents feared that the International Longshoremen's Association would not unload their shipments at U.S. ports if their ships participated in trade with Cuba.

— As a result of all this, with the exception of socialist block ships, the number of vessels that called at Cuban ports had decreased from 337 in the first three months of 1962 to 62 in same period in 1963 (12 in January, 22 in February, 28 in March). With respect to the latter figures, import levels remained similar in those first three months because of the number of ships that called at Cuban ports to pick up sugar.

— Of the 78 vessels that had called at Cuban ports up to April 17, 1963 —that is, until the very day before the report was drawn up, which shows us just what level of intelligence on this activity existed— 32 were English, 20 Greek, 6 Norwegian, 6 Lebanese, 4 Italian, 4 Yugoslavian, 2 Spanish, 1 West German, 1 Japanese, 1 Danish and 1 Moroccan.

— Serious problems faced by the United States as a result of the strict application of Section 107(b) were pointed out, in terms of what "to allow" and what "economic assistance" meant.

113

These ambiguities could even result in the need to suspend assistance to British possessions such as Kenya or British Guinea, or to Greece. The freight contracts that facilitated access to Cuban ports to most or all ships that sailed under the Greek flag —one Italian— and those that did so under Italian, Japanese, Danish and West German flags, were expected to expire; what remained were 32 English and 6 Norwegian ships.

— The only public measure that could be adopted was to extend the provisions of National Action Memorandum N° 220 of February 5 to the owners of those vessels, which would not cause too serious a problem in the relations with Morocco, Yugoslavia and Poland, but which could cause a favorable internal and international psychological effect. Instructions had been given the Maritime Administration, specifying what measures would be applied and what their effects would be. According to preliminary studies, these would be negligible.

— The CIA director considered it was not advisable to adopt other public measures during James Donovan's negotiations with Cuban authorities on the exchange of prisoners taken during the Bay of Pigs invasion.

— The recommendations made were: to continue pressuring the British, Norwegian, Italian and Spanish authorities to reduce the number of visits made by ships under their flags to Cuban ports; to prepare documentation to make the measures of Memorandum N° 220 more restrictive and to give a 45-day "grace period" for the elimination of such trade; as well as to pressure U.S. owners or people in control of oil companies to refrain from supplying oil to Cuba, a practice which persisted in some Central American ports.[27]

Proposed New Covert Policy and Program Towards Cuba

On April 18, 1963, the Interdepartmental Coordinating Committee on Cuban affairs (Cottrell Committee) presented the Special Group with the document that this group had requested from the

[27] Ibid., pp. 766-769.

Department of State and the CIA following the discussions about secret anti-Cuban operations held on the 11th.

The document, titled *Proposed New Covert Policy and Program Towards Cuba*, contained six guidelines for action, three of which directly referred to economic warfare issues: propaganda activity to encourage passive resistance and low-level sabotage by the population; the placing of incendiary or explosive devices in the hulls or inside the cargo of Cuban vessels to damage or sink them in the high seas; and the use of abrasive or other materials to damage propulsion, communication or other mechanisms and render the vessels inactive. Another guidelines, which called for the intensification of espionage activities, also had a severe impact upon the Cuban economy and exacerbated the effects of the blockade and other economic actions.

According to the document, the United States believed that the elimination of the Revolution was the task of Cubans. They could not, however, refrain from carrying out subversive actions to prevent its consolidation and had to offer assistance to those who worked in that direction in the country, despite the fact that, if captured, they would reveal this support, something with less than considerable repercussions.

Expanding on the proposed actions, the document sketched out the following aspects:

1. To place explosive loads with timers in the hulls of vessels anchored in Cuban or foreign ports. They would have underwater demolition groups by the month of June and would be able to carry out attacks starting July, on a monthly, planned basis. These measures were supposed to increase the stress on Cuba's marine transport and demoralize its crews. The Soviet reaction would be propagandistic and would involve motions at the UN. Similar reprisals or other strong reactions were considered unlikely.

2. Gun-boat attacks against Cuban vessels in the country's territorial waters, in ports or adjacent keys. It was believed that Cuban exile paramilitary forces trained for this purpose could carry out these marine actions, from vessels equipped with rifles and 20-mm cannons. The first attack on sailing vessels could be carried out in the month of May, and attacks would continue in subsequent months. The first attack on vessels in Cuban ports would be take place in the month of June. These actions would

disrupt coastal traffic transport. The United States would be accused, and Cuban reprisal measures could be taken. The USSR would also blame the United States, although Soviet response measures outside of Cuba were unlikely, and they would possibly offer Cuba a means to repel this kind of aggression.

3. Actions, by forces from abroad, against ground targets such as molasses containers, oil tanker wagons, fuel stations, refineries and electric power plants.

    Trained commandos would carry out these operations. The first attack could be carried out in the month of April, and similar attacks could be executed every month. Their results were hoped to bolster the morale of exile groups and contribute to the disruption of the economy. The United States could be accused of sponsoring these attacks. They could also contribute to the strengthening of Cuban security and protection forces. The Soviet reaction could be propagandistic and involve political motions in support of Cuban patrolling.

4. To support the internal counterrevolution, supply it materially, guide it and give it the capacity to carry out diverse sabotage and harassment operations.

    The supply of resources for these actions would be introduced into the country through marine infiltrations, through the diplomatic channels, or concealed via the mail; means obtained in the country could also be used, cases for which instructions would be given. The first acts of sabotage could be carried out within 30 days. This program was expected to produce a maximum of damage and raise morale. The repercussions envisaged included an increase in security measures and a Soviet propaganda and supply reaction.

An annexed note said that the document included already approved and other new sabotage plans which, in and of themselves, would not cause the destruction of the Revolution, but would undermine its consolidation and contribute to its destabilization. Actions were expected to reach a higher stage in a matter of six months.

Nothing is more revealing and incriminating than the closing paragraph: "A source of additional agent personnel is from Cuban

116

personnel trained in the U.S. Military Forces under the recent programs, but released to civilian status".[28]

This document was discussed at the April 25 Special Group meeting, which concluded:

1. Not to object to the use of mines, which should be technically enhanced, against Cuban vessels.
2. Boat attacks against sailing or anchored vessels were not particularly attractive.
3. Commando attacks against ground targets seemed worthy of consideration and could be carried out in May, following authorization at the highest level (President Kennedy). Refineries and electric power plants were particularly good targets. Such operations were particularly valuable, especially if they were executed in conjunction with other resistance activities.

The meeting of the Special Group (recently reorganized as part of government structures) discussed a document drafted by President Kennedy's Special Assistant McGeorge Bundy, entitled *A Sketch of the Cuba Alternatives,* which developed different alternatives for destroying the Revolution. Among the seven tasks derived from that discussion, the fourth was: "Measures to disrupt the economy of Cuba."[29]

On April 30, 1963, the agenda distributed by the president's Special Assistant for National Security McGeorge Bundy at the NSC Standing Group meeting held on this date contained a second item titled *Programs which might be initiated by the United States Government with both immediate and long-run objectives.*

Its second epigraph referred to the intensification of economic actions, including the execution of sabotage actions a much larger scale than ever before. "Within this category additional possible gambits are of great interest to higher authority and it is hoped that some may be offered". According to a footnote, below this paragraph, McGeorge Bundy wrote the words "sugar, petroleum, oil, lubricants, money."[30]

[28] Ibid., pp. 769-772.
[29] Ibid., pp. 780-782.
[30] Ibid., pp. 794-795.

For the meeting, the CIA prepared a document on the possible forms of effective interference in Cuba's economic life through sabotage and other means. Special attention was being given to petroleum-related problems, and the first report of a study in this connection would be available the following week.

Approval of the *Proposal for Covert Policy and Integrated Program of Action towards Cuba*

On June 8, 1963, the CIA presented the document *Proposal of a New Secret Policy and Integrated Action Program on Cuba* to the National Security Council Special Group,[31] which was approved by President Kennedy at the June 19 National Security Council meeting.[32]

It consisted of three items and a special annex on sabotage.

The first item stated that this was the proposal for covert actions —a number of them already approved— that the CIA was in a position to execute.

Emphasis was made on the close relationship between the six proposed measures, whose combined execution would make their impact all the more deeply felt. As an example, it was said that the results of espionage should allow for the planning of "economic denial" measures and the identification of sabotage targets; that only after the effects of the economic measures and sabotage were "deeply felt" by the population and "elite groups," would there be hopes of transforming the disaffection of the armed forces and other centers of power into militant action against the regime, in which the CIA-controlled exile organizations or other autonomous organizations would play their role; and that this interrelation would make it possible to obtain more and improved intelligence.

The proposed policy was to use all available means, save military force, to bring as much pressure to bear on Cuba as possible, with a view to preventing the pacification of the population and the consolidation of the "Castro-communist" regime. The ultimate goal of the *Proposal* was to encourage dissidence in the military and other centers of power capable of overthrowing the Revolution.

[31] Ibid., pp. 828-834
[32] Ibid., pp. 837-838.

It was stated that, without action, the regime would gain in administrative efficiency and the security institutions in experience; and the enhancement of partisan and government institutions would spell having to accept, for an indefinite period of time, the presence of a communist regime in Cuba.

The second point further explained the six proposed measures, which were: 1) Covert collection of intelligence, both for U.S. strategic requirements as well as for operational requirements; 2) Propaganda actions to stimulate low-risk simple sabotage and other forms of active and passive resistance; 3) Exploitation and stimulation of disaffection in the Cuban military and other power centers; 4) Economic denial actions on an increased basis; 5) General sabotage and harassment; 6) Support of autonomous anti-Castro Cuban groups to supplement and assist the above courses of action.

Covert collection of intelligence/espionage should continue to be one of the main missions of the CIA; and, without affecting strategic intelligence efforts, emphasis should be made on increasing the volume and quality of information for the planning and assembly of operations included in the program, on regime defections and penetration measures in particular; *as well as those relating to damaging the economy and sabotage actions against its vulnerable sectors.*

As regards propaganda, its full name of *propaganda actions to encourage simple low-risk sabotage and other active and passive forms of resistance* refers to the role it was given as part of the economic war on Cuba. It was stated that it should also encourage and aggravate tensions inside the regime, and between Cuba and the socialist bloc, highlighting Sino-Soviet differences, calculated to create a psychological atmosphere that would facilitate the execution of other courses of action in the program.

With respect to *actions to damage the economy*, it was stated that *open U.S. official sanctions, along with secret economic hindrances, would have an adverse effect on the Cuban economy, whose impact would be maximized if combined with sabotage actions. An inter-agency committee with the authority to call for prompt action by the participating agencies would enhance those actions.*

Sabotage and harassment were considered an economic weapon as well as a stimulus for resistance. They would be an economic weapon if supplemented by and coordinated with the economic hindrance efforts. They were perceived as a stimulus for resistance since they

119

were a dramatic symbol of the people's increased opposition to the Revolution.

All these operations would be carried out through external means –which they had—as well as internal means –which were to be created. The CIA-trained and controlled external means could be used as autonomous exile groups. Initially, the emphasis would be placed on external means, and on internal means when possible.

The types of sabotage actions considered appropriate were:

1. Large-scale simple, low-risk sabotage, encouraged by previously approved radio propaganda already in place.
2. Sabotage against Cuban vessels in international waters, also already approved and in place.
3. Attacks from abroad by terrorist groups, upon selected, mainly economic, targets.
4. Supporting elements of the internal resistance, giving them materials and personnel to carry out sabotage and harassment actions.

It was recognized that no single act of sabotage by itself could affect the economy, or encourage significant resistance, but "a well planned series of sabotage efforts, appropriately executed, could, in time, produce the desired effect."

With respect to the *support of autonomous anti-Castro Cuban groups to supplement and assist in the execution* of the courses of action set out, it was argued that up to that point in time the CIA had used completely controlled groups of agents, to prevent unilateral and irresponsible actions by exile groups, but that if sabotage and resistance actions were to be undertaken on a large scale, it was necessary to run the risk of using autonomous groups that were not under the CIA's direct control, but such actions were to be organized and carried out outside U.S. territory, and the U.S. government should be prepared to publicly deny any link to them.

The third item of this *Proposal* offered recommendations, stating that actions had been previously authorized.

Annex A of the document we are summarizing expounded on the category of targets that were to be included in plans for sabotage and harassment actions, prioritizing those related to electric power generation; petroleum, oil and lubricants; transport and production and processing factories.

120

As regards *electric power generation,* it was remarked that deactivating any of the electric network components could effectively damage or destroy the power generation facilities, or the critical distribution line substations. The significant economic and social repercussions of this would be all the more severe because electricity was not available in many areas, or its supply did not suffice to satisfy the demands of industry and the population. Small acts of sabotage and harassment as, for instance, throwing chains onto high-voltage lines to break them, would increase the existing deficit and its cumulative effects could cause a prolonged collapse of the electric system, if, in addition to this, there was already a deficit of spare parts or replacement pieces.

With respect to *petroleum, oil and lubricants* (POL), it was stated that the damaging or destruction of POL production or storage facilities could seriously affect all aspects of the Cuban economy. The power industry depends almost entirely on POL, as do the sugar industry and inter-provincial transport. Production and storage facilities are susceptible to external attacks with heavy weapons and to the subtler methods used by the internal fifth column, which can achieve an appropriate degree of accessibility. The loss of refining facilities can be compensated for through increased imports of refined products from the socialist block, but their substitution requires a readjustment period that would heavily stress the economy. The additional burden on the Bloc's refining capacity would remain until the capacities damaged in Cuba were restored.

In the area of transportation, damaging or destroying railroads and transport means or main bridges could weaken regional economies that were dependent, to a large extent, on imported products. Processing and export of the vitally important sugar crop also depended entirely on transportation. These actions were not expected to cause enough damage to bring about the collapse of the economy or society, but it was thought they could adversely affect the standard of living and economic yield, two important factors for the stability of the regime. A wide range of actions can be carried out, from an exquisitely sophisticated attack with external or internal means against transportation, important bridges or repair facilities, to simple acts such as the derailment of trains or littering the highway with piercing objects.

In reference to production and manufacturing installations, it was stressed that, although the economy depended on the import of food products and the export of sugar, there was a wide range of other facilities that could be targeted and whose undermining would weaken the economy and foster discontent among the people. These targets included the Nicaro nickel complex, cement producing plants, distilleries and a wide range of related industries that produced food, clothing and construction materials. It was pointed out that these targets were particularly susceptible to attack by external and internal means because they were numerous and of relatively low strategic importance and, consequently, not protected sufficiently.

The specific sabotage targets, and the tactic to be used, were to be decided bearing the following in mind:

— The extent to which the target could be physically damaged.
— Resulting effect on the economy.
— Cost to and effort required from the Socialist camp to repair the damages.
— Psychological effect on the population.
— Adverse reactions that could be anticipated.
— CIA Operational capacities and limitations

On June 14, 1963, the CIA prepared a National Intelligence Estimate that served as a reference framework for the *Proposal for Covert Policy* mentioned in the previous point.[33]

In a White House meeting held on June 19, 1963, President Kennedy approved the *Proposal for Covert Policy* presented by the CIA on the recommendation of the National Security Council Special Group. The president showed special interest in the externally organized sabotage operations and was shown maps detailing typical program targets, and the advantages and disadvantages their sabotage entailed. McGeorge Bundy described the integrated nature of the program presented, pointing out that the Special Group would revise it on a weekly basis. Kennedy wanted to know how soon actions could begin, insisting on the need for speed in the matter.[34]

On June 20, 1963, the State Department Bureau of Inter-American Affairs drew up a document entitled *Future relations with Castro*, which concluded that an essential component of economic warfare

[33] Ibid., pp. 834-836.
[34] Ibid., pp. 837-838.

was legislative action by Congress. Unfortunately this policy trend would continue, with even more force after 1992, thirty years later.

On June 22, 1963, the CIA director and other high officials took part in a meeting held in the office of the State Secretary to specify actions related to the Proposal for Covert Policy approved by the President. According to CIA director McCone, the objective was to pressure the State Secretary who, apparently, did not look too kindly upon terrorist attacks prepared from abroad because of how vulnerable these actions made the State Department.[35]

July 1963 marked the beginning of the CIA plan –ultimately frustrated– to sabotage the Cuban economy by counterfeiting its currency and introducing it in large quantities into the country.

Establishing the fundamental elements of the blockade. Close of the initial cycle in the systematization of economic warfare actions against Cuba

On July 8, 1963, on the basis of the Trading with the Enemy Law of 1917, the United States Treasury Department substitutes its Cuban Import Regulations with the Cuban Assets Control Regulations (31 CFR; 515.101-515.808). These were to establish the fundamental features of the blockade, including:

1. Freezing of all Cuban assets in the United States
2. Prohibition of all financial and commercial transactions that are not under license.
3. Embargo of Cuban imports.
4. Prohibition to set up non-authorized negotiations in Cuba with U.S. dollars, regardless of the person's nationality or location.
5. Article 515.533 incorporated the Commerce Department's export regulations into these regulations.

At the July 19, 1963 meeting of the National Security Council Special Group, CIA Planning Director Desmond FitzGerald reviews the actions of the *Integrated Program of Action towards Cuba* carried

---

[35] Ibid., pp. 842-844.

out in the preceding three weeks, explaining that two were to be executed on July 26. Debates centered on what to tell the press when it asked about sabotage and harassment actions. All connection with these was to be denied.[36]

The most important blockade measures since 1963

Although very well known by our people, it would be worthwhile to briefly go over the most important U.S. public measures, pursued after the economic blockade assumed its basic form in 1963.

— On May 1964, the total prohibition of the shipment of food, medicine and medical equipment is decreed although, in truth, these shipments had been suspended prior to the decree.
— During the Ninth Advisory Conference of the OAS, held in Washington on June 26, 1964, Latin American governments were called upon to interrupt direct or indirect trade with Cuba.
— On October 6, 1964, the Commerce Department prohibited foreign ships from stopping at U.S. ports to refuel if their destination was a Cuban port or if they had stopped at one on or after January 1, 1963.[37]
— On October 1964, on the basis of a 1949 law, Congress approved the Program of liquidation of Cuban claims to set up a mechanism to justify or certify claims in connection with losses suffered by U.S. citizens in other countries, receiving these in the pre-established period between November of 1965 and May 1, 1967. In that period, there were 8 816 claims made by private persons or corporate bodies for a sum total of 3 226 631 898 dollars. Concluding its work in 1972, the commission certified only 5 011 claims for a value of 1 851 197 358 dollars. According to the law, only individuals who were U.S. citizens at the time of nationalization could make claims. [38]

[36] Ibid., p. 848.
[37] Michelle Abdo Cuza: "Impacto de la Ley Helms-Burton en las relaciones jurídicas y financieras internacionales. Medios para enfrentarlo" ("The Impact of the Helms-Burton Act on international juridical and financial relations. Means to confront it"). Masters Thesis, Universidad Nacional Autónoma de México, Facultad de Derecho, División de Estudios de Post-Grado, 1997, p. 62.
[38] Ibid., p. 848.

— On October 7, 1964, Congress approved the Hickenlooper Amendment, according to which no U.S. court could pass sentence in favor of other States in the case of the nationalization of U.S. properties, not even if such a key principle of International Law as the doctrine of sovereign right was invoked (curiously enough, after events since January 1, 1959).

This was in answer to the U.S. Supreme Court decision of March 23, 1964, in connection to the "Sabbatino Case", as to who was to be paid for a sugar shipment sent to the United States when the sugar mill was nationalized. The Supreme Court ruled that the nationalization was valid and expressed the obligation of all States to respect "the independence of each and every other sovereign State and, consequently, the courts of a given country cannot judge another government's actions, made within its own territory [...] maintaining intact the doctrine on actions by a sovereign power".[39] This moment of lucidity with respect to Cuba experienced by a U.S. state authority was short lived; the Hickenlooper Amendment was passed in spite of the words of the only Judge who opposed the decision (Judge White). According to Olga Miranda: [...] the voice of the highest court is silenced, its dignity trampled on [...] and, thereby, the famous ruling handed down in the Sabatino Case was betrayed, sold out and silenced".[40]

[39] The legally preposterous treatment of this decision in the Helms-Burton Act is best grasped by reading the concluding report published by the Claims Commission in 1972, which expressed that "the aim of Congress was to certifiably stipulate before the Secretary of State, the sum total of losses, for the purposes of supplying this official with the appropriate information that could be used in future negotiations towards an agreement on the liquidation of claims with a friendly Cuban government when diplomatic relations are re-established. Consequently and in effect this program can be considered as a prior liquidation of the claims for the purposes of determining the total losses suffered by U.S. citizens and to supply an instrument through which our government can use it in deals with the Cuban government in the future, concerning this important inter national issue." See words by Olga Miranda In the Instructive Round Table on July 6, 2000. Special Tabloid No. 18, *Abajo el bloqueo*, p. 7.

[40] See Olga Miranda Bravo: "Las nacionalizaciones cubanas, los tribunales norte-americanos y la Enmienda Hickenlooper", ("Cuban nationalitations, US. courts and the Hickenlooper Ammendnent"). in Colectivo de Autores: *Agresiones de Estados Unidos a Cuba Revolucionaria* p. 213.

— In 1964, aided by their veto power at the international Monetary Fund, the United States managed to separate Cuba from that financial institution, depriving it of funds from the World Bank and, thus, of all possibilities of using these international financial mechanisms of the capitalist system.
— In 1965, the Department of Commerce's group system of nations was divided into groups T,V,W,X,Y and Z. Cuba was placed in the most restrictive category, group Z.[41]
— In 1969, the Department of Commerce amended its rulings on exports, expressly declaring that its policy was to deny all requests to export merchandise and technical data to Cuba, " [...] except in the case of humanitarian transactions".[42]

After the Nixon and Ford administrations and the beginning of the Carter administration, the international situation, primarily in the Caribbean and Latin America,[43] drove the United States to search for means that, without affecting the blockade, would allow their future insertion in potential Cuban economic spaces. This led to a lifting of travel restrictions. Remittances to families were authortized, as was the supply of fuel to ships from third world countries trading with Cuba; Cubana de Aviacion was allowed to fly over U.S. territory and the country was allowed to trade with United States subsidiaries (something which did not take effect until 1981 due to the imposed restrictions, which included the prohibition to finance operations by U.S. firms; Cuba was not allowed to use dollars in the transactions, the products obtained could not have more than 20% U.S. content, etc); the "black list" was discontinued; Interest Sections in both countries opened and sea and fishing limits agreements signed.[44]

The extreme right's neo-conservative current that took control of the White House during the Reagan administration in 1981

---

[41] Michael Krinsky and David Golove: ob. cit., p. 114. Also inn Michel Abdo Cuza: ob. cit., p. 62.

[42] Michael Krinsky and David Golove: ob. cit., p. 116.

[43] Diplomatic isolation measures set down by the United States at the hemispheric level were significantly undermined in 1972: towards the end of that year, diplomatic relations with Cuba were renewed by several countries of the region: Barbados, Jamaica, Trinidad and Tobago. In 1975, the OAS decided that every country was free to establish diplomatic and trade relations with our country in spite of efforts by the United States to prevent this.

[44] Special Newspaper Supplement. No. 18, p. 11.

rapidly dispelled these winds of change and stepped up aggressive actions to turn these into a reactionary tempest which has not ceased raging since.

The main measures adopted included:

— Creation of the Cuban-American National Foundation as the representative instrument of Cuban-born reactionaries to act, in close coordination with the U.S. far right, as a pressure group for the management, approval and execution of measures to overthrow the Revolution.

— From April to June 1982, the process of dismantling everything the Carter administration had achieved in terms of trips to Cuba began. New regulations re-establish the specific licenses of old and stricter regulations begin to govern expenditures. In 1989 measures of this nature are taken again, in relation to costs and the control of flights to Cuba that, up until then, had been authorized.

— In August 1986, the President approves new measures to improve the effectiveness of the blockade and a list of "designated Cubans" is drawn up. It includes private persons and corporate bodies, in any part of the world, with whom any individual or entity under the jurisdiction of the United States is barred from entering into any kind of commercial relationship. Designed to discourage trade relations with Cuba, it was a new kind of "black list", based on practices inherited from the Second World War. Between 1986 and 1989, the Treasury Department issued seven consecutive lists of "designated Cubans", for a total of 230 listed entities.

— On August 23, 1988, congress approved an amendment that, once again invoking the Trading with the Enemy Act, instructs the administration to issue recommendations to tighten measures against Cuba. According to experts, this legal invitation paved the way for a new period of renewed efforts to intensify the blockade.[45] Four recommendations were presented to Congress in November 1988 by United States trade representatives; the first was to apply penal and civil provisions under the Trading with the Enemy Act to those who violated the measures set down; the second was to have the Office of Foreign Assets Control

[45] Michael Krinsky and David Golove: In p. 120.

(OFAC) broaden its interaction with other federal agencies to train these and directly help strengthen the blockade; third, that OFAC work directly with government agencies (CIA? FBI? – INR – State Department?) in gathering all available information on Cuba's international trade network to allow for the more effective identification of entities controlled by Cuba and monitor their transactions and, fourth, to intensify efforts by OFAC and other federal agencies to develop joint and integrated programs to effectively strengthen the "embargo".[46]

— The incredible and criminal strengthening of U.S. control over our international economic relations since then is exemplified by the fact that, on October 1989, Congress' Conference Committee approved increasing OFAC's staff by 40 an the allotment of an extra 2 million dollars for its activities.[47]

Espionage on Cuba's economic performance and measures to undermine it were rapidly stepped up, not by chance, but as part of a political and subversive strategy meant to exacerbate the effects of the disintegration of the Socialist block and later collapse of the U.S.S.R.

This period saw a strengthening of the extraterritoriality of the blockade measures and actions to prevent Cuba from trading with the rest of the world. One of the most vivid examples was OFAC's increased hindering of Cuban sugar and nickel exports, which relied on the "blockade by agreements" learned from the English during the First and Second World Wars. This was brought about through bilateral agreements by which their trade partners, who also traded with Cuba, certified that none of their exports to U.S. territory had Cuban parts or raw materials.

With regards to nickel, the United States entered into these kinds of agreements, which are still in force, with Italy, Holland, France, Japan and even the Soviet Union, shortly before its collapse.[48] According to testimony given by a foreign trade expert in the suit for economic damages brought against the United

---

[46] María de la Luz B'Hamel: Round Table, July 7, 2000; Special Newspaper Supplement No. 18, p. 12.

[47] Special Newspaper Supplement No. 18, p. 11.

[48] Ibid., p. 12.

States, these agreements prevent the access of Cuban nickel to 40% of the world market.[49]

As for sugar, this measure was taken after the Food Security Act was passed in 1985, and violations are punished with exclusion from the quota system.

In 1989 and 1990, when the Mack amendment was unsuccessfully advanced in Congress, a more serious step towards extending the extraterritoriality of the blockade was essayed. The amendment sought to bar companies in third countries, branches of U.S. companies, from all forms of economic and trade operations with Cuba, to deal a coup de grâce to Cuban foreign trade (90.6% of trade with U.S. subsidiaries abroad, for a total of 719 million dollars in 1991, was in food and medicines) and strangle the economy when the European socialist block was on its last leg.

Although it reached the president in 1990, the amendment was not approved because of its insertion in very complicated projects, and was objected to by Bush because of its extraterritoriality and the adverse effects it could cause in third countries. Another amendment from the same period which was not approved was the Smith Amendment; in addition to Mack Amendment provisions, it included the confiscation and seizure of all ships arriving at a U.S. port that had touched a Cuban port less than 180 days prior.[50]

Torricelli Act

Against this background and in order to secure the votes of Florida's Cuban community in that year's presidential elections, President Bush approved the "Cuban Democracy Act" (Torricelli Act) on October 1992. This act had the same criminal intent as the Mack and Smith amendments, as, with the collapse of the socialist block, Cuba needed to reorient its trade towards capitalist markets (Europe, Canada and

[49] Testimony by María del Pilar González Rodríguez, international salesperson of Empresa Cubana Exportadora de Minerales y Metales (CUBANIQUEL).
[50] Remarks by Ana Mayra Rodríguez during the Round Table discussion of July 7, 2000; Special Newspaper Supplement N° 18, p. 13.

Latin America). There was growing trade with the subsidiaries of U.S. companies; there was also a need to move to chartered fleets and use other shipping companies that were not those previously used for trade with European socialist countries.

Under its basic blockade-related provisions, trade with Cuba by branches of U.S. companies based in other countries was prohibited; ships were forbidden to touch Cuban ports for trade purposes; any ship that had touched a Cuban port less than 180 days before was barred from touching U.S. ports; and countries that offered assistance to Cuba, as per the penalties included in the Trading with the Enemy Act, were sanctioned.

Through semantic juggling, the authors of this act named it the "Cuban Democracy Act", a title justified by the inclusion of measures to assist in a transition towards "democracy" in Cuba. Thus, they publicly acknowledged, through what would later assume the form of the act's lamentably well-known Track II, what had been implicit since the beginning of the blockade, born of the secret Operation Mongoose: the subversive nature of U.S. policy, aimed against the political superstructure of Cuban society.

As we shall explain below, these propagandistic efforts to present what is black as white, interference in the internal affairs of other countries or the eagerness to restore neocolonialism as "contributions to democracy" are, in fact, examples of another form of subversive activity: political-ideological subversion, lies and deceit in the field of ideas; attempts to deceive public opinion about its true objectives, shamelessly using the means and methods necessary.

Finally, to soften the opposition of its allies regarding the extraterritoriality of the act and following the debates prior to approval, they introduced the article titled "Aid to the Cuban people", a hypocritical exercise in charity towards the very people the act has condemned to death by hunger and disease.

Helms-Burton Act

While the Torricelli Act aimed to brutally damage Cuba's trade with Western countries at a time when this trade was growing following the collapse of the East European socialist block, the Cuban Freedom and Democratic Solidarity Act, or Helms-Burton Act, made one of its main objectives that of preventing the participation of foreign investment in the country's economic reanimation process.[51]

In 1994, with a Republican majority in both the House and Senate, the extreme right set out to reverse Cuba's economic reanimation. At the beginning of 1995, it already had a proposal which synthesized all anti-Cuban legal texts being processed into one. In this connection, the administration had given its consent towards the end of that year and signed it in March 12, 1996, using, as pretext, the incident involving the violation of Cuban airspace by and the downing of the planes deployed by the counterrevolutionary organization "Brothers to the Rescue". The act came into force in September of that same year.

As with the Torricelli Act and, in general, all anti-Cuban activities since 1959, the legal abomination embodied by the Helms-Burton Law combines, in one legal corpus, economic warfare measures with those aimed at encouraging internal subversion and our country's return to capitalism.

An example of the many political maneuvers the U.S. Congress uses to implement economic warfare actions is the manipulation of information about Cuba, described as a promoter of terrorist activities against U.S. properties and interests, the category under which we were included in the State Department report to Congress of 1982 and from which, since then, we have never been excluded,[52] even though many acknowledge that the United States is not driven so much by objective reality but by the political pressure of anti-Cuban representatives in Congress.

On the basis of this, Congress has approved laws to ratify or take advantage of this classification in order to step up anti-Cuban measures; prime examples are the Torricelli and Helms-Burton Acts, as well as the great majority of acts against international trade and sanctions imposed on Cuba. Through this discriminatory treatment,

---

[51] The fall of the economy in 1993 was halted and there was a small growth of 0,7. In 1995 this growth was of 2,3.

[52] In the Law of Export Control of 1979, State Department was required to present an annual report to Congress about terrorism (Title 22, United States Code, Section 2656[a]) and, in 1981 the first Annual Report was published on International Terrorism prepared by the Office of the Coordinator of Counterterrorism of the State Department

grounded in Cuba's inclusion in this category, Cuba is subjected to measures to prevent trade in medicines and food. In addition to this, it blocks access to international funds, depriving us of funds frozen in the United States and prohibiting Cuba from exporting technology. Previous blockade measures were apparently not enough.

In Chapter VI, where we deal with Cuba's condemnation of the blockade and, more generally, with the economic war waged through the United Nations General Assembly since 1992, we will again refer to the Torricelli and Helms-Burton Acts and to subsequent legal initiatives that have continued to intensify the economic war against our country.

March 18, 1960

MEMORANDUM OF CONFERENCE WITH THE PRESIDENT
2:30 PM, March 17, 1960

Others present: Vice President Nixon, Secretary Herter,
Mr. Merchant, Mr. Rubottom, Secretary Anderson,
Secretary Irwin, Admiral Burke, Mr. Allen Dulles,
· Mr. Richard Bissell, Colonel J. C. King, Gordon
Gray, Major Eisenhower, General Goodpaster

After Mr. Herter gave a b[rief] ⸻ning use of the OAS
in connection with the Cu[ban] ⸻ reported
to the President an action
covert operations to effe
will be to form a moder:
take about one month.
tion" which Castro has
to carry out gray or bl
lished, probably on Sw
United States), in two
affected elements wil'

To a question by the
tion would probably
be better if they col
Venezuela would be
government could
Rica may be a pos

Mr. Allen Dulles
will begin outside
of leaders toget
might take som

The President
with this situal
of security.

- 2 -

heard of it." He said we should limit American contacts with
the groups involved to two or three people, getting Cubans
to do most of what must be done. Mr. Allen Dulles said
this, and reiterated that there should be only two or three
governmental people connected with this in any way. He understood that the effort will be to undermine Castro's position and
prestige. Mr. Bissell commented that the opposition group
would undertake a money-raising campaign to obtain funds on
their own -- in the United States, Cuba and elsewhere.

The President indicated some question about
The President

Mr. Gray commented that events may occur rapidly in Cuba,
and force our hand before these preparations are completed.

Secretary Anderson stated that Castro is in reality financing
his operations out of the funds of the U. S. companies that are
operating in Cuba. He suggested that the Administration might
take steps to bring business leaders together with elements
of our government to consider what course the businesses --
which are now being milked of their assets -- should take. He
said he had received a report that Castro is trying to inflame
Cuban opinion and create an incident against the Americans
which would touch off attacks on Americans in Cuba which might
result in the death of thousands. The President stated that
once the operation Mr. Douglas had proposed gets started, there
will be great danger to the Americans in Cuba. Mr. Rubottom
said that the "warning phase" of our evacuation plan is already
in effect, and that many Americans are leaving, with almost
no new ones going in.

Mr. Anderson said he thought that if we were to cut the Cubans
off from their fuel supply, the effect would be devastating on
them within a month or six weeks. There is some question
whether other countries would join in denying fuel oil -- especially
Venezuela. Mr. Anderson added that if Cuba is to seize the
Nicaro plant or other U. S. Government property, we could not
stand on the sidelines. In reponse to a question by the President,
it was brought out that there is no treaty on this, and that Cuba
of course has the right to confiscate the plant so long as compensation is given. Mr. Rubottom stated that if we wanted to cut

On 17 March 1960, U.S. President Dwight D. Eisenhower approved a CIA plan which, culminating in the Bay of Pigs invasion, systematized economic measures against Cuba. (Original source: Eisenhower Library, Project "Clean Up", Records, Intelligence Matters. Top Secret).

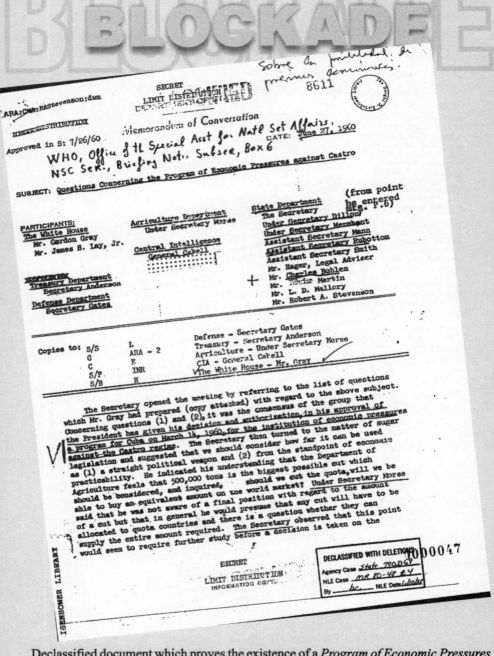

Declassified document which proves the existence of a *Program of Economic Pressures* against the Cuban revolution, elaborated by the U.S. government and approved with the *Covert Actions Program* of 17 March 1960. It refers to a top level government meeting which approved anti-Cuban economic measures. (Original source: Department of State, S/P Files: Lot 67 D548, Cuba 1959–1961. Secret; Limit Distribution).

UNCLASSIFIED

TENTATIVE

F. SABOTAGE SUPPORT PLAN

ACTIVITY	PURPOSE	CONSIDERATIONS
1. Sabotage Cuban supply of nickel to Soviets.	To deny supply to Soviets and to hinder Cuba's ability to pay for Bloc imports.	(blacked out)
2. Sabotage fuel supply.	To cripple transportation.	(blacked out)
3. Sabotage communications.	To dramatize and encourage the spirit of resistance.	Prime targets for hit-and-run teams based outside Cuba are CMQ TV and the Czech radio transmitter (believed now used to jam U.S. broadcasts). Attacks mounted only when operationally feasible. The G-2 micro-wave net should be dealt with when there are sufficient assets inside to make sabotage coincide with a critical need, in August-September.
4. Sabotage power supply.	To increase strain on regime and bring daily business to a standstill, by dramatic action all people will note.	This should be a concerted attack, as feasible in July-August, on power plants at Havana, Santiago, Cinfuegos, Vicente, Santa Clara, Cuatro Caminos, Matanzas. It is of a type requiring detailed planning and special equipment, and can be mounted from outside Cuba.

Operation Mongoose entailed a scorched earth policy towards the Cuban economy. This document details a number of measures included in a plan to sabotage prioritized sectors. (Original source: Kennedy Library, National Security Files, Meeting and Memoranda Series, Special Group (Augmented), Operation Mongoose, 2 / 62-4 /62. Top Secret; Sensitive. Supplement).

Sabotage/Harassment Program

The broad target categories against which the sabotage/harassment operations would be mounted and a preliminary evaluation of their effect, can be summarized as follows:

A. *Electric Power*

Disruption of any of the existing power grids which might be effected by damage to or destruction of the generating facilities or of the critical sub-stations in the distribution network, would significantly weaken the existing economic and social structure, particularly in view of the fact that in many areas the power now available is not adequate to meet the demands of industrial and public consumers. Smaller acts of

sabotage/harassment by the populace such as throwing chains over high tension lines to short them out, would also exacerbate the current power shortage, and the cumulative effect of all such actions could cause a prolonged breakdown of the power system as there is already a shortage of spare parts and replacement matériels.

B. *Petroleum, Oil and Lubricants (POL)*

Damage to or destruction of POL production and/or storage facilities would seriously affect almost all aspects of the Cuban economy. The electric power industry depends almost entirely upon POL as fuel for the generating plants and the sugar industry depends upon POL powered processing and transportation facilities as does all intra-province transportation. Production and storage facilities are susceptible to external attacks by heavy weapons or by more subtle methods if internal assets having an appropriate degree of accessibility can be developed. The loss of refining facilities could be offset by increased Bloc shipments of refined products but such a shift would require a period of readjustment during which there would be a heavy strain on the Cuban economy. An additional burden on the Bloc refining capacity would also exist until Cuba's refining capacity is restored.

C. *Transportation*

Damage to or destruction of railway and/or highway rolling stock or the destruction of key bridges would lead to breakdowns in the regional economics which to a large degree are dependent on the distribution of imported products. The processing and export of the vitally important sugar crop is also entirely dependent on transportation. It is not anticipated that we could achieve that degree of disruption which would cause a collapse of the economy or social structure, but even a minor degree of disruption will adversely affect the standard of living and the output of the economy, both of which are key factors in the stability of the regime. The type of operations envisioned in this category would range from fairly sophisticated attacks by external or internal assets against the rolling stock, key bridges and repair facilities to simple low risk acts by the populace such as the derailing of rail transportation or placing tire puncturing material on highways.

D. *Production Processing and Manufacturing Facilities*

While the Cuban economy primarily depends on imports for indigenous consumption and even though the sugar crop is by far the most important item in Cuban exports, there are still a number of other facilities such as the nickel complex at Nicaro, cement plants, distilleries, and the myriad industries associated with the provision of food, clothing and shelter, which are worthwhile targets in that stopping or lessening their output will weaken the economy and breed discontent against the regime. These targets are particularly susceptible to attack by external or internal assets in that due to their profusion and their relatively low stra-

In June 1963, at the instance of the CIA, President Kennedy approved the document titled *Proposed Covert Policy and Integrated Program of Action Toward Cuba,* which came to substitute the ill-fated *Operation Mongoose.* The document highlights prioritized sectors to be sabotaged. (Source: Department of State: *Foreign Relations of the United States,* vol. XI, document 346).

BLOCKADE

The National Security Act of 1947 which officially established the CIA invoked, as the fifth duty of this agency, a broad and vague field of "covert actions" which were detailed in 1948, when the execution of economic warfare actions against other nations was explicitly mentioned. According to the policy of "plausible denial", covert actions had to be undertaken such that no one could implicate the government of the United States. The photo shows the Central Intelligence Agency's headquarters in Langley, Virginia.

In his book/denunciation *CIA Diary*, published in 1975, Philip Agee, an ex official of this espionage and subversion agency, refers to two types of economic warfare actions: direct sabotage of key economic sectors and covert measures to prevent the country from importing essential supplies.

In a televised interview about clandestine actions against Cuba, ex CIA sub-director (1962 - 1966) Ray S. Cline described forms of "subtle sabotage" as follows: a piece of equipment imported by Cuba, apparently in excellent conditions, could contain ball bearings that had been tampered with to render the machine inoperative after a short period of operations. In the lower photo, Cline, in 1956, appears with then CIA director Allen Dulles and another undercover agent. A mere two years later, they would become key actors in the dirty war against the Cuban revolution.

The CIA has devoted scrupulous efforts to destroy important economic targets through acts of sabotage. According to declassified U.S. government documents, one of the conditions sabotage actions had to meet was that their effects had to be significant and lasting.

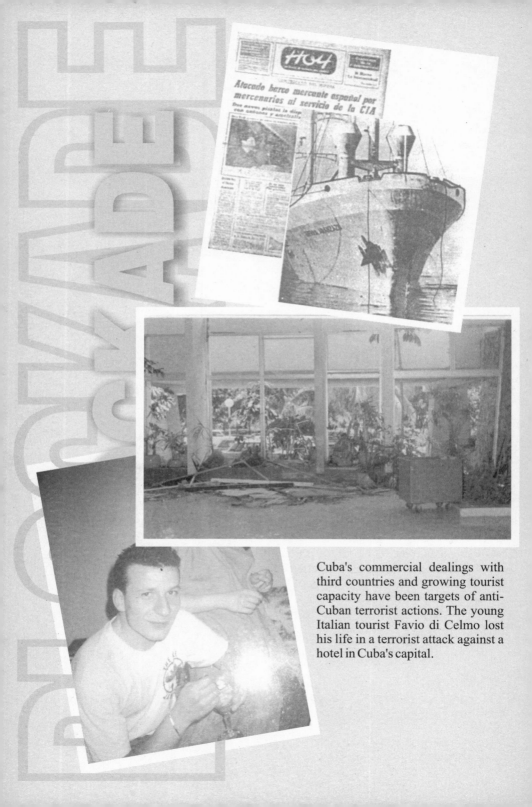

Cuba's commercial dealings with third countries and growing tourist capacity have been targets of anti-Cuban terrorist actions. The young Italian tourist Favio di Celmo lost his life in a terrorist attack against a hotel in Cuba's capital.

Acts of biological aggression are part of the economic war against Cuba. In the photos, Cuban-born counterrevolutionary Eduardo Arocena confesses, in 1984, that he had introduced pathogenic germs into Cuba. African porcine fever, dengue fever and *Thrips palmi* are some of the many pathogens that have been used against our country. Cuban experts provided a well-documented analysis of the use of biological warfare as witnesses during the suit brought against the United States for economic damages to Cuba.

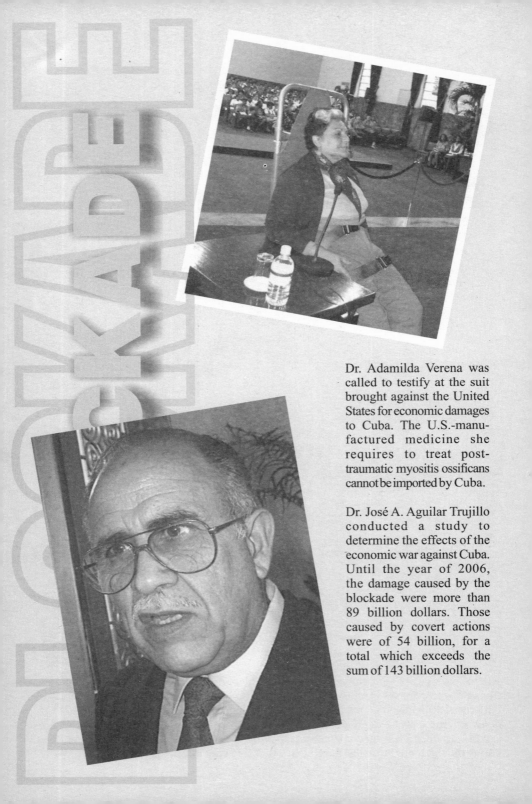

Dr. Adamilda Verena was called to testify at the suit brought against the United States for economic damages to Cuba. The U.S.-manufactured medicine she requires to treat post-traumatic myositis ossificans cannot be imported by Cuba.

Dr. José A. Aguilar Trujillo conducted a study to determine the effects of the economic war against Cuba. Until the year of 2006, the damage caused by the blockade were more than 89 billion dollars. Those caused by covert actions were of 54 billion, for a total which exceeds the sum of 143 billion dollars.

CHAPTER IV Espionage and its use in the planning and execution of sabotage actions against the Cuban economy

The approval of the Helms-Burton Act in 1996 in the United States publicly revealed the existing link between *subversive activity* and *open state policy towards* Cuba. Documents to be declassified in the United States in 2020 will by then (!) allow us to study the complexity of this relationship, as was possible in the previous chapters that dealt with the decade of the 60s.

However, we needn't wait for their declassification to identify the general components of this relationship. The very text of the Helms-Burton Act, especially Section 108, officially prioritizes acts of espionage which must be executed in Cuba to evaluate the effects of this piece of legislation.

This section, entitled "Reports on commerce with, and assistance to, Cuba from other foreign countries", established annual reports, by the President to Congress, containing a description of the bilateral aid received by Cuba during the period in question; a description of Cuba's commerce with foreign countries, including an identification of Cuba's trading partners and the extent of such trade; a description of the joint ventures completed, or under consideration, by foreign nationals and business firms involving facilities in Cuba, including an identification of the location of the facilities involved and a description of the terms of agreement of the joint ventures and the names of the parties that are involved, as well as a determination as to whether or not any of the facilities described is the subject of a claim against

Cuba by a United States national; a determination of the amount of debt of the Cuban Government that is owed to each foreign country; a description of the steps taken to assure that raw materials and semifinished or finished goods produced by facilities in Cuba involving foreign nationals do not enter the United States market and a description of the military supplies, equipment, or other material sold, bartered, or exchanged between Cuba and such countries.[1]

These documents' information requirements, entrusted to the CIA and State Department, explain the constant search for information on these areas undertaken in our country, or anywhere in the world, by open or covert U.S. espionage services, designed to apply measures to foil all efforts made by Cubans to survive.

Cuba has systematically denounced these actions before the international community. It has not ceased doing so since the passing of these acts, by presenting the General Assembly of the United Nations with a draft resolution calling for an end to the blockade.

Because of the importance of this point, we must quote the National Assembly of the People's Power expert on the United States Ana Mayra Rodríguez extensively. During a Round Table discussion televised on July 11, 2000, she expressed:

"[...] espionage [...] is conducted by U.S. government agencies to monitor Cuba's economic and commercial activities around the world.

"This, of course, does not begin with the Helms-Burton or Torricelli acts, it is something that began at the very triumph of the Revolution; but this time what Congress achieves with the acts is to force the government to give an account of its actions in these reports.

"And I want to quote a declaration of a Department of State official, Michael Ranenberger, of March of 1998, when he said that, on June 1998, January 1997 and January 1998, the government had submitted to Congress the reports required by the Helms-Burton Act, saying the following: 'The required information continues to be available only from sources that we are bound to protect, so we have provided classified reports to Congress'. *There is no more convincing evidence that this is the result of an intelligence activity, of an activity of persecution that, in this case, pursues a second objective, that is, to report to Congress; but, until that time, its intent had also been to sever any kind of relationship we could have with a*

---

[1] *Cuban Liberty and Democratic Solidarity Act,* Helms-Burton Act, Section 108.

foreign entity, a foreign government, a company or anyone.[2] (The italics are ours).

The president of the National Assembly of the People's Power provided additional information on this point during the same Round Table discussion, when he expressed that: "Of course, there is another section of the Helms-Burton Act that also refers to resources. It is perhaps the most discreet phrase in the act, Section 115: "Nothing in this Act prohibits any lawfully authorized investigative, protective, or intelligence activity of a law enforcement agency, or of an intelligence agency, of the United States."[3]

According to documents revealed in another cycle of Round Table discussions, televised on January 23 and 26, 2001, entitled **U.S. subversive actions against Cuba**, diplomatic staff and their families and a group of officials in transit, who visit our country for short periods of time and on a regular basis, offer a large part of the information sought by U.S. espionage services.

These include officials, analysts and technicians from CIA headquarters in Langley, Virginia, whose "presence in the country allows them to evaluate, in situ, the internal situation and support other illegal actions". In 1998, 1999 and 2000, *the country was visited by more than 540 officials in transit; almost 30% were identified as holding posts in or suspected of being in the service of U.S. intelligence agencies*.[4] (The italics are ours).

Background

The United States was already an expert in the kinds of practices it implements against Cuba in this area when the Revolution triumphed.

Referring to the espionage activities behind the economic measures implemented during the Second World War, Gordon and Dangerfeld's book on these subjects mentioned above, describes

[2] Ana Mayra Rodríguez: remarks during informational Round Table discusión of 11 July 2000, Special Newspaper Supplement N° 18, p. 21.

[3] Ricardo Alarcón: ibid., p. 21

[4] "Las acciones de subversión política del Gobierno de Estados Unidos contra Cuba" ("The US government's politcal subversion actions against Cuba". Document presented at the Round Table broadcast of January 2001, p. 11.

the abundant use of agents recruited within these economic, commercial and financial mechanisms, who even actively participated in the activities on which they had to report; the gathering of market studies to find out on what opportunities the adversary could be prompted to act; the study of cargoes to detect product substitutions prohibited by others and many other practices.

"These intelligence actions are top secret", the authors explain, noting the close relationship established by the Office of Strategic Affairs (OSS, predecessor of the CIA) and the FBI with British Intelligence, for their execution during the war.

Though careful in covering up the subversive actions taken on the basis of the information acquired, other revealing aspects of U.S. espionage on the economic status of countries of interest is found in the work of Sherman Kent, considered one of the architects of the United States intelligence community and a key figure of the CIA apparatus during the tense moments of the Cold War, when he headed his Office of National Estimates.[5]

Published in 1949, Sherman Kent's **Strategic intelligence for American world policy,** containing the experience acquired by the United States during the Second World War, continues to be a key text studied in U.S. universities that treat the subject.[6] Kent describes three moments in espionage activity: an initial basic description offering all the information available at a given moment; a systematic informative element used to keep the existing information up to date and, finally, a speculative-evaluative and analytical element based on the previous two that would give the United States government the possibility of being "prepared [...] prepared for the future [...] protected against contingencies [...] prevent surprises by unexpected events [...]".[7]

The need for encyclopedic information can at times reach aberrant levels. According to Kent, in his explanation of the initial basic descriptive point: "Take the chapter on 'transports' [...] the section roads begins with a map of the road network; it is then followed by a description, kilometer by kilometer, of the main roads with observations on the surface, width, slopes, curves, gravel roads,

[5] Donald Steury: Sherman Kent. Center for the Study of Intelligence.
http://www.cia.gov/csi/books/shermankent/intro.html.

[6] Idem.

[7] Sherman Kent: *Strategic intelligence for American world policy,* second edition, pp. 29-59.

detours, cuts and bridges; then, it offers a general appreciation of the route in question."

Regarding railroad transportation: paths, the number of tracks and routes [...] a kind of map detailing each kilometer, terminals, workshops [...] and inventory on the type of locomotive and rail stock [...]."

With respect to ports: "[...] the area of protected waters, depth of the water [...] dams and depth of the water on either side [...] dam cranes, means of transport to free the dams and port area, port deposits and storage facilities."[8]

According to the author, *complete descriptive knowledge of the economy of the adversary* is needed for military operations,[9] economic warfare actions, the administration of occupied territories[10] and as a daily update for those who plan subversive activities in other countries. The characteristics of the electricity supply in any business neighborhood, the output of copper mines at a given moment, or the particularities of water supply in the city of interest, all these details may prove useful to intelligence work, as the work we are mentioning appears to indicate.[11]

Referring to the work of systematically gathering information to bring available information up to date, Sherman Kent explains:

"[...] information work has the responsibility of being up to date regarding economic development [...]. It should note the formulation of new economic doctrines and theories [...]; it should note the changes in government economic policy, policies that affect industry,

---

[8] Ibid., pp. 31-32.

[9] "Before the planes took off on their first systematic destruction mission, those planning the bombing of Germany had to have extensive knowledge of the production of ball bearings, synthetic rubber and fuel [...]. The decision to send in B-29s against Japanese aviation, motor factories, arsenals, electronic plants, oil refineries [...] was supported by a similar 'stock' of encyclopaedic knowledge. Sherman Kent: p. 37. In the first chapter, when we referred to the British Economic War ministry we mentioned that the activity included evaluating the enemy's war potential and advising military actions to identify industries targeted for destruction. Following this, the ministry worked to prevent enemy countries from obtaining the means to set these industries in motion again.

[10] Title II of the Helms-Burton Act includes, to a certain extent, guidelines to guide US actions during a hypothetical occupation of Cuban territory, as does the document issued by the United States President on January 1997 entitled *Support for a democratic transition in Cuba*.

[11] Sherman Kent: p. 47.

the organization of businesses, agriculture, the banks, finances and foreign relationships. It must be aware of changes that occur in the volume and distribution of wealth and national incomes, of changes in the "standard" of living, working hours and jobs. It must monitor new harvests and the development of new methods in agriculture, changes in farm and cattle farming equipment, the use of land, of fertilizers, crop projects. It must keep a close eye on new industrial processes, the creation of new industries and excavation of new mines. It must closely follow the development of new public services and the increase of already established ones. It must inform on changes in techniques and distribution tools, on new transportation routes and changes in the inventories of transport bases (cars, trucks, locomotives and boxcars, airplane transportation, canal cargo freighters and transoceanic merchant ships) [...]".[12]

Referring to the analysis of information gathered and asking what should be found out to reveal the adversary's greater vulnerabilities, the author states: "[...] one must have all the kinds of encyclopedic knowledge described and be capable of choosing, through an analytic process, those factors of life [...] that are vulnerable to the weapons possessed. These weapons [...] can be of many different kinds: psychological, political, economic, military".[13]

For the United States, acquiring the kind of knowledge described was only possible by illimitably extending espionage activities around the world and, at the same time, impelling and organizing a vast system of foreign studies in their universities and other research centers created for that purpose (the think tanks). This is precisely what occurred in the post-war period, with the rapid expansion of "area studies", conducted on the basis of intelligence gathered during the war by the OSS Section of Information Analysis (SIA), which studied countries that were military operations theaters or of interest for other reasons.

During the war, this espionage organization was based in the Library of Congress and, by 1945, it is estimated that the service was staffed by 1, 600 psychologists, economists and other professionals who supplied intelligence on all parts of the world, for its subsequent use in the planning and execution of U.S. foreign policy.[14]

[12] Ibid., pp. 53-54
[13] Ibid., pp. 77-78.
[14] Nikolai Yaklovev: *La CIA contra la URSS (The CIA against the USSR)*. Editorial Progreso, Moscow, 1983, pp. 80-81.

The evaluation of this process by the OSS chief's biographer, William Donovan, is significant indeed: "For academic history it is a curious fact that the first great comprehensive study center in the United States was founded not in a university by in the Office of Strategic Studies during the Second World War. The study programs (about other nations) set up in universities after the war were largely directed or stimulated by graduates from the OSS institution [...] partially made up by agents and scientists. Today, it is also true, and I believe it always will be, that between the universities and the Information Services of the United States there is a high degree of interpenetration."[15]

Public Information

This process had important consequences in two areas: in a broader sense, in setting up and improving a system of foreign affairs in universities, created to address the establishment's need to strengthen and broaden world capitalist leadership; and, in a narrower sense, in the study of other countries undertaken by members of the U.S. intelligence community.

The USSR and other socialist countries, as we can logically infer, were the prioritized objects of study. *Sovietology* was given renewed impetus[16] with the creation of the Russian Institute at Colombia University in 1946 and a similar center in Harvard University in 1948. Renowned sovietologists were responsible for the creation of the strategic doctrines that characterized political, economic and military actions of *contention* or *liberation* aimed at the socialist community; of a *differential treatment* towards some countries, designed to separate them from the USSR; the later strategies of *extending bridges, eroding socialism from within* and, more recently, the *democratic project* as the banner of the neo-conservative foreign policy that reached the White House with the Reagan Administration, to decisively combat and bring about the disappearance of socialism in Eastern Europe and the USSR.

---

[15] C. Ford: *Donovan of OSS*. Boston, 1970, pp. 149-150. Quoted by. Yaklovev: In p. 81.

[16] In 1919 the Hoover Institution on War, Revolution and Peace had been created. According to its founding charter, it was created "to reveal the evil of Karl Marx's doctrine".

By the end of the 50s and beginning of the 60s, renewed impetus was given U.S. area studies. Without abandoning their priorities of old, these began paying closer attention to a Third Word which, at the time, had witnessed the break up of the old colonial empires and was showing signs of a collective awakening,[17] of which Cuba was one of the most important examples in the Hemisphere.

As a result of this, U.S. universities began giving priority to Latin American studies. In 1959, Congress approved the National Defense Education Act, under which Latin American studies began to be included in government-funded university research work,[18] rapidly steered towards an evaluation of the region's existing revolutionary potential.[19] Studies on Cuba, which began shortly after the revolutionary triumph in 1959, coined the term **cubanology**.

This was the stage in which studies on the Cuban economy began at universities and other research centers in the U.S. Later, we will refer to cubanology's contribution to the sphere of propaganda. Now, we are only interested in pointing out two of its facets: its contribution to the establishment's more complete knowledge of the Cuban economy's internal situation and its prospects.

We are not claiming, not even remotely, that researchers on Cuban economic affairs could be accused of consciously participating in actions that damaged or could damage Cuba. The methods are much more subtle; the system creates conditions (providing funding, for example) to prioritize research on those aspects that are of greater interest for Cuba policy decision makers. In this manner, the analysis of any piece of data on the development of any of the country's economic areas offered by Cuban publications,

---

[17] Recall that, already in the Bandung Conference of 1955, there were signs of what would become the Non-Aligned Movement in 1961, a necessity for those emerging States, and that the U.S. political and military doctrine that was gaining strength was that of flexible reaction, designed to confront the liberation struggles that were later classified as *low intensity conflicts*.

[18] We could ask ourselves: did the struggle in the Sierra Maestra have any bearing on the adoption of this decision?

[19] The most relevant and controversial of which was what became known as the Camelot Plan, unmasked in the Chilean Senate in 1965 and considered the vastest plan of *sociological espionage* ever undertaken. Its purpose was to evaluate the degree of revolutionary infection in Latin America (comparing it to the Cuban situation), the basis for adopting more appropriate counterinsurgency measures. It was a time when continental counterrevolution sharpened its teeth to prevent the repetition of processes similar to Cuba's.

140

any evaluation or point of view about any fact expressed on a radio or television broadcast, as trivial as it may seem, rapidly becomes raw material for the analysis of development trends in a given field or the results of investments in a certain sector. Without going into these mechanisms in detail, we wish to point out how U.S. intelligence and subversion services are intertwined with and use public studies on the Cuban economy for their own purposes.

For the search, processing and evaluation of public information on Cuban issues and to academically evaluate information gathered from public sources, the CIA created its own Center for Cuban Studies. According to reliable sources, by the mid 80s, that Center's catalogue included the most important studies on Cuba in existence in the United States, and its staff of highly qualified researches far surpassed, in number and experience, those of the most outstanding universities, including Pittsburgh University's Center for Latin American Studies which, at the time, had the most impact in the university scene.

The CIA has offered the use of public information it gathers to other government agencies and, in general, to those interested in the subject. In the area that interests us here, the report "The Cuban economy: a statistical Review"[20] is a telling example.

The data offered in this publication, gathered exclusively from public sources, refer to the management of the sugar industry, agriculture (with the exception of sugar cane) other industrial productions, oil production; energy consumption and construction material estimates; the transportation sector, distribution; finances; foreign trade and statistics on the population and work force. The figures offered have such a degree of detail that they tell us, for example, the percentage of sugar found in sugar cane fields each year; viand and vegetable production levels or the total number of passengers traveling in the country by type of vehicle. This recalls the systematic updating of data that, according Sherman Kent's book, U.S. intelligence services require.

In these times of Internet surfing, the CIA has not lagged behind and, through this medium, offers navigators worldwide similar statistics, assuming a role of world encyclopedia which no one asked it to assume. Before him, as he writes these lines, the author has the statistics on

---

[20] Central Intelligence Agency: Directorate of Intelligence: *The Cuban Economy: A Statistical Review.*

Cuban imports for the 1990s (Table 122, Cuban imports, according to data from the Cuban government and official figures from its trade partners).[21] Contemplating the more pronounced fall observed in the 1992-1994 period, he asks himself: following the collapse of the socialist block, to what degree did the Torricelli Act contribute to the sharp decline of these figures? Similarly, looking at Table 121 on Cuban exports during the same period,[22] the question arises: How did U.S. harassment affect the sale of Cuban nickel in the world during the sharp fall that began in 1990 and became steeper after the disappearance of the USSR? What we have before us, thus, is a unique source of statistics, capable of anything to change what is not to its liking.

Espionage on the Cuban economy through subversive means and methods

On referring to public sources through which U.S. espionage and subversion services obtain information of interest on the Cuban economy, we have simply relied on an opinion widely accepted by experts on these subjects: the greater part of the information those services require are obtained from public sources. This has special repercussions for Cubans: all who, because of their work, must handle economic information that can be used by the CIA and other U.S. agencies to tighten the blockade or plan sabotage or other measures to undermine the economy, must rigorously protect this information.[23] The security of the Homeland is at stake.

But this information is complemented by what they obtain clandestinely through their agents in the country. And, if we ask ourselves what these two types of surveys pursue, we dredge up those sordid details which cannot be divulged over the Internet, where

---

[21] Handbook of International Economic Statistics, 1977, Economic Profile, table 122. http.//.cia.gov/cia/publications/hies97/j/tab122.htm

[22] Ibid., table 121. Expressed in sugar, nickel, tobacco, medical products, fish and shellfish, citrus fruits and others.

[23] In the 70s, the national press published an article, entitled: "Without leaving the office", which became study material in some institutions. It offered an interesting evaluation of how the espionage services of developed capitalist countries use information obtained from public sources.

the idyllic vision of a bespectacled university professor, evaluating the drop in Cuban imports following the collapse of the socialist block and the USSR in a scholarly manner, finds itself substituted by an army of officials scattered across the world's trade centers, resorting to blackmail and pressures to prevent the sale of Cuban products or the purchase of products for the country, by agents recruited to bomb vital industries for the country or to arm launches for terrorist actions and foreign mercenaries, hired to place bombs in Cuban hotels.

The acts of espionage against the Cuban economy that the CIA and other espionage services have conducted and continue to conduct cannot be thought of as the romantic adventure portrayed in spy films. It is not a *duel between gentlemen*, as some literary works portray acts of espionage. Invariably, the search for information on the Cuban economy by U.S. services has always been aimed at hindering, damaging and delaying its development. For this reason, espionage has always been accompanied by direct subversive actions against the economy, which make negotiations abroad more difficult or prevent them altogether, or which resort to sabotage, terrorism and the introduction of plagues and diseases into the country as part of biological warfare efforts or others aimed at the internal economic infrastructure. For the wide public, many of the facts that we will deal with below might seem something out of a *suspense novel*. Actions undertaken in different periods have been chosen as examples of the persistence of this criminal policy of direct espionage and subversion of the economy.

Unfortunately for the Cuban people and to the satisfaction of those in the United States who have directed and executed this policy of subversion and crime, the measures aseptically reported on in official U.S. documents that we read in the previous chapter resulted in very concrete and far from aseptic actions, through complex plots that for many are the stuff of movies but that Cuba has had to endure as the harshest of realities.

Oil Case

In the previous chapter, we saw that at the April 10, 1963 meeting of the Coordination Committee for Cuban Affairs, held to discuss proposals for covert actions against Cuba that would be evaluated in the following meeting of the National Security Council Special

Group, CIA Plans director Desmond FitzGerald commented on planning an action against "the most important sabotage target" which would seriously damage Cuba but that, because of its degree of complexity, the action "could take eight months to execute". We considered that it could refer to the CIA-planned sabotage action against the "Ñico López" refinery. We have no doubts about the matter and could not be more categorical: assuredly it referred to this macabre plan.

What did it entail? What actions were undertaken to execute it?

The agent had been recruited in the United States during the second half of 1961 while completing his engineering degree at the University of Louisiana. Following his return to Cuba as a repatriate in 1962, he had begun working in that refinery as Department Head of Maintenance, where he began his initial espionage activity in the oil refinery sector, detected towards the latter part of 1963. Thanks to the work of Cuba's State Security agencies, it was discovered that he had received instructions from the CIA to paralyze production in the "Ñico López" refinery for no less than a month, a task for for which four collaborators had been recruited.[24]

The shortest period of time for which the industry was to be paralyzed coincided with statements by the U.S. Treasury Secretary, in the discussions at the March 1960 National Security Council meeting on the *Program of Economic Pressures against the Castro Regime*, which was the starting point of the economic war against our country. He had stated that if oil supplies were suspended in Cuba, "the effect would be devastating on them within a month or six weeks". It is evident that, by striking at the most important refinery in the country through its agent, the CIA intended to fulfill a dream it had nurtured since March 1960.

Congruent with these interests, dating back to 1960, and the 1962 Cuba Project that spawned Operation Mongoose, the desired effects of this terrorist design scrupulously mirror the targets envisaged by and the requirements approved at the highest U.S. government level through the *Covert Policy and Integrated Program of Action Toward Cuba* of June 1964, extending these in a way that proves methodologically insightful.

The interest in striking at such a sensitive product as lubricants was evident since the first moments of work on this case, upon

[24] MININT Archives: *Oil Case*

learning of the request sent to the agent to take samples of Soviet MARK 20 and MARK 22 lubricants received in the country, and of the different formulas and additives used. In page 35, the agent's confession about his activities reads (all these quotes are taken from the archive files): "In the second message of January, 1964, I sent the report of lubricant production and, if memory serves me right, asked them to tell me what to do with the samples if I managed to get them out of the refinery [...]."Among other things, the ninth radio message received in mid September 1964 expressed:

"NINE X [...] IMPORTANT RECEIVE AS SOON AS POSSIBLE INFORMATION ON [...] NEW FORMULAS FOR LUBRICANTS X PLANS FOR PRODUCTION THIS YEAR [...] INFORMATION ABOUT SOVIET LUBRICANTS [...]".

Apparently, to confirm the results of actions undertaken to undermine trade in this important product with the USSR, a radio message received by the agent during the early part of October 1964 said:

"ONE ONE X FOLLOWING INFORMATON URGENTLLY NECESSARY, COLON, REPORT IF RUSSIANS ARE HOLDING BACK OR DECREASING DELIVERY OF LUBRICANTS PROMISED ACCORDING TO CONTRACT FOR SEPTEMBER OF 1964 X IF SO, IDENTIFY THE LUBRICANT AND HOW THEY ARE HOLDING BACK DELIFERY X SEND SPECIFIC DATA ON NORMAL DELIVERIES PROMISED AND MONTHLY DELIVERIES THAT ARE NOW BEING CARRIED OUT FOR EACH TYPE OF LUBRICANT SHOWING CHANGES OR DECREASES [...]."

How closely the CIA monitored the internal situation of that target in order to damage it can be appreciated in the requests contained in the tenth radio message received towards the end of September 1964:

"ONE ZERO X GLAD TO RECEIVE VALUABLE REPORT AND EXPECT FURTHER REPORTS SINCE WE NEED CONTINUOUS INFORMATION ABOUT THE STATE OF THE REFINERY AND PRODUCTION X SEND TWO WEEKLY MESSAGES X REPEAT X TWO WEEKLY MESSAGES WITH INFORMATION YOU AND YOUR AGENTS CAN REPORT ON [...]."

An example in this connection appears in the eleventh message received in early October:

"DESCRIBE ALL CHANGES IN THE OPERATION OF THE CATALIZING CRACKER IN THE ÑICO LÓPEZ REFINERY AND REASON FOR THESE CHANGES X EXPLAIN SITE X PROBLEMS WITH THE GAS COMPRESSOR X REPORT TIME CATALYTIC CRACKER WAS HALTED AND REASON IN THE LAST SIX MONTHS AND KEEP US INFORMED ON THE STATE OF THE FOLLOWING UNITS X CATALYTIC CRACKER X FORMER POWER X HYDROFINER X PLAT FORMER [...]."

A fifth radio message received during the early part of August 1964 requests information to tighten the blockade:

"FIVE X [...] REPORT IMPORTANT CHANGES IN SUPPLY OF SPARE PARTS AND BRIGHT STOCKS X FULLY IDENTIFY SHIPS AND PORT OF ORIGIN X REPORT CRITICAL SCARCITY OF PARTS AND RAW MATERIAL IN REFINERY [...]."

Similarly, message fourteen of early November read:

"ONE FOUR X [...] INSIST ON WEEKLY REPORTS ON VALUABLE INFORMATION TO WHICH YOU HAVE ACCESS AND WE NEED ON A DAILY BASIS X [...] DESCRIBE CRITICAL PARTS THAT REFINERY NEEDS GIVING NUMBER X MANUFACTURER X HOW THEY ARE SHIPPED AND RECEIVED X FOR WHICH UNIT REQUIRED X IF POSSIBLE OBTAIN ORDER AND IN STOCK COPY [...]."

The purpose of these data was revealed in message eighteen, received towards the end of November 1964, when, repeating the previous request, it explains:

"[...] NEEED SPECIFIC DATA FOR EFFICTIVE BLOCKADE[25] OF SUPPLY OF CRITICAL PARTSS [...]."

---

[25] The italics are ours. Note the use of espionage for the purposes of sabotage and strengthening the blockade.

146

However, the most dangerous actions appear in part of a message sent at the end of March 1964:

"[...] OUR INTEREST IN CARRYING OUT INTENSE SABOTAGE TO PARALYZE THE REFINERY AND DESTROY STORAGE TANKS STANDS [...]."

The radio messages received from that point on are an eloquent example of this monstrous form of state terrorism.

The fourth radio message received on July 6, 1964 caused no small measure of surprise:

"FOUR X SEND COMPLETE DESCRIPTION OF AUTOMOBILE AT YOUR DISPOSAL, INCLUDING BRAND, COLOR, YEAR AND NUMBER OR SIZE OF TIRES [...]."

This message was explained months later, after the information requested had been sent, when the twentieth message was received on December 14 that year.

"TWO ZERO X COLLECT SABOTAGE MATERIAL HIDDEN IN CONSUL CAR TIRE BURRIED SIX INCHES IN THE EARTH BETWEEN SHORT PALM (CANA) AND TALL PINE TREE CLOSE TO NUMBER 8 POST OF WIRE FENCE OF THE NEARBY STREAM ACCORDING TO MAP SENDT WITH SECRET WRITING [...] TWO FIVE (25) METERS NORTH OF THE NORTHERN CIRUCIT HIGHWAY BETWEEN CONSOLACIÓN DEL NORTE AND LA MULATA IN PINAR DEL RÍO [...]."

The plotting of sabotage actions can be appreciated, in its different variations, in different messages sent to the agent. Part of radio message number 19 of early December stated:

"KEEP US INFORMED ON SECURITY MEASURES IN THE ÑICO LÓPEZ REFINERY X FIND SAFE PLACES IN THE REFINERY TO BEGIN MOVING SABOTAGE MATERIAL AND HIDE IT THERE UNTIL THE APPROPRIATE TIME COMES [...] X STUDY AND REPORT IN DETAIL ON THE PLACES X EQUIPMENT X UNITS THAT CAN SABOTAGED CAUSING GREATER

DAMAGES WITH INCENDIARY AND EXPLOSIVE DEVICES
[...]."

Tying them to his legs and following precise instructions from the
CIA, the agent gradually introduced explosives and incendiary devices
into the installation.

The final instructions for the sabotage were received in mid
February of 1965. Radio message number 29 reads:

"NECESSARY TO SABOTAGE REFINERY IN THE EVENING
OF MARCH SIX (6) [...] MATERIAL SHOULD BE PLACED
DURING USUAL WORK HOURS AND SET THE YELLOW
DETONATORS TO THE MAXIMUM TIME BEFORE LEAVING
WORK [...]."

How the CIA treated its agents as mercenaries is revealed in a part
of the same message:

"WE WILL GIVE YOU A TEN THOUSAND DOLLAR BOND IF
THE SABOTAGE PARALYSES THE REFINERY FOR THREE
ZERO (30) REPEAT 30 DAYS X A GREATER BOND DEPENDING
ON DAMAGES CAUSED [...]."

The CIA also began to indicate which specific places were to be
targeted for sabotage by the agent from message 33 of 25 February
on. The message read:

"[...] IN CONTROL ROOM PLACE CLIPS ON CONTROL
PANELS WITH SENSITIVE IRREPLACABLE CONTROLS X
PREFERRABLY CRITICAL CONTROLS THAT CAN CAUSE
SECONDARY DAMAGES IN WORKING UNITS X SELECT
THREE OR FOUR KEY OBJECTIVES FUNCTIONING IN THE
REFINERY AND USE TWO TO FOUR CLIPS FOR EACH TARGET
[...]."

Message 34 of February 27, whose instructions were later
repeated on more than one occasion, instructed:

"[...] SALT WATER TANKS PLACE MAGNETIC CLIPS DIRECTLY
ON THE FRAME X POSSIBLY HIDDEN INSIDE INSPECTION

REGISTRIES X MANAGE TO DAMAGE MOVABLE PARTS TO CAUSE SECONDARY DAMAGES X IF DAMAGE IS TO BALL BEARINGS YOU WILL PUT OUT THE HIGH SPEED ALIGNMENT AXIS [...]. PLACE CLIPS ON BOILERS WHERE THERE IS GREATER HEAT AND PRESSURE TO CAUSE SECONDARY EXPLOSIONS X ALTERNATIVE TARGETS COULD BE ELECTRIC TRANSFORMERS IN THE REFINERY [...] SELECT CRITICAL PARTS THAT CAN CAUSE SECONDARY DAMAGES [...]."

Despite the enemy's efforts and the meticulousness with which sabotage actions were plotted and executed, the vigilance of the Cuban people was mightier and prevented one of the most dangerous acts of sabotage ever organized by a government against another with whom it is not officially engaged in war.

The sugar agro-industry

Undermining Cuban sugar production and, more generally, the country's sugar export revenue in foreign currency is one of the oldest of U.S. government aims, plans and actions. These actions have gone from the burning of sugar cane crops and bombing of industrial installations in the sector began in the last quarter of 1959 to the plan submitted to President Eisenhower by the CIA director in the first days of January 1960, recommending a broadening of the plan. General Edward Lansdale was tasked with directing Operation Mongoose in the second half of 1961 and with preparing a wide-encompassing operation aimed at increasing sugar production in other locations and artificially lowering its market price. All of this was aimed at preventing foreign currency from entering Cuba at a time of rising sugar prices in the world market, as we saw in Chapter 3. This included contaminating the product in foreign ports, introducing plagues to damage the crops and many other actions.

Milkman case

We have selected the Milkman Case from among the many files, kept in Ministry of the Interior archives, on the criminal actions perpetrated in the sugar sector by the CIA. Thanks to *CIA Diary*, a book/indictment published in 1975 by a former official, Philip Agee, who was sickened by the subversive actions of his government[26], we have a glimpse of CIA actions in this area.

Referring to the time he was assigned to the CIA station in Montevideo on April 3, 1964, Agee points out:

"My first Cuban recruitment looks successful. A trade mission arrived from Brazil and will be here until sometime next week. An agent of the Rio station had reported that Raúl Alonzo Olive, a member of the mission and perhaps the most important because he is a high-level official in the sugar industry, seemed to be disaffected with the revolution. In order to protect the Rio agent against provocation and because of the confusion in Brazil this past week,[27] the Rio station suggested that a recruitment approach be made here or in Madrid which is their last stop before return to Havana.

"The AVENIN surveillance team[28] followed him after arrival and at the first chance when he was alone they delivered a note from me asking for a meeting. The note was worded so that he would know it came from the CIA. After reading it he followed the

[26] Philip Agee: *Inside the Company: CIA Diary*. Penguin Books, 1975.

[27] Military coup against Joao Goulart.

[28] Visual observation team set up by the CIA in countries it operates to control persons of interest. Quoting Agee extensively is useful to understanding the methods used by the CIA to control Cuban officials abroad: "The station has two surveillance teams [...] The team consists of seven surveillance agents, one agent in the state-owned electric company, and one agent in the telegraph company [...] Most of the surveillance agents [...] are employees of the Montevideo municipal government. The team is well trained [...] Vehicles include two sedans and a Volkswagen van equipped with a periscope photography rig with a 360-degree viewing capability for taking pictures and observations through the roof vent. Concealed radio equipment is also used for communication between the vehicles, between the vehicles and the OP at the Cuban Embassy, and between the vehicles and the people on foot. These carry small battery-operated trans mitter-receivers under their clothing and can communicate with each other as well as with the vehicles. They are also trained and equipped for clandestine street photography using 35-mm automatic Robot cameras wrapped to form innocuous packages. [...] The AVENIN agent in the electric company is valuable because he has access to lists of persons who are registered for electric service at any address in Montevideo [...] also provides on request the architect's plans for any building served by the electric company and these plants are used for planning audio installations or surreptitious entries for other purposes". Philip Agee: p. 344.

instructions to walk along a certain street where I picked him up and took him to a safe place to talk. Headquarters had sent a list of questions for him, mostly dealing with this year's sugar harvest, efforts to mechanize cane cutting, and anyone else he might know was dissatisfied. We spoke for about two hours because he had to rejoin his delegation, but we'll meet again several times before he leaves for Madrid. Contact instructions just arrived from the Madrid station".

"He said sugar production form this year's harvest should be about five million tons and he rambled on at length about the problems with the cane-cutting machines, mostly caused when used on sloping or inclined surfaces. What was surprising was that he knows so many government leaders well even though he wasn't particularly active the struggle against Batista.

"I recorded the meeting, which he didn't particularly like, and reported by cable the essentials of what he said. He thinks he will be in Madrid for most of next week, or perhaps longer, so communications training can be done there. Strange he agreed so readily to return to Cuba and for his salary to be kept safe for him by the CIA, but he seemed honest enough. In Madrid he'll get the polygraph, which should help to resolve his *bona fides*."[29]

In the notes Agee took on April 24, he wrote: "Desmond FitzGerald is very pleased over the recruitment of the Cuban but fears it may be a provocation based on the high yield of this years sugar harvest that he revealed. Instead of five million tons, this year's production would be less than four million, according to FitzGerald."[30]

And on June 6 he wrote: "[…] the new Western Hemisphere Division Chief, Desmond FitzGerald […] was pleased with the Cuban recruitment but suspects he may have been a provocation because of his high estimate of the sugar harvest. Instead of five million tons, according to FitzGerald, production this year will probably be less than four million."[31]

But, in truth, the agent recruited had knowingly accepted working for the CIA, which was quick to perceive this and began to use him as a valuable source of information on the sugar and agricultural sectors in general.

[29] Ibid., pp. 362-363.
[30] Ibid., p. 366.
[31] Ibid., p. 377.

In the CIA message of January, 1967, this agent reported: "Mechanical cane cutters have been provisionally set aside [...]. All emphasis is given to collection and cranes. The harvest can reach six million five hundred thousand tons. The higher yield of sugar cane is the result of heavy rains [...]."

In March 1968, he reported: "[...] MINAZ estimates harvest at five million two hundred thousand tons but this figure may not be reached. In Oriente cane will be planted for mechanized cutting [...]. A crop of about 656 hectares is planned for this year".

It was evident that the activity of this enemy agent included the sending of information to frustrate Cuban negotiations with third countries. In a message dated September 1968, he reported: "Cuba is interested in purchasing Australian cane cutting equipment. A mission will be sent for the first contacts [...]."

In an April 1969 message: "The gentleman [...] will visit Zaragoza to purchase farm equipment [...]. The Engineer [...] will soon travel to Japan to buy pesticide products for agriculture [...]." Shortly after sending this message, the agent was discovered, arrested in December 1969 and taken to court. In view of his age and educational level, he was given administrative tasks in prison. He was freed well before the completion of his sentence. After his release, he remained in Cuba, where he died a few years ago.

Actions against maritime transportation and fishing

In Chapter III we looked at the debates of the U.S. State Department Coordination Committee on Cuban Affairs during the early part of 1963, where different options for the destruction of Cuba's maritime trade fleet were discussed. As in all other sectors, many were the actions carried out.

In an interview with Major General Manuel Fernández Crespo who was responsible, since the early part of the 60s, for directing investigations into subversive activities against important sectors of the economy, including maritime transportation, we were able to gather interesting testimonies about how these actions were perceived in Cuba. According to our interviewee:

"At the time, we had no doubt that the CIA had set out to destroy our merchant fleet. It was logical because, with the blockade law and so-called 'black lists' of ships touching Cuban ports, they had managed to prevent capitalist ship companies from trading with Cuba: the next step was to prevent our ships from setting sail.

"I was quite an impact for me, when I recently read declassified U.S. documents, to remember how, in effect, during those years we were faced with so many incendiary bombs placed by their agents inside the cargo or with motors that broke down for no apparent reason, leaving the ships at the mercy of the ocean. More than once we had to go and tow a ship back. Mines were also placed in the hulls several times.

"I remember when we worked in the *Two Brothers* case. It was during the interrogations of one of the mostly deeply involved people, a man who had acted as machine chief in a ship of relative importance and who was used by the CIA to gather information for sabotage by other agents, that we learned – and he knew of this through his CIA superior – that the substance being usedwas made in Company laboratories to prevent the analysis of the oil of the destroyed motors from detecting abrasive substances and thus eliminate any evidence of sabotage. It was a means of guaranteeing impunity for the collaborators and, consequently, of convincing them to carry out these actions.

"Since those first years of the 1960s, the aggressiveness of actions against our ships and crews was stepped up to an incredible extent. In the main European ports —and practically anywhere in the world where our ships docked—were the CIA men, looking for the slightest opportunity to sabotage our ships and to try and recruit our officials and crew [...].

"The declassified documents make no mention of something else they systematically did to deprive us of our crew: encouraging desertions in foreign ports. They organized parties and other activities for our crews and officials to prevent them from boarding the ship when it set sail and told them: 'look, if you go back to Cuba you will be shot, so you best stay and work in ships under other flags'."[32]

An important example, related to this account, was the sinking of fishing boats in the port of El Callao, in Peru, in 1977. In his testimony before the Provincial People's Court of Havana, in the suit Cuba brought against the U.S. government for economic

[32] Testimony by Major General Manuel Fernández Crespo, 2003. Author's file.

damages in March 2000, Lieutenant Colonel Francisco Gómez Pons was very clear on this point:

"For 14 years, I acted as head of the fishing sector for MININT counterintelligence [...]. During that time, we learned of the information interests of U.S. special services, particularly the CIA, in this sector which, at the time, was the main source of foreign currency and was an important source of food for the population [...].

The 70s, when TACSA 96 ships were purchased, saw the modernization of Cuba's Fishing Fleet which, at the time, sailed the Atlantic and Pacific Oceans. These were large trawlers with the most advanced technologies of the time.

"In 1977, fishing activity in the Pacific was extended when an agreement was signed with the Republic of Peru and a base of operations and repairs was established in the port of El Callao, west of the capital. This is when we detected that the CIA stepped up its search for information on our fishing activities. What they were going to do with that information we soon found out.

"In June 22, 1977, when the *Río Jobabo* was docked, an explosive charge was placed at the back of the engine room, sinking the fishing boat. This action was well planned because the explosive charge was set in the exact place where it could cause the most damage.

"On October 7 that same year, when the operation to refloat the *Rio Jobabo* was nearing its end, an explosive charge was placed in the flour factory of the *Río Damují* motor boat, a less than ideal place in terms of causing maximum damage, probably because of the speed with which this action had to be carried out owing to the crew's increased vigilance.

"Investigations by salvage teams and criminologists sent from Cuba demonstrated the participation of frogmen in the placing of explosive devices in the hulls of ships. Later investigations, patiently but fruitfully, proved that terrorist commandos that answered to the CIA were the ones responsible for the sabotage actions [...]."[33]

[33] Testimony by Lieutenant Colonel Francisco Gomez Pons, before the Provincial People's Court of Havana on March 7, 2000. Some points were cleared up in an interview held in February 2003. Author's file.

Public exposure of CIA espionage and subversion in 1987

In the summer of 1987, the acts of espionage and subversion against Cuba conducted from the Local Station of the U.S. Interest Section in Havana were brought to the light of day on a series of television programs aired over several consecutive days, a blistering denunciation with no precedent anywhere in the world.[34]

The Cuban people were able to watch secret films by Cuban State Security bodies, covering several years of clandestine activities by CIA officials who supplied sophisticated means of communication, encryption codes for information, high sums of money and other materials to a large group of supposed agents, selected in different sectors and institutions. These agents, directed by the Security Organs, had managed to penetrate CIA structures to unveil and prevent aggressive designs against Cuba.

Acting in the guise of diplomats and a high number of officials in transit, allegedly representing the State Department or other departments and agencies, agents from CIA headquarters in Langley, Virginia participated in the official subversive actions of the Local CIA Station based in the U.S. Interest Section in Havana. Incredible as it may seem, patient intelligence work unmasked the subversive actions of 89 (!) of these alleged diplomats.

---

[34] The Cuban press gave broad coverage of the denunciation made. Cuban television aired a series entitled The CIA's war against Cuba, which began on July 6, 1987, the day the denunciation was made, and concluded on August 11. During this time, the newspapers printed articles by Roberto Álvarez Quiñones, Emilio del Barrio, Dantes Cardosa, Nidia Díaz, Orlando Gómez, Gladys Hernández, Héctor Hernández Pardo, Nicanor León Cotayo, Gardenia Miralles, Gabriel Molina, Joaquín Oramas, Raisa Pagés, Raúl Palazuelos, Roberto Paneque, Orfilio Peláez, Diana Sosa, Reynold Rassi, Mirta Rodríguez Calderón, Alberto Rodríguez Fernández, Alexis Schlachter and Juan Varela Pérez, who reported on details of the denunciation, some of which will be discussed below. In spite of its significance and worldwide repercussions as an unprecedented and documented revelation of subversive actions and support and backing of terrorism by the CIA – an important part of the plans revealed were aimed at the elimination of Fidel Castro – the international press ignored these charges, save for a few short reports that were quickly silenced by their central offices. All in the interests of preserving "freedom of the press", no doubt. Almost certainly, the United States public never learned of Cuba's denouncement.

The testimonies of 29 persons from different walks of life were the irrefutable proof of these actions; supposedly recruited by the CIA, they were, in fact, patriots who had become aware that they could be of great use to the homeland, by learning about the enemy's interests and preventing the damage it could cause.

Some were already working with State Security bodies as, early on, the country saw itself forced to defend itself, from such enemy actions as those that culminated in the Bay of Pigs invasion, Operation Mongoose and the *Covert Policy and Integrated Program of Action Toward Cuba*, approved by President Kennedy in June 1963. With the experience it had accumulated since then, the country had created conditions to confront the CIA and which equipped it for the early detection of enemy actions.

There are other examples. Of note is that of Italian citizen Mauro Casagrandi, who was approached to work for the CIA and against the Cuban Revolution and saw this as an opportunity to contribute to the defense of one of the purest social projects in contemporary history, placing his determination and intelligence, even at the risk of his own life, at the service of the Revolution, whose destruction the United States government called for.

Subversive actions against the Cuban economy that we will look at below are consistent with those carried out by the United States against Cuba since the early years of the Revolution. The greater number of "agents" they thought they had in Cuba had been selected by the CIA in different sectors of the economy, complying with subversive plans inherited from the first years after the revolutionary triumph in 1959.

A newspaper article published in the summer of 1987 clearly summarized the moment: "It doesn't mean, of course, that the CIA will disappear because of this; we cannot even expect a reduction in its activities against Cuba. It is simply that everything our people know now and the barrage of proof and evidence placed before the eyes of international public opinion are such a complete document revealing the tenacity with which imperialism has worked to strangle our country and its revolution that, if anyone still has any doubts, this example should have been enough to open many eyes."[35]

---

[35] Mirta Rodríguez Calderón: "Serviré a la misma causa" ("I shall serve the same cause"). Account of CIA infiltration by a Cuban Security agent and Italian citizen, Mauro Casagrandi. *Granma* newspaper, June 29, 1987, p. 3.

Interests in maritime, air and fishing sectors

The Angel Matthew. That is how the press, invoking the bible, referred to one of the patriots[36] who managed to learn of important information requirements and enemy plans in a broad sphere of national affairs because **Juan Luis Acosta Guzmán**, captain of the Cuban Tuna Fleet, had been assigned the alias *Angel* by the CIA but was, in fact, *Matthew* in his work with Cuban Security. His wife, **Teresa Martínez,** employee of the fleet's Finance Department, according to CIA officials, could also be useful. This is why they suggested that *Angel* "recruit" her, not knowing that *Maite* was, in fact, here husband's comrade in the ranks of Cuban Security.

The CIA supposedly recruited Matthew in 1974 in the Rompeolas hotel in Las Palmas, Canary Islands, through a personal contact by the then head of the CIA station in Spain, Alberto Allen Morris. For his apparent work against his country, they began paying him 250 dollars a month and systematically raised his wage because of the "quality" of information supplied. His salary, which was deposited in a U.S. bank, reached the high figure of 1 700 dollars a month. The final balance of his account at the time of revelation was close to a hundred thousand dollars.[37]

In addition to personal contacts when he traveled abroad, he was trained in the use of invisible writing methods to hide "information" in normal letters for his work in CIA espionage. He was also given a sophisticated RS-804 radio at the time valued at a quarter of a million dollars, capable of sending coded messages directly to CIA headquarters through geo-stationary satellites of the FITSATCOM system operated by the U.S. Defense Department, whose functions include serving as a CIA channel for secret communications around the world.[38] It was precisely upon installing these conveniently concealed devices in the outskirts of the capital, for their subsequent pick-up by their "agent", that several "diplomats" of the U.S. Interest Section were filmed and publicly exposed.

[36] Gabriel Molina: "El Ángel Mateo" ("The Angel Matthew"). *Granma* newspaper, June 9,1987, p. 3. See also Agencia de Información Nacional (AIN): *La Guerra de la CIA contra Cuba (The CIA's war against Cuba)*. Havana, 1988, p. 15.

[37] The national press at the time offered extensive coverage of the details, CIA information requests and monitoring of a broad sphere of interests. See *Granma* daily of June 6, 1987 and following days.

[38] Agencia de Información Nacional (AIN): p. 34.

Antonio García Urquiola, captain of the Empresa de Navegación Mambisa (Mambisa Navigation Company) was recruited by the CIA in Amsterdam in 1978 by an alleged U.S. diplomatic official accredited to the United States Embassy in Holland. He was assigned the alias of *Alejandro,* although, in truth, he was agent *Aurelio* of Cuban State Security.

The harassment of Cuban crews was accurately described by the press when it reported on this "recruiting" process and on how, at many ports our ships touched, particularly in the Netherlands and Spain, CIA officials and agents, both from the United States and native Cubans who were used as a means of approaching old colleagues, approached our seamen to encourage them to desert and accept work as spies.[39]

The broad spectrum of CIA interests, both with respect to details about the national maritime fleet's work, particularly their movements and cargo, and many aspects of life in the country, were supposedly satisfied through personal contacts made in different parts of the world, in those countries whose ports were visited by ships captained by *Alejandro* / *Aurelio,* in the Japanese cities of Osaka, Kobe and Tokyo and in Mexico City, Tampico, Veracruz, Panama and Tarragona, Spain.

Alejandro was the first alleged CIA agent assigned what was then one of the most sophisticated communications equipment used by the CIA; a new type of rapid plant, designated CDS-501, for agent-to-center communication, which transmitted to the Local CIA Station on the fifth floor of the U.S. Embassy in Havana. He also used invisible ink.

In 1966, the CIA "recruited" Cubana de Aviacion instructor **Ignacio Rodríguez-Mena Castrillón.** He was assigned the name *Julio.* For Cuban State Security, he was *Isidro.* In addition to numerous requests for information on diverse matters, including the prioritized and urgent request for all information on Fidel Castro's trips abroad, he received numerous demands for data on the technical situation of our aviation, the total number of planes and their functioning.

On October, 1979, when African porcine fever reappeared in the country, the CIA showed great interest in knowing whether Cuban planes were transporting products to combat the disease.

---

[39] Gabriel Molina: "Nuestro hombre en la CIA" ("Our CIA insider"). *Granma* Daily, June 11, 1987, p. 2.

To gather more complete information on the functioning of the "José Martí" airport in the capital, the CIA suggested he recruit his wife, **Mercedes Herrera López,** who also worked there. She became agent Marlen. She recalls talking with a CIA official who began directing her through personal contacts established in Panama, in June of 1985: "The interest of this official centered on my work, in the "José Martí" International Airport, in the movement of flights [...] on communications, extra flights [...] and other factors of flight movement".

An example of the CIA's interest in additional information is a message received by *Marlen* that read:

MSJ TWO EIGHT X INTEREST IN DETAILS ABOUT CONSTRUCTION OF NEW AIRPORTS, EXPANSION OF EXISTING ONES IN VARADERO AND CARBONERAS X WHAT HAS BEEN BUILT UP TO NOW X HOW LONG UNTIL CONCLUSION X PROBLEMS [...].

Agro-industrial sectors. Biological warfare

Orlando Argudín was advisor to the first vice minister of the Ministry of the Sugar Industry and agent Rolando of State Security. After his supposed recruitment in London in 1970, under the alias of *Oscar Lopez*, the CIA tasked him with gathering economic, political and military information.

One of his most important actions was unmasking the CIA's attempt to sabotage the entry into Cuba of ammonium tanks for fertilization purposes. These tanks were offered at very tempting prices by a specialized foreign company; about 40 to 50% cheaper than other suppliers. According to his testimony in the denunciation aired on television, ammonium is caustic and highly toxic and, because it is a gas, it must be manipulated under pressure using special tanks and equipment that, if built following the specifications, are not at all dangerous.

Agent *Rolando* explained:

"Towards the end of 1984, having signed a contract for an ammonium system with a capitalist company, I met with a CIA official in Madrid who called himself *Peter*. This man informed me that they were aware of negotiations in Cuba with capitalist firms to acquire

159

these systems and told me that CIA headquarters would send me a message about the matter.

"This message requested I use my influence as a high level official, without blowing my cover, to achieve two things: that negotiations be maintained with the company of their interest and also that technical supervision be as superficial as possible so that any problem in the equipments being built for Cuba would pass unnoticed."

Upon his return to Cuba, the alleged CIA agent received a message from Langley headquarters.[40]

MESSAGE FOUR ZERO X IT WAS A PLEASURE TO SEE YOU X AS ALWAYS WE WELCOME YOUR INFORMATION X NECESSARY TO KEEP US INFORMED OF CONSTRUCTION AND DELIVERY OF AMMONIUM SYSTEMS X REGARDS X.

Through another supposed agent of theirs, **Jose Abel González López**, *Pepe Serrano* for the CIA, agent *Alejandro* of State Security (in fact), director of supervision in the State Committee of Economic Cooperation, they also sought to back this criminal act of sabotage.

According to his testimony: "In April of 1985, I had came into contact with a CIA official, Maria Elena, who required information on my work in the ammonium tanks. After explaining my task she told me she was interested that supervision of this equipment be as superficial as possible and to try to ignore any problem they had and to keep her informed if any defects were found."[41]

With this information, special attention was given to the construction of these tanks. The supervising commission detected several irregularities that included the falsification of documents that certified the quality control procedures required. The final report of the supervising commission stated:

"These tanks have a capacity for 110 000 liters of water with 56 tons of ammonium. Defects were found in the soldering, lack of thickness in the laths; Also found were security irregularities in some of the valves, made o f copper alloys whose use in the handling of ammonium is prohibited.

[40] Agencia de Información Nacional (AIN): p. 51.
[41] Ibid., p. 51-52.

"An important number of these valves had to be changed, as they were not suitable for work this substance.

"This defect, coupled with the others listed above, could have had such consequences as the filtering out of ammonium, including explosion of the tanks that would have called for the immediate evacuation of nearby persons and animals, who risked sure death, and a long time would have been necessary to evacuate the rest of the population living in areas where the ammonium cloud was headed."[42]

The CIA planned to use their agent *Oscar López* to search for information on plagues affecting sugar cane crops. Towards the end of the 70s, the CIA official responsible for him intensified requests for information on this matter and on other crops. They trusted Oscar Lopez so much that the official confided in him that, "in the fight to the death with Cuba and the Revolution, we also introduce certain diseases and plagues to attack persons and animals [...]".

Shown an aerial photograph taken by a spy plane, he was asked to account for the existence of clearings observed in cane fields in a given region, specifying the causes and the date these clearings had appeared. The interest in confirming the results of actions undertaken was obvious. There was also an interest in finding out the results of Cuba's research work, aimed at obtaining sugar cane varieties resistant to the climate and certain plagues, as well as in knowing who was responsible for this research.

In 1981, the CIA station in the U.S. embassy in Havana expressed an interest in receiving information from the head of pesticides of the Ministry of Agriculture, agronomical engineer Angel Lopez, about the country's phytosanitary state; the main plagues attacking tobacco and citrus plantations, the chemical products used to combat them and the foreign companies supplying them, in an obvious attempt to prevent their supply. Through Lopez Núñez, agent Callejas of Cuban Security, the CIA expressed an interest in having one of their officials visit the agricultural station in Pinar del Rio, in a region of exceptional importance for tobacco production, as well as the province of Matanzas. In other contacts, they expressed an interest in receiving tobacco leaf samples, one of the main exportable goods of the country.

[42] Ibid., p. 52.

Dulce María Santiesteban Loureiro, (*Regina* for the CIA and *Amy* for Cuban Security), was recruited in 1976 by the CIA when she visited Spain as a member of the Central Board of Planning.[43]

Before scientifically proving the deliberate introduction of hemorrhagic Dengue virus into the country during the first half of 1981, an action which caused the death of 158 persons, and months before the onset of symptoms, she reported that the CIA was planning biological warfare actions against the country.

Message 40 of February 1981, sent by the CIA to agent Regina, read:[44]

MESSAGE FOUR ZERO X POSSIBLITY OF KNOWING WHAT STRAINS OF DENGUE ARE KNOWN IN CUBA X DETAILS OF VIRAL DISEASES THAT AFFECT THE POPULATION X MEDICINES CUBA IMPORTS X COUNTRIES X GREETINGS X JULIA X

On April 6, 1981, when Cuba had not yet detected that dengue had been introduced into the country and the 101 children who perished still lived, CIA agent Regina received message 45, similar to the previous one[45]. It read:

MESSAGE FOUR FIVE X WHAT ARE THE MAIN DISEASES CIRCULATING IN CUBA X DO YOU KNOW PEOPLE WIITH CONJUNCTIVITIS X LOCALITIES X LISTEN CAREFULLY TO CONVERSATIONS ABOUT INFECTIOUS DISEASES X JULIA X

Only five months after this "innocent" request, the hospitals in the capital and one of the central provinces reported the appearance of many cases of epidemic hemorrhagic conjunctivitis, a disease that spreads easily and produces alarming symptoms. Between September and December that year, there were 600 000 cases. By

[43] See Alberto Ferrera Herrera: *Yo fui Regina para la CIA.* ("*I was Regina for the CIA*") Capitán San Luis Publishing House, Havana, 1997.

[44] Agencia de Información Nacional (AIN): p. 40.

[45] Ibid., p. 43.

the end of the following year, the number had grown to a million persons infected.

Message 97 to this "agent" read:[46]

MESSAGE NINE SEVEN X DETAILS OF HEPATITIS INSTALLATIONS IN ISLE OF YOUTH X ABOUT OUTBREAK OF CONJUNCTIVITIS X SCARCITY OF MEDICINES AND MEDICAL EQUIPMENT X BEST WISHES X JAMES X

No comments are necessary.

Other requests for information received by this agent, while employed in the country's main planning institution referred to economic issues in a broader sense, cooperation programs, the development of the oil industry and other matters related to practically all aspects of life in the country.

Dr. Eduardo Sagaró González, a specialist in infantile gastroenterology, was apparently recruited by the CIA as agent Antonio, during the early part of 1979, while heading the Cuban mission in Mozambique. In 1981, as a result of the Dengue epidemic, the CIA requested an evaluation of its results and of Cuba's means to combat the disease. Between 1980 and 1986, this alleged CIA agent received over 200 requests for information on the health sector.

Trade, financial and economic cooperation relations

José Abel González López had been recruited by the CIA during a trip to Spain in 1977. When assigned the alias of *Pepe Serrano*, he had been agent *Alejandro* for Cuban Security for several years.

For the ten years of his apparent collaboration with the Agency, a great deal of information was requested from Alejandro. This included information on Cuban trade relations with foreign companies and the types of contracts our country entered into. He was also asked for information on the internal functioning of what was then the State Committee for Economic Cooperation, its payroll and the characteristics of its staff. As explained above, he contributed to preventing the entry of sabotaged ammonium tanks into the country.

[46] Idem.

Pedro Ramón Calcines Pérez, representative of Cuban companies in Japan, was recruited by the CIA in 1980 during the Kobe Trade Fair and was assigned the alias of *Rodríguez*. As a result of the requests for information from the Agency he received and as agent *Saturno* of Cuban Security, it was possible to learn that the CIA was carefully reviewing Cuba's trade with all her trade partners and seeking to prevent its fruition. The last request made in May 1987 was to deepen knowledge on the state of Cuban trade in the spheres of nickel, coffee, cement and electronic articles.

From an interview held with the agent at the time, we selected the following points:

"[…] I was working in the Cuban commercial office in Japan […] and their main interest was in learning about our trade with that country and the progress it was making.

"First, they wanted to know of our nickel sales to Japan, what companies imported it and what it was used for.

"The reason they wanted this information was to prevent the import into the United States of vehicles with that raw material, to guarantee Japan would not purchase it from us anymore, as they are their main market.

"To check our exportable volumes they wanted to know about the projects to repair the Moa, Nicaro and other new construction plants.

"They sent specialists to those countries to check and set up production controls to deprive us of that market.

"When I started to work at CubaExport, they were very interested in the balance of trade between Cuba and Japan and to learn which companies were re-adopting a more favorable position towards our country and also about associations such as the Cuba-Japan Economic Society and others created in certain regions.

"The position Cuba would assume regarding the foreign debt was a constant in their inquiries. They wanted to know which company or bank gave us credit and under what credit conditions they traded with other States.

"Other important matters such as sugar and coffee were the object of their inquiries, as was the cement industry. Their interest in the latter was related to production volume, varieties, if any special kind of cement was being manufactured, what our markets were and at what prices we were selling the product.

"They insisted on knowing if we had triangular oil transactions, with whom and how much we had in reserve.

"The acquisition of new technologies was always a forced subject in each contact, as was their permanent concern over the creation of new companies or corporations.

"In other words, they were snooping around in all fields, and even though their main interest in approaching me was to gather information on our trade with Japan and those corporations and my evaluation on other factors, they missed no opportunity to obtain information that, although obtained from other agents, allowed them to cross check the data."[47]

This CIA agent received camouflaged communication means in an artistic cedar cabinet. A secret compartment had been made in its lower part for the purpose.

José Senén Meléndez Álvarez was apparently recruited by the CIA in Japan in 1981, while working as vice president of the Nipon Caribbean Shipping Company, then responsible for the transportation of Cuban sea cargo. He also represented other Cuban companies that included Navegacion Mambisa and CUFLET. For the CIA, he was agent *Guillermo Peña*; for Cuban Security he was *Gallego*. In a televised interview, he expressed: "What they were after was economic information on Cuba's foreign trade, about negotiations in Japan and the companies and banks that gave credit to our country and what kind (short or medium term) as well as what kind of companies shoed a more aggressive management towards Cuban trade."[48]

Through him, the CIA was interested in keeping up to date on that company's trade transactions. They undertook maneuvers to sabotage sugar and nickel negotiations as well as the purchase of medicines and equipment for the Hermanos Amejeiras hospital then under construction. Pressures to hamper negotiations with Japanese companies to acquire microprocessors were felt. He was also instructed to find information on the nuclear power plant being built in Cienfuegos. He was also trained in secret writing techniques.

Through contacts with **Jesús Francisco Díaz Agregan**, Director of the joint venture company CARIB MOLASSES, the CIA showed an uninterrupted interest in the sugar trade. Recruited in Paris in 1982, through contacts begun at the U.S. embassy in Paris

---

[47] Casilda Pereira: "Curiosos en acecho". *Moncada* journal, Havana, December 1987, p. 11.
[48] Agencia de Información Nacional (AIN): p. 78.

165

when he requested a visa to attend a meeting of sugar businesspeople in New York, he was assigned the alias of *Julio Méndez*. He was in fact *Dionisio* of Cuban Security.

He was asked for information on sugar contracts between Cuba and the Soviet Union and on how Cuba was fulfilling those commitments. They also inquired into the sale of sugar to Arab countries, particularly to Egypt, as part of their interests to hamper any negotiations and prevent the intake of foreign currency by our country. At the same time they were interested in monitoring the "Julio Antonio Mella" plant, which was being set up to obtain high quality sugar.

Finances

Miguel Ángel López Escobar who, in 1987, was the National Bank of Cuba's (BNC) General Business Director and in charge of bank contacts with North America and Asia, had worked for five years as head of BNC offices in Tokyo and London. The CIA had recruited him to satisfy its information needs in the finance sector, including data on credits requested, to whom and under what conditions, financing received, foreign investments being negotiated, strategies for negotiating and renegotiating the debt in the Paris Club, possible Cuban maneuvers in response to important import reductions as well as perspectives in the broad field of foreign finances.[49]

At the beginning of 1987, the CIA requested he obtain information on the capitalist countries that had agreements with Cuba to supply spare parts, raw materials as well as about contracts to repair ships, both fishing and merchant marine vessels.

One priority they gave him was to send all available information concerning Cuba's internal economic situation and day-to-day difficulties, as, with this data, their analysts "could give ideas and different alternatives about the targets or localities where the most damage could be done [...]. They emphasized that the strategy used against Cuba was total economic war [...]".[50]

[49] See Miguel A. López Escobar: *Objetivo Langley. Veintiséis más uno.* ("Target Langley. Twenty-six plus one") Capitán San Luis Publishing House, Havana, 1989.
[50] Agencia de Información Nacional (AIN): pp. 49-50.

It is well worth reiterating that the Central Intelligence Agency's espionage work is not a passive monitoring of the Cuban economic situation but rather a condition for the planning and execution of measures aimed at obliterating this economy. This is clearly evident in an instruction received by López Escobar, allegedly agent Miguel, in which that U.S. service requested he hamper contracts that would strengthen the national rayon industry, which were being negotiated with India and in which he would participate.

Similarly, through the Management Director for the western region of the BNC, **Raúl Fernández Salgado**, recruited by the CIA in Madrid in 1977 as agent Paul (agent Bello for Cuban Security), preventive measures were taken to counteract measures to hinder and prevent the use of credits granted to Cuba in capitalist countries. Their aim was also to create difficulties with creditors in the renegotiation of the foreign debt.

On May 20, "agent" Paul received the following message:

MESSAGE FIVE X INTERESTED TO KNOW IF CUBA TRIES TO CHANGE PLAN FOR PAYMENT OF HER DEBT TO ANY WESTERN BANK X DETAILS X WHO WERE THE BANK OFFICIALS OF WESTERN EUROPE VISITED IN APRIL AND MAY X FOR WHAT PURPOSE X RESULTS X IF WESTERN BANKS HAVE BEEN ASKED TO REPROGRAM PAYMENT OF CUBAN DEBT X WHAT BANKS AGREED X REGARDS C THOMAS X

Calixto Marrero, *Robert* for the CIA and *Ramon* for Cuban Security, was recruited by the CIA in Paris while heading an export company of sea products for the French market, CARIBEX.

The information requested from all agents in this economic spheres – including other matters – was, for the most part, about countries that offered loans to Cuba and the conditions of those loans, what reasons and issues Cuba invoked in its efforts to renegotiate its foreign debt and the working order, tasks and results of the Central Group, the state entity that, at the time, took the important economic decisions in the country.

The Italian **Mauro Casagrandi,** who had settled in Cuba in the early sixties, was the representative of Cogis, an import-export company that sold Alfa Romeo cars and Olivetti typewriters. He was also an advisor of the Order of Malta. He was "recruited" by the CIA on December 10, 1975, during a visit to Spain, to obtain information about the country living situation through his access to trade and the diplomatic channels in which he moved.

A man with a deep sense of ethics and progressive ideas, he understood that it was an opportunity to serve a just cause, to play along with this intelligence and subversion service, in order to learn of its criminal interests with respect to Cuba. Consequently, he approached Cuban State Security to become agent *Mario,* when, for the CIA, he was agent *Luis.*

In his declarations, he explained:

"It seems that the CIA was interested in me because of my possibilities in Cuba, because of my position, which, owing to the type of commercial and economic activities I was involved in, allowed me to come in contact with many companies and State institutions and leaders. I had a certain knowledge of the persons who made the decisions concerning planning in Cuba and how foreign trade functioned.

"The CIA wanted economic and financial information about the organization of trade abroad and even wanted to know how decisions were made in the Central Board of Planning, which persons made them and how...

"[...] I had many contacts with different CIA officials in Europe, in the United States, in South America and their interests continued to center on economic and financial issues, because I also had a good relationship with the National Bank of Cuba [...].

"In time, there was a qualitative jump in the CIA's information requests and there were varied interests. From the economic point of view they expressed an interest on the manner in which Cuba obtained credit abroad, which were the Western banks and companies with which Cuba maintained relations."

Communications

At the time, **Eduardo Leal Estrada** was the Deputy Director of the Cuban Telecommunications Company (EMTELCUBA) attached to the Communications Ministry and in charge of efforts to modernize communication through the installation of coaxial cables in the country. He was "recruited" by the CIA in 1982 during a visit to Washington. For the CIA he was *José Luis Tamayo;* in fact, he was *Alejandro* of Cuban State Security.

168

The post he occupied was, in the eyes of the CIA, an opportunity to satisfy their interests on a broad spectrum of topics in this important field. For five years, this U.S. service inquired into all matters related to the modernization of communications through the use of the coaxial cable and the dates on which each of the phases were to be concluded, as well as about matters on diverse areas. The most sensitive requests were those inquiring into the communication systems used by Fidel Castro.

"As part of these broad requests for information on communications made by the CIA, the agent assigned to me instructed me to prioritize [...] the coaxial cable project [...].

"Requests for information included data on the technical characteristics of the cable, the depth it was installed at, the places where cable substations were located, ramifications constructed and plans to connect communication centers, both civilian and military, as well as existing security measures in these cable substations and stations throughout the country.

"The official explained [...] that the request for information stemmed from his interest in being able to intercept [...] information transmitted in that manner."[51]

It was not exclusively through this agent that Cuba learned of these interests. It was also learned that two CIA officials allegedly accredited as diplomats of the United States Interest section in Cuba, since there arrival in Cuba, were intent on studying the location of the coaxial cable and registry cabins corresponding to the joints they filmed dealing with these matters in several opportunities.

Then CIA Director William Casey suggested rewarding "agent" José Luis Tamayo for his apparent good work. This was done in Room 503 of the Anthony House Hotel in the U.S. capital. Participating in this activity, also, was his superior, *Albert and* the CIA deputy director of operations Robert Edwards, who told Leal Estrada that they would increase his bank balance in the United States by 10 000 dollars. When the denunciation was made, the agent had received about 200 000 dollars for his "good work" in this service.

This concludes the brief summary of the details of espionage activities undertaken as part of the economic war against Cuba, as reported on in the denunciation of CIA actions CIA made in our country in the summer of 1987.

[51] Ibid., p. 53.

One of the most important evaluations of the whole process described was made thirteen years later, on the occasion of the suit brought against the United States by the Cuban people for economic damages, reviewed by People's Provincial Court of Havana.

In March that year, when evidence for the proceeding was being prepared, Lieutenant Colonel Leorenzo Aguiar Arredondo was invited to offer witness testimony. Over a period of thirty-two years, he had been part of a State Security team responsible for following espionage and subversive actions against the economy, preventing and neutralizing them. In that post, he played a key role in the evaluation of the inquiries into the Cuban economy described above.

During his extensive testimony before the court, based on information about CIA economic espionage and subversion known, Lorenzo Aguiar offered a detailed description of the harassment of Cuban trade throughout the world and the search for information to favor actions against it, of the *modus operandi* employed to sabotage our negotiations, be it by disassembling machinery, contaminating our sugar exports with undetectable chemical substances, adulterating lubricants to damage equipment or falsifying the technical specifications of products obtained. All this was done covertly, under the principle of ***plausible deniability,*** so that the CIA would not be unmasked as the true author of these actions.

CHAPTER V Other components of economic warfare

Terrorism as an economic weapon

According to experts, one can find hundreds of definitions of terrorism, which differ in dependence of the emphasis given its aims, means and methods or other components related to its execution.

In this book, terrorism is understood as those actions which, in addition to causing direct damage in the individual object targeted, are aimed at evoking feelings of insecurity, terror and panic, with a view to producing subsequent effects, particularly the severing of those links which are identified as the reason behind the terrorist actions.

Terrorism was used as a weapon against Cuba from very early on, by an organized fifth column equipped and directed by the U.S. government through the CIA and other agencies, in actions aimed at alienating the people from the Revolution and undermining the growing support that revolutionary measures found in the great majority of Cubans.

As explained in chapters two and three, acts of sabotage in the country's main economic sectors, organized by the CIA and approved by the National Security Council during Operation Mongoose and later periods, were designed to cause direct economic damage in the various areas targeted, and open blockade measures were combined with these actions to prevent or delay the repair of the sabotaged targets.

171

It was precisely after Operation Mongoose that, under orders from Attorney General Robert Kennedy, the green light was given to actions by émigré counterrevolutionary organizations that were to maintain the appearance of autonomous action, with no ties to the government. These groups, however, responded to a strategy designed at the highest government level and were supplied with and trained in the use of diverse means for their actions.

The Attorney General's call for deploying terrorist organizations in the émigré community as part of the economic war on Cuba did not take long to materialize.

On March 17, 1963, the Soviet cargo ship *L'Gov* was shot at by a pirate vessel belonging to the terrorist organizations Alpha 66 and Segundo Frente Nacional del Escambray (Second National Escambray Front). The Soviet ship was docked at the port of Isabela de Sagua, in the province of Villa Clara, hitting the chimney and one of the ship's fans.

A State Department communiqué dated March 19 expressed "the Department's strong opposition" to those actions, which were under investigation to "determine if U.S. laws had been violated". Readers should not forget that the Coordinator for Cuban Affairs, responsible for both open and covert actions against Cuba – and this attack was one such covert action – was part of that same Department of State. Worse yet: in a press conference held on March 21 that year, President Kennedy stated that the information at his disposal was that "they did not come from the United States", adding that the United States "did not support the group and had no connection with it". When, on March 19, Undersecretary Johnson held talks with his colleague Ball and stated that the United States had no links with the counterrevolutionary organization Alpha 66, a position which was apparently conveyed to the president, Ball replied that "nobody is going to believe this".[1]

To complicate matters even more, there was a pirate attack against the port of Caibarién, in the province of Villa Clara, shortly after. The attack was against the Soviet ship Baku, which had a sugar cargo. The ship received many impacts from 20 mm cannons and 30 and 50 caliber machine guns. As a result of the explosion of a magnetic mine, a four-meter long and half-meter wide hole was blown open on the ship's hull. The group "Commandos L", an Alpha 66

---

[1] Department of State: volume XI, 1996, p. 728.

splinter organization headed by the terrorist Antonio Cuesta Valle, was responsible for this action. The degree of impunity these actions enjoyed is proven by the fact that a Life magazine reporter, who had taken part in similar actions in the past, was part of the attacking group.

In this connection, the State Department sent the President a communiqué on March 28, pointing out that these actions worked against U.S. policy towards the USSR and the issue was discussed at a meeting of the National Security Council Executive Committee on March 29.[2]

The discussion was thorough, demonstrating the support of these terrorist actions by many of the participants; in the end, however, the President's decision was to take measures to keep these actions under control. In the following meeting, the Attorney General met with the Defense Secretaries, the CIA director and other officials, who agreed to immediately send a group of officials to Miami to approach the CIA, the FBI, the Coast Guard, Immigration and other agencies to gather as much information as possible on Cuban counterrevolutionary groups, improve the exchange of information between the CIA and FBI at that level, improve ties with customs and the coast guard, warn groups about similar actions and about the stockpiling of war material and other measures to dissuade their actions. In the end, what concerned U.S. authorities were the repercussions of these actions on relations with the USSR and not the terrorist actions against Cuban targets.[3]

It is important to know of these government-level instructions, as they are proof that the government could not, from that time on, claim ignorance of the innumerable anti-Cuban terrorist actions which continued to be carried out. A study of declassified documents demonstrates that it was not only an accomplice but that its policy was to encourage actions by these groups.

Some of the most important of the first terrorist-styled counterrevolutionary organizations during the early 1960s were the Movimiento de Recuperación Revolucionaria (MRR –Movement for Revolutionary Recovery), Movimiento Revolucionario del Pueblo (MRP – Revolutionary Movement of the People), Directorio Revolucionario Estudiantil (DRE – Revolutionary Student Directorate),

[2] Ibid., pp. 738-746.
[3] Departament of State: volume XI, 1996, document 304, pp. 744-745

Movimiento Insurreccional de Recuperación Revolucionaria (MIRR – Insurrectional Revolutionary Recovery Movement), Alpha 66, Movimiento Nacionalista Cubano (MNC – Cuban Nationalist Movement) and others. Later the list was expanded with Brigada 2506, the Junta Revolucionaria (JURE – the Revolutionary Junta), el Movimiento 30 de Noviembre (M-30-11 the November 30th Movement), el Ejército Secreto Anticomunista (ESA – the Secret Anti-Communist Army) and others.

Since 1963, attacks on Soviet ships and those of other nationalities forced the government to try to maintain more direct control over the activity of these organizations, although this control was relatively limited as a result of the double standard maintained and the fact these actions were in line with government objectives.

FBI documents declassified by the National Security Archive of the George Washington University in May 2005, during the heated polemic stirred up by the entry of international terrorist Luis Posada Carriles into US territory on board the Santrina —an action tolerated by the authorities— reveal a plan, in which Posada Carriles was involved in July 1965, to blow up a Cuban or Soviet vessel in the port of Veracruz, Mexico. Posada was receiving funds for this action from Jorge Más Canosa, later president of the Cuban American National Foundation, on behalf of the counterrevolutionary organization Revolutionary Recovery in Exile (RECE). For this act of sabotage, Posada had 100 pounds of C-4 plastic explosive and magnetic mines, to be placed in the hull of the targeted vessels, at his disposal, a procedure familiar to us, approved in the United States at the highest goverment level in the first half of 1963, as we saw in the previous chapter. (Nacional Security Archive, George Washington University: *Nacional Security Archive Electronic Briefing Book No. 153. Luis Posada Carriles. The declassified Record CIA and FBI documentos Detail Career in International Terrorism; Connection to U. S. Document 6: FBI, July 7, 1965, "Luis Posada Carriles".* May 10, 2005.)

If the execution of sabotage actions against Cuba's more important and complex economic targets continued being directed, for the most part, by the CIA, which relied on its own forces and means to do so, these other actions were to have an illustrative effect aimed at consolidating the international economic isolation of the Revolution. More and more, these actions were the patrimony of counterrevolutionary organizations which, *in view of the ends sought, were by definition terrorist organizations*, with allegedly no ties to the United States government but, under the table, financed and supplied by it. Thus, already from 1963 on, an alternative system of terrorist actions against the Cuban economy had been set up. Its main representatives were the figureheads and members of far-right counterrevolutionary organizations mainly based in the United States.

It made use of terrorism to serve economic warfare purposes, as opposed to other activities in other spheres.

José Luis Méndez'[4] book *Salvar al mundo del terrorismo (Saving the world from terrorism)* offers a detailed account of actions which targeted Cuba's economy. Referring to the actions undertaken between 1963-1967, he states: "During those years, the placing of bombs in Cuban entities abroad and *ships trading with Cuba* was the most common form of terrorist activity", later substituted by acts of terrorism "against facilities, interests, Cuban personnel and friends of the Revolution"[5] abroad. He expands on this idea further on when, referring to the same period, he expresses: "The actions of terrorist organizations were aimed at *strengthening the blockade, especially against the interests of countries that traded with Cuba* [...]"[6] adding a list of other targets. (The italics are ours).

As a way of limiting the actions of these terrorist organizations inside the United States, with a government policy of *laissez faire* (as long as these actions were perpetrated in other countries), the period known as the "war in other countries of the world" began with the 1970s. Not exclusive of direct actions against the national territory (which continued until 1974),[7] this war was taken to all parts of the world where Cuban interests, particularly economic interests, could be damaged. In the final and most important phase of this "war", an important role was played by CORU, created in June 1976 by the Cuban-born pediatrician who became one of the most dangerous terrorists in the Hemisphere: Orlando Bosch Avila. CORU was made up of such organizations as Brigada 2506, Movimiento Nacionalista Cubano (Cuban Nationalist Movement), Omega, Movimiento Insurreccional Martiano (Marti Insurrectional Movement),

---

[4] José Luis Méndez: *Salvar al mundo del terrorismo.* Editora Política, Havana, 2003.
[5] Ibid., p. 8.
[6] Ibid., p. 11.
[7] Ibid., p. 15.

Alianza Cubana de Organizaciones Revolucionarias (Cuban Revolutionary Alliance), Comandos Pedro Luis Boitel, Movimiento La Estrella (Star Movement) and Frente Revolucionario (Revolutionary Front).[8]

Numerous official US documents reveal the links of the main perpetrators —particularly Luis Posada Carriles—tho the CIA. Posada Carriles, like Orlando Bosch Avila, also an international terrorist, today freely walks the streets of Miami.

The first action that marked the beginning of this stage was a message sent to Canadian entrepreneurs who traded with Cuba. On April 4, 1972, a terrorist attack destroyed Cuba's commercial office in Montreal, Canada, causing the death of Cuban diplomat Sergio Pérez Castillo. "A prelude to the final stage of the war around the world"[9] according to Méndez Méndez, another message to potential customers of Cubana de Aviacion and, in general, to all those interested in visiting Cuba and beginning any kind of business relation with the country was the mid-air bombing of a Cubana airliner which took off from the Barbados airport on October 6, 1976, causing the death of 73 persons on board. There were no survivors. This event was poignantly remembered in 2005, when Luis Posada Carriles, one of the masterminds behind the attack, sought legal residence in the United States.

To illustrate the extent of these actions, suffice it to note that numerous terrorist actions were carried out between these two events as part of the economic war on Cuba. These included the sinking of the Cuban fishing boats *Aguja and Plataforma IV*, off the coast of the Bahamas (October 1972); the attack on the fishing boat *Plataforma I*, of the fishing cooperative of Caibarien and the placing of a bomb in the *Mereghan II* (January 1973), the launching of bombs into the residences of Cuban commercial representatives in Chile (June, August, September, 1973) and the bomb placed on a Cuban fishing boat in the Bahamas, which caused the death of fisherman Roberto Torna Mirabal (October, 1973).

Other actions included bombs placed in the offices of Cubana de Aviacion in Mexico (March 1974) and the Bahamas' Eastern Steamship Lines (November 1974) the Bahamas lines shipping company (December 1975); the placing of a bomb in a Cuban plane

[8] Ibid., pp. 103-104.
[9] Ibid., p. 21.

in Kingston, Jamaica (January 1975); the murder of a technician of the Cuban fishing fleet in port Chimbote, Peru (January 1976); the attack on a Soviet ship in the Bahamas (February, 1976); the sinking of *Ferrocemento* 119 and damages to *Ferrocamento* 123; the murder of fisherman Bienvenido Mauris Dias (April1976); bombs placed in the luggage department of Cubana de Aviacion at Kingston airport, Jamaica; in the Cubana offices in Barbados and in the British West Indies of Barbados, for servicing the Cuban airline; in the offices of Air Panama in Colombia; in the offices of Cubana de Aviacion in Panama and in the airport of Tocumen (July and August, 1976).[10]

The U.S. far-right, then represented by the neoconservatives, took the reins of power in the U.S. with the election of republican Ronald Reagan to the presidency in January 1981.

To push ahead the anti-Cuban policy like the first anti-Cuban actions approved by Eisenhower in March 1960 they needed a "responsible exile community" that would give credibility to the idea that these actions responded to the interests of Cubans themselves, and to have this community act as a pressure group for the approval of policies towards Cuba that was part of the republican platform for the 1980 elections, summarized in the Santa Fe Committee document.

In this manner, the creation of the Cuban American National Foundation (CANF) in July of 1981 as a kind of "think tank in charge of taking Cuban reality to Washington" signaled the emergence of the most important of all anti-Cuban terrorist organizations in history, able to wash over the contradiction of "U.S. government vs. counterrevolutionary organizations" that began to surface after 1963. For it was at once an allegedly Cuban counterrevolutionary organization and a representative of the U.S. far-right, whose spiritual inheritance it professed.

From the very beginning, its members included former CIA agents, participants of the terrorist actions of the teams involved in coastal attacks and the infiltration of weapons and military supplies in the stage prior to the Bay of Pigs invasion and those with intimate ties to the defeated Batista dictatorship. CANF began to fully participate in the three basic lines of action that, since its inception, characterized U.S. policy toward Cuba, regardless of the partisan veneer of the White House tenant in power: economic warfare, actions aimed

[10] Ibid., pp. 215-220.

at the international isolation of the Revolution and attempts to resurrect the counterrevolutionary opposition in the country that had vanished by the mid 60s.

CANF was particularly active in setting U.S. economic warfare mechanisms in motion from that time on. If at first it played a doctrinal function, offering, in its publications and conferences, arguments for the strengthening of the blockade to block the entry of foreign currency into the country, it would later be known for its lobby power in Congress and for pushing for the approval of the harshest of anti-Cuban laws. At the same time, and more intensely since the fall of the Socialist block and the USSR, it became the spearhead of the U.S. government in the blackmail of entrepreneurs and governments that tried to offer loans to, purchase products from or make investments in the country.

But, though the methods used during the first decade were openly terrorist, the new situation Cuba had to face in the 90s influenced that organization to try to precipitate events they thought imminent – the fall of the Revolution – taking terrorism to the extreme.

According to José Luis Méndez, in1992 "[…] the terrorist content and strategy of CANF became official with the creation of a structure and assignation of a millionaire budget for its actions. With the creation of the so-called Security Commission, and the selection of members from Cuban residents in the United States with experience in this type of crime, a program is begun to pursue two specific aims: the physical elimination of the Cuban President *and directing actions to affect the flow of foreign currency into Cuba, specially, through the tourist industry.*"[11] (The italics are the author's).

The new situation faced was the disappearance of the country's main trade partners. If Cuba's survival strategy was trade with U.S. subsidiaries in third countries, timidly begun towards the end of the 1970s, the Torricelli Law of 1992 would be responsible for making such trade disappear.

This is the reason behind the development of the tourist industry as the only viable alternative for the future of the country, which needed a sector capable of driving the rest of the economy in a necessary recovery process and in a world where it no longer had its traditional economic counterparts. Hampering this development

[11] Ibid., p. 130.

and preventing the sector from fulfilling this role became the main objective of the Cuban-American National Foundation. Due to their open character in the sector, these actions could be executed with relative ease; they could have a demonstrative effect on possible visitors and investors, negatively influencing their willingness to approach the country and thereby deprive the economy of enormous resources.

The year 1997 marked a relevant turn in that direction. The first explosions in hotels in the capital began during the first months; others occurred in the summer in similar facilities in the city and the Varadero resort, the most important in the country.

Events that year, according to a source that cannot be accused of partiality —the special rapporteur on mercenary activities of the United Nations Commission on Human Rights, during a visit to Cuba on September 12 to 17, 1999– pointed to the Cuban-American National Foundation and one of its most important actors: the terrorist Luis Posada Carriles, one of the confessed perpetrators of the bombing of Cubana de Aviacion commercial airliner, off the coast of Barbados, in October of 1976.

According to this UN expert on mercenary activities:

a) "Arnaldo Monzon Plasencia, member of the board of directors of the Cuban-American National Foundation, together with Gaspar Jiménez Escobedo and Guillermo Novo Sampoll recruited, hired and financed Santos Armando Martínez Rueda and José Enrique Ramírez Oro to place a 1,38 kilogram plastic C-4 explosive in a hotel in Varadero. These persons entered Cuban territory with forged Costa Rican passports and were paid 8 000 dollars for their services.

b) "The United States paid Cuban citizen Orfiris Pérez Cabrera 20 000 to poison cattle, carry out acts of vandalism against foreign cars and attack tourist centers in Havana.

c) "On April 12, 1997 a bomb made of plastic C-4 explodes in the bathroom of the Ache disco in the Melia-Cohiba hotel in Havana. On the 30th of the same month another was detected, this one made of 401 grams of C-4 plastic explosive and left on the 15th floor of this hotel.

d) "Four persons were injured on July 12, 1997, as a result of almost simultaneous explosions in the reception halls of the Capri and Nacional de Cuba hotels.

e) "Another bomb was set off (sic) on August 4, 1997 in the reception of the Melia-Cohiba hotel.

f) "On August 22, 1997, a bomb exploded in a hallway of the Sol Palmeras hotel in Varadero.

g) "Italian citizen Favio di Celmo died on September 4, 1997, and seven other persons were injured as a result of explosive devices set off in the Copacabana, Tritón and Chateau-Miramar hotels and in the Bodeguita del Medio restaurant.

h) "An artifact made of 170 grams of plastic explosive was found and de-activated on October 19, 1997 inside a tourist microbus.

i) "Lastly, on October 30, 1997 another bomb was discovered and de-activated under a stand in the 'José Martí' International airport."[12]

The use of terrorism as an economic weapon is described in other parts of the Rapporteur's report:

— The planning of actions relied on a "central unified brain", the clandestine structure of the Cuban American National Foundation.
— The tourism sector had been chosen because it constitutes the country's main source of revenue, with plans to go from 340 000 tourists in 1990 to 1,7 million in 1999.
— This sector is very sensitive to the spread of information and publicity. The hotels chosen belonged to important chains such as the Melia-Cohiba, or were other world famous tourist centers such as the Bodeguita del Medio, for a stronger propagandistic impact.
— Bombs were not placed in rooms but in areas such as receptions to make the repercussions of the attacks more extensive.[13]

The foreign mercenaries hired for these actions were the Salvadorians Raúl Ernesto Cruz León and Otto René Rodríguez Llerena and the Guatemalans María Elena González Meza, Nader Kamal Musalam Barakat and Jazid Iván Fernández Mendoza.[14]

---

[12] United Nations Organization: "Report of the special rapporteur on mercenary activities of the UN Commission on Human Rights who visited Cuba from September 12 to 17, 1999". *Granma* daily, special supplement, April 8, 2000, p. 3.
[13] Ibid., p. 4.
[14] Report of the Ministry of the Interior, Granma daily, October 29, 1998.

The analysis and investigation conducted by the special U.N. rapporteur identified the following important points that cannot be considered maneuvers by Cuban authorities:

— The attacks with explosives occurred. In their magnitude, they constituted terrorist actions designed to cause damage by spreading terror indiscriminately, regardless of its effects on human lives.
— They were part of a vast plan against Cuban tourism complexes and against the safety of its population and visiting tourists.
— The damages caused included the killing of the Italian citizen Favio di Celmo; considerable injuries and emotional and psychological damages to several persons as well as significant material damages. The report points out, however, that the greatest and unquantifiable damage caused by this chain actions was creating the sensation abroad that Cuba is not a safe place, the victim of uncontrollable terrorist attacks.
— The mercenaries were foreigners who accepted money to commit these actions but responsibility was shared by those who recruited them, paying for, financing and planning the criminal act. As such, a heavy burden of responsibility falls upon the Salvadoran Francisco Chávez Abarca and Luis Posada Carriles.
— With respect to the aim of the attacks, why they were committed and what they hoped to achieve, the rapporteur concludes that the attacks were aimed at affecting the climate of tranquility that is one of the first requirements to attract tourism, substituting normal and daily tranquility with collective insecurity and thereby causing an international impact to discourage tourists from traveling to Cuba.
— The persons who did the recruiting and the organizations on behalf of which the mercenaries were acting have, perhaps, greater responsibility than the material authors of the crime.[15]

The plans were not only aimed at attacking the tourist sector. According to Méndez Méndez: "In 1995, CANF broadens its terrorist plans, and, to this end, diversifies the targets to be destroyed within Cuba. As part of this escalade, *industrial centers* and points where

15 UN Organization: p. 6.

181

tourists concentrate are targeted. *The refinery in Cienfuegos, the Matanzas thermoelectric plant[16] and Tropicana cabaret in the western part of the capital, are chosen.* The location of these places was transmitted to CANF headquarters through a sophisticated Global Positioning System (GPS), equipment given by this organization to several of its agents in Cuba [...]"[17] (The italics are ours)

Attacks against other sectors did not remain in the planning stage. According to Jose Luis Méndez, before the attacks on hotels in the capital: "On January 12, 1996, two assassins were captured while moving C-4 plastic explosive and other materials for terrorist actions in Cuba. A month later, on February 11, three more were captured after an action in Bahía de Cárdenas, Matanzas. All three were members of PUND, with ties to CANF [...]. On September 17, there is an infiltration near Punta Alegre in the Chambas municipality, in Ciego de Avila, where a Cuban-born Miami resident is detained after introducing weapons, ammunition and other articles of war into the country."[18]

The actions mentioned above are the most important terrorist actions or attacks perpetrated against the Cuban economy. Other actions, carried through or not, had remained unknown to the public until the recent publication of the book by Jose Luis Mendez, whom we have quoted at length. Of the book's revelations, we will quote a number corresponding to the decade of the 1990s, all related to the use of terrorism as an economic warfare weapon.

— In July 1993, Posada Carriles is known to have visited the San Pedro Sula airport to study the arrival times, taxiing and departure sites of the Cuban transport and cargo airlines Aerocaribbean and Aerogaviota.
— In June 1994, Posada Carriles was in Costa Rica with the Cuban-born counterrevolutionary Miguel Mariano Merino Vázquez, studying the situation in Limon port with a view to attacking a Cuban ship that frequently docked there for loading.

---

[16] High priority target in sabotage plans approved by the U.S. National Security Council during Operation Mongoose (1962) and in Proposed New Covert Policy and Program Towards Cuba of June 1963.
[17] José Luis Méndez: p. 133.
[18] Idem.

His presence in that country was due to the resumption of Cubana de Aviacion flights to that destination, which finally came to fruition on December 3, 1995.

— In March 1995, he was in Honduras organizing terrorist actions against entrepreneurs in that country who traded with Cuba. He was accused of placing several bombs in Tegucigalpa.

— At the time, he had close ties to the terrorist organization Movimiento de Solidaridad con Centroamerica (MOSCA – Solidarity with Central America Movement), in existence since 1994, which was the owner of SOSA airlines, some of whose planes had visited the "José Martí" International Airport in Havana, preparing subversive attacks.

— At the end of that period, in 1996, Posada Carriles prepares the terrorist attacks that shake the Cuban capital in 1997 and those attempted in 1998; he recruits his direct executors, training them and offering means for their execution, all through funds provided by the Cuban American National Foundation.

Other similar intentions had been kept in the shadows until then. In the trial against Central American terrorists hired by CANF through Posada Carriles, the prosecutor presented a witness whose testimony made a deep impression: It was the Guatemalan citizen residing in Cuba, Percy Alvarado Godoy, who revealed he had received an offer of 60 000 dollars through contacts with CANF for placing bombs in the Tropicana nightclub and other tourist centers; actions that were neutralized because Alvarado Godoy was an agent of Cuban security, working under the alias of *Fraile*.[19]

Propaganda as part of economic war

There is an important aspect of CIA subversive activity that is often ignored when speaking of economic war against the Cuban Revolution and which cannot be left aside if a comprehensive evaluation of the phenomenon is sought. This component is related to political-ideological subversion in economic areas or sectors and

[19] Percy Alvarado: *Confesiones de Fraile. Una historia real de terrorismo.* ("Fraile's Confessions. A true story of terrorism") Editorial Capitán San Luis, Havana, 2002.

includes a broad variety of propaganda and subversive actions aimed at strengthening the iron siege on our country established through economic warfare measures designed to bring about the economy's collapse.

Slanderous propaganda was used against the Revolution since the first moments following its triumph in January of 1959. Used by the U.S. press and the official government-sponsored Voice of America radio broadcast, it focused on the just execution of murderers and torturers of the overthrown dictatorship, fomenting anti-communist sentiments or harassing and slandering revolutionary leaders. Propaganda operations against the Revolution followed the schemes inherited from the Cold War and were used as spear heads in the most unimaginable plans to steer the Cuban population in their aim to weaken support for the triumphant revolutionary process and to undermine support and sympathy towards this process within the United States, Latin America and all over the world.

According to Fabian Escalante: "A giant propaganda campaign was unleashed. Arguments such as that Cubans would nationalize large land holdings without compensation, indiscriminately punished Batista murderers, aimed to export revolutions, sent children to Russia to be indoctrinated and thousands of more lies, aimed by the mass media against a population of scarcely six million inhabitants, made of Cuba the most dangerous enemy of the Western world in the continent.[20]

Propaganda by radio means

These efforts were strengthened by the organization of actions that culminated in the Bay of Pigs invasion. In addition to sending lecturers to participate in conferences all over Latin America and spread anti-Cuban propaganda in the continental mass media, the United States set up a radio station on Swan Island that took its name and that went on the air on May 17, 1960. Its aim was to create a psychological climate to garner support from the Cuban people for those being trained abroad to put an end to the Revolution.

Merely two months later, the first pirate[21] anti-Cuban station, named Radio Cuba Independiente, began transmissions aboard the

[20] Fabián Escalante Font: p. 10.
[21] Illegal stations with that name or counterrevolutionary symbols.

yacht Calypso, anchored in Sal keys, off the Bahamas, and operated by a counterrevolutionary émigré who would later be in charge of directing communications for Brigada 2506.[22]

Radio Swan not only aimed to secure the population's passive support for the actions undertaken by forces organized and trained by the CIA but, with growing intensity, also called for terrorist actions against the economy. According to experts on the subject:

The contents of Radio Swan broadcasts became increasingly aggressive, calling for subversion and sabotage. An announcement, with the traditional format of a commercial advertisement, clearly illustrates the aims of the project.

The narrator, whose voice was well known in Cuba's commercial radio, would say: "Worker, you know your machine, destroy it, who better than you to destroy it in such a way that the communists don't notice [...] don't oil it, drop sand into its mechanisms [...].[23]

Radio Swan's propaganda activity was complemented by other commercial stations in southern Florida (WRUL, WGBS and WMIE in Miami; WKWF In Key West) and WWL in New Orleans. Apparently independent, they were directed, under the table, by the CIA , and their programs complemented counterrevolutionary messages.

After the Bay of Pigs fiasco and as part of Operation Mongoose, propaganda campaigns against the Revolution were stepped up. New resources from the United States Information Agency (USIA) were added to what was secretly done by the CIA and, to a limited extent, by Voice of America. These institutions were responsible for the "psychological" tasks of Mongoose, aiming, through failed attempts, to isolate the Revolution internationally, achieve internal support for

---

[22] Narciso Viera: *"La estimulación radial de la contrarrevolución en Cuba"* ("The encouragement of counterrevolutionary activity in Cuba via radio means"). Havana, 2000. Unpublished.

[23] Arnaldo Coro Antich, José R. Cabañas and Félix Raúl Rojas Cruz: "La radio de Estados Unidos como instrumento de agresión contra Cuba" ("U.S. radio broadcasts as an instrument of aggression against Cuba"), in Colectivo de Autores: El conflicto Estados Unidos-Cuba (The U.S. – Cuba conflict). Félix Varela Publishing House, Havana, 1998, pp. 233-263. Through radio-technique observations, the first author made a copy of the mentioned transmission during its broadcast.

their aim and to create an internal fifth column that would respond to their terrorist interests. Economic subjects were openly manipulated and the calls for sabotage in economic sectors reached a peak. This was one of the reasons behind the substantial increase in this kind of enemy action during the Operation.

A memorandum from USIA deputy director Donald M. Wilson to Operation Mongoose chief General Lansdale dated June 20, 1962, stated that propaganda on economic matters was aimed at highlighting the deterioration of the economic situation, the government's alleged incapacity to satisfy the basic needs of the population; poor administration of the economy and a supposed mirroring of the economic situation in the USSR and China. What is revolting about this is that these matters about the deterioration of the Cuban economy, supposedly caused by the Revolution, were selected by the very same people who had declared war on the country's economy and were going to unspeakable extents, as part of Operation Mongoose, through open and covert means, to turn the country into scorched earth.[24]

Economic matters were not the only ones that were manipulated. The following, described by Fabian Escalante, is a telling example of the criminal nature of these actions: January 1962 marked the beginning of a radio campaign called Operation Plunder (Operacion Botin) whose aim was to push for the assassination of revolutionary leaders by offering rewards as high as one hundred thousand dollars, depending on the posts occupied by the victims.[25]

The October Crisis occurred during the high point of Operation Mongoose. This resulted in an intensification of anti-Cuban radio propaganda, with the quick installation of two new medium-wave transmitters in Marathon and Sugar Loaf keys in southern Florida.

According to the abovementioned experts, these installations began a new phase of radio war against Cuba, "by taking the United

---

[24] Department of State: volume X, 1997, p. 858. Also in Jon Elliston: *Psywar on Cuba. The declassified history of U.S. anti-Castro propaganda.* Ocean Press, 1999, p. 106. See also, Jacinto Valdés-Dapena: *"La propaganda radial en el esquema de las operaciones de subversión político-ideológica de la guerra psicológica contra Cuba"* ("Propaganda over the radio within the political and ideological subversion schemes of the psywar on Cuba"), Havana, 1999, p. 35. Unpublished paper.

[25] Fabián Escalante: p. 34.

States' direct acts of aggression to hectometric and medium wave lengths, where they expected to capture significantly larger audiences in our country".[26] This meant a dramatic increase in radio broadcasts calling for internal subversion and acts of sabotage against the Cuban economy, direct participation in its organization and promotion by U.S. high agency officials for propaganda.

According to U.S. writer Jon Elliston, author of the book *Psywar on Cuba*, in which he quotes many declassified government documents on these subjects: "The USIA's role in the anti-Castro psywar, which had grown during Operation Mongoose and become predominant during the missile crisis, remained significant as the crisis subsided".[27] The author offers the example of a memorandum from USIA director Edward R. Murrow to CIA director John McCone, offering recommendations about a better use of Cuban émigrés in radio broadcasts directed at Cuba and pointing out their important role in urging"[…] *economic sabotage and passive resistance* […]"[28] (The italics are ours)

In his communiqué to the CIA director, Murrow explained that the exiles chosen to participate in these transmissions had to have "a reputation and credibility" in each of the sectors to which their broadcasts were directed, pointing out what, in his opinion, should be the main subjects broadcasted on and, as can be seen, that they were uncomplicated and safe acts of sabotages which, if carried out at a mass scale, could cause serious damages: the Cuban audience should be urged to work at snail's pace to increase inefficiency, to waste means and to carry out relatively safe acts of sabotage, for example: dropping glass and nails onto the highway, wasting water in public buildings, dropping sand into machines to damage them, wasting electricity; invoking an illness to skip work, damaging sugar warehouses during the harvest and other acts of sabotage.

It additionally explained that these broadcasts should be strictly attributed to Cuban exiles to prevent public knowledge of the participation of USIA or of any other government agency. If results were obtained, USIA would re-transmit them as an alleged example

---

[26] Arnaldo Coro Antich, José R. Cabañas and Félix Raúl Rojas Cruz: p. 241. The statement is based on a letter from William Rust, dated 1963, to the U.S. Federal Commission of Communications.

[27] Jon Elliston: p. 153.

[28] Idem.

of opposition to the Revolution and broadcast them around the world, carefully hiding that the U.S. government was the true source. The memo concluded expressing that the proposal would contribute, among other factors, to United States economic measures against Cuba and encourage the population to carry out necessary acts of sabotage.[29]

Proof that these terrorist actions against the Cuban economy were always directed at the highest U.S. government level was the December 10, 1962 meeting of the National Security Council Executive Committee, in which President Kennedy approved the Murrow proposal and directed the CIA to hire the Cuban exiles for this program,[30] a policy that was only surpassed by the setting up of a subversive radio station in January of 1985.

For decades, Cuba has continued to bear the heavy weight of propaganda against its economy by many radio and television stations that, in an affront to our nation, use the name of our National Hero. These have included commercial stations and counterrevolutionary programs.

According to a recent study[31], from 1990 to 1999, in addition to the radio stations inaptly called "Jose Marti", 6 medium-wave anti-Cuban stations, one in FM and a total of 65 counterrevolutionary programs participated in anti-Cuban propaganda campaigns, for a yearly average for each of the latter of 731,8 hours, 62 from U.S. territory and one in Puerto Rico, Guatemala and El Salvador. Three transmitted in radio ham wavelengths, while the remainder did so in the wavelength of official radio broadcasts.

The counterrevolutionary transmissions called for acts of economic sabotage as part of its regular programs, calling on listeners to damage machinery, transportation means, crops and, in general, anything the could be destroyed on a daily basis. The main economic sectors, those of greater importance for the economic development of the country, were preferred targets in these calls for destruction. In the period mentioned, these included the sugar agro industrial process, nickel production, tobacco plantations and production and the tourist industry.

---

[29] Ibid., pp. 154-155. Also in Department of State: volume XI, 1996, p. 605.

[30] Departament of State: volume XI, 1996, p. 608.

[31] Narciso Viera: *"La estimulación radial de la contrarrevolución en Cuba"*. Havana, 2000. Unpublished work.

To the above list, we must add Miami channels 23 and 51, which devote spaces in their programs to propagandize terrorist organizations abroad and anti-Cuban actions in general.[32]

In 2007, through a recently concluded legislative process, the US Congress approved a monetary package of 33 million destined to radio and television broadcasts aimed at Cuba's radio-phonic space, a new violation of the international norms established by the International Telecommunications Union.

Studies on the Cuban economy in U.S. academic circles. Ideological U.S. "support" for the "transition" to capitalism in Cuba

Nourished by the works of émigrés Felipe Pazos, Rufo López Fresquet and Jose R. Álvarez Díaz and European economists Karol and Dumont, the work of Cubanologist, Carmelo Mesa Lago rapidly acquired preeminence in the United States. Together with Jorge Pérez López, Sergio Roca, Andrew Zimbalist and others, he set the interpretative framework for studies on the Cuban economy in the United States and around the world.

With an important role in the University of Pittsburgh and many other universities and "think tanks" in the United States (Rand Corporation, Heritage Foundation, American Enterprise Institute, Center of Foreign Relations, among many others) and even abroad, studies on the Cuban economy gained in preeminence as part of what we referred to before as the "wide track" of academic studies on Cuba, to differentiate them from those conducted within the intelligence community.

Referring to these studies, the Cuban academician, Jorge Hernández, has said:

"It is not that [...] there is a necessary, general and automatic subordination of these studies to U.S. policy – although that also happens – but rather that there is the common premise which is that socialism in Cuba will invariably and eventually fall. This is combined with several factors, of an intellectual and political nature: the traditional anti-Marxist positions, the disenchantment of those who believed in the Revolution and socialism and conservative intolerance.

[32] Idem.

"Although these studies were not subordinated to each U.S. administration, academic circles refract the socio-political context they are in. It happens, therefore, that in line with the generalization of the dominant ideology of all class societies, they often reflect and socialize a negative outlook about Cuba that has existed in government circles and in the policy applied for over thirty years."[33]

Until the latter half of the 1980s, the main cubanology theses on the Cuban economy contributed to propaganda campaigns and to the reduction of foreign support for the Cuban revolution, thus becoming part of economic war actions. They were:

— Absence of real economic development in Cuba, challenging, as is logical to assume, the country's development strategy, economic policy and official statistics.
— Existence of social development without an economic basis and even denial, by ignoring the facts, of the levels of development achieved.
— Criticism of Soviet "subsidies" and "dependence" on the then existing USSR and socialist bloc.[34]

The disappearance of the socialist block and belief in the rapid fall of the Revolution gave new overtones to evaluations of the Cuban economy during the early 1990s. Stress is then placed on an analysis of the real economic situation and what would be needed to speed up a transition to a market economy after the hypothetically imminent fall of the Revolution. The subject of a transition from socialism to capitalism in Cuba, for which programs and projects were created in several universities, began gaining in prominence.[35]

According to Jorge Hernandez: "[…] the discussion of a transition towards a new society or what has been called post-Castroist Cuba,

---

[33] Jorge Hernández Martínez: "Miradas desde afuera: política y estudios sobre Cuba en los Estados Unidos" ("Foreign gazes: policy towards and studies on Cuba in the United States"). Temas magazine, N° 2, 1995, p. 49.

[34] José Luis Rodríguez García: Crítica a nuestros críticos (Critique of our critics). Editorial de Ciencias Sociales, Havana, 1988, p. 15.

[35] The most well known study is that of the Association for the study of the Cuban Economy (ASCE) created in 1990. Through the publication, in association with the International University of Florida, of Cuba in Transition, this institution publishes articles and presentations made in its yearly meetings.Another important study, entitled Transition in Cuba, was conducted by Lisandro Pérez, CRI-FIU, 1993.

190

is at the core of efforts that have been underway since the beginning of the current decade in the sphere of social sciences. In this manner, the objective diagnosis and characterization of the processes studied tend to be substituted, in the mentioned studies, by others based on forecasts and prescriptive formulas that would set down rules to be followed in the future reordering of Cuban society."[36]

With such a prescriptive focus, similar to what occurred during the 1960s, when studies on Cuba[37] gave the Eisenhower administration an ideological pretext for what later became the Bay of Pigs invasion, the theory of "a betrayed revolution", placing the accent on the inevitability of a return to capitalism in Cuba, studies undertaken in the 1990s simply served to sanctify a government policy reflected in the Torricelli Act of 1992; the Helms-Burton Act took this policy to new heights in January 1997, with the document entitled "Support for a democratic transition in Cuba" which, backed by millions of dollars, outlined a political-ideological subversion scheme for the country to encourage the resurgence and strengthening of counterrevolutionary forces capable of appearing as valid alternatives to power.

Some authors not only justify the inevitability of change but also actively participate in attempts to encourage efforts by forces that, according to the transition program, would do away with the Revolution, acting in connivance with internal counterrevolutionary factions that, in turn, act under the orders of the U.S. Interest Section in the country.

A good example is the article which appeared in volume 4 of the Association for the Study of the Cuban Economy, where, below the name of Rolando H. Castañeda and member of the ASCE Executive Committee George P. Montalban, some principles, expounded on there, were said to have been received from representatives of the internal counterrevolutionary opposition, which expressed the need of sectors linked to foreign investment in Cuba to speed up changes towards capitalism.

In spite of the above, sometimes the opinions of experts on Cuban issues did not always go hand in hand with the express interests of the President and Congress. According to the article by Jorge Hernández mentioned above, "[...] the opinions of academics who

---

[36] Jorge Hernández Martínez: p. 50.
[37] Particularly the works of Theodore Draper.

have participated in congressional hearings have, at times, been in conflict with that consensus and, at others, have been dismissed". In a footnote, he explains that Jorge Domínguez and Anthony Maingot, in a hearing of the Senate Select Committee on Intelligence held on July 29, 1994, "believed that the United States had not applied an adequate policy towards Cuba and proposed, among other things, to partially eliminate certain clauses of the blockade policy. The two experts agreed that the U.S. government needed to rectify false concepts about the Cuban leadership and redesign its policy towards the island."[38]

According to this author, during the 90s, studies on Cuba in the United States paid close attention to the effects on the Cuban economy had by the disappearance of the socialist bloc, and arrived at the basic and inevitable conclusion that the same steps taken in Eastern Europe and the USSR, which restored the economic models of market society in those countries, were to be followed. As a corollary to this, they stressed the obsolescence of the prevailing political system and, noting the combination of these two factors, insisted on Cuba's supposed need to return to capitalism.

Among the theses that supported this position, we will mention only those referring to a change in the economy:

— Cuba should start changes [...] in its forms of economic organization, with a view to getting in step with the need to rescue the country from the gradual and inexorable deterioration it is facing. This goes hand in hand with changes in internal organization that would garner international respect and support.[39]
— The aim of regaining equilibrium within the logic of continuing within the framework of the Revolution is not viable. Change is only possible by breaking existing schemes, both economically and politically [...].[40]
— It is necessary to rethink not only nationalism but also the question of equality. The ideological platform of the past three

[38] Jorge Hernández Martínez: op. cit., p. 52.
[39] Jorge I. Domínguez: "Cuba y el Mundo" ("Cuba and the world") (presentation), 16th Congress of the Association for Caribbean Studies, Havana, May, 1991. Quoted by Jorge Hernández Martínez: p. 54.
[40] Guilliam Gunn: "Will Castro Fall?", Foreign Policy, summer, 1990, and "Cuba in Crisis", Current History, March, 1991. Also Juan del Águila: "Why Communism Hangs on in Cuba", Global Affairs, winter, 1991. Jorge Hernández Martínez: idem.

decades is of no use for the future. It is necessary and fruitful to think of a possible transition to a market economy in Cuba.[41]

— U.S. policy towards Cuba relies on the premise that the current Cuban situation is untenable in the long range; thus, it is a question of speeding up inevitable changes at an acceptable cost to that policy.[42]

The picture in the mainstream press

The problems faced by Cuba's economy in the 1990s were reported in the same manner in the mainstream press of the United States. In a well-documented article[43], Alfredo Prieto González discusses the issue and gives us the key to identify one of the methodological suppositions that encumbered – and continues to encumber – the objective analysis of Cuban reality, thereby contributing to the economic war against our country.

The first question the author asks is: Does the image of Cuba in the U.S. press reflect reality? He quickly answers: perceptions of Cuba's reality reported are either distorted because of several reasons or turn into problems issues that are not so for Cubans.[44]

Another point to clarify is that there is no homogenous and monolithic press in the U.S., as it responds to different sectors of the dominant class that are neither. It is "[...] a diffuse complex conceived and formulated for the political class and the more educated, higher income sectors of society. Its ultimate purpose is to contribute, as much as it can, to the reproduction of the ideological-cultural system that

---

41 Marifeli Pérez-Stable: "Towards a Market Economy in Cuba? Social and Political Considerations", in Cuba in Transition, volume 1 Papers and Proceedings of the First Annual Meeting of the Association for the Study of the Cuban Economy (ASCE), Florida International University, Miami, August, 1991, Florida International University, Miami, 1992. Jorge Hernández Martínez: idem.

42 Jorge I. Domínguez: "La política de EE.UU. hacia Cuba y las relaciones con América Latina y el Caribe" ("U.S. policy towards Cuba and relations with Latin America and the Caribbean"). Seminar, Elections of 1992 and Relaciones Interamericanas, CEA-Universidad de Columbia, Havana, July 3 to 5, 1992. Jorge Hernández Martínez: Idem.

43 Alfredo Prieto González: "Cuba en los medios de difusión norteamericanos" ("Cuba in the American mainstream press"). Temas Magazine, N° 2, Havana, 1995, pp. 13-21.

44 Alfredo Prieto González: "Cuba en los medios de difusión norteamericanos". Temas Magazine, N° 2, La Habana, 1995, pp. 13-21.

makes it possible and to the construction of hegemony". It is important to highlight the growing influence of a "[…] new theory of public relations, in the style of Goebbels, who maintained that if a lie is repeated with sufficient conviction and emphasis it will be believed to contain a certain degree of truth".[45]

According to this author, the critical focus on Cuba that appears in this press – repeated without substantial differences in other countries, thus becoming a global referent – took shape at the beginning of the 1960s. If at that time the topics were the "questionable and excessive execution of war criminals", "the revolution betrayed", "Soviet beachhead" or "USSR satellite", despite the changes that have taken place in the international arena, the content of all critiques continue to be stereotypes inherited from that period.

For the U.S. press, the main aspects of the Cuban problem since the beginning of the crisis of the 1990s — in line with government policy[46]—are factors of an economic nature.[47] And here we arrive at the subject we are interested in expounding upon, because of its direct relationship to the economic war against Cuba.

The negative view of Cuba's economy divulged till then was strengthened by the sharp fall of indexes during the first half of that decade, immediately after Cuba lost its main trade partners and sources of foreign funding. This reality had an objective explanation that was systematically silenced by the press, in correspondence with official policy, which was aimed at finding a justification for encouraging processes of political change in the country.

According to Alfredo Prieto:

However, in the informative model employed, we find no explanation of the circumstances that led to the problems or the policies confronting them.

Informed by alleged ideologues, *the mainstream discourse basically emphasizes factors connected to the collapse of trade*

45 Ibid., pp. 13-14.

46 "[…] (objectivity) together with the need to preserve social access and prestige, leads the mass media to divulge and even depend on the perceptions of power and the communiqués of its agencies, considered to be objective and reliable sources. This results in the socialization of its conjectures as assured truth and, above all, a molding of the parameters of debate". Ibid., p.17.

47 Other factors are the political system and human rights.

194

with the USSR. The main objective is obvious: to stress the idea of a subsidized country and, this way, the parasitic character of Cuba's socialist system, incapable, according to this discourse, of guaranteeing the simple reproduction of citizens, in such a way that all responsibility falls on the political system, which is condemned in advance. (The italics are the author's).

Concluding with a scathing comment, the author remarks:

The dark side of the formula is the specific weight of the blockade that, in contradiction with statistics, is presented as a screen used by the Cuban government to conceal its own problems and incapacities [48] (the italics are the author's).

For the readers who have followed the thread of our argument to this point, one question: Can anyone who has systematically followed Cuban political and economic issues and their relationship to the United States over the past forty years honestly ignore the heavy burden that the U.S. blockade represents for the economy of the island? Can they claim ignorance of the clandestine actions against the island's economy? Can they ignore the final result of the interaction between the blockade and these covert operations that have been systematically applied, since June of 1963, against the island?

Consequently, we have but one alternative: to identify the propagandistic actions that "obscure" important aspects of the problem, not those of a poorly informed observer but of someone interested in keeping some elements of the equation in the dark, to identify, this way, another component of the economic war, of a propagandistic nature, whose function is to minimize this war, to hide it and make believe it does not exist.

Another alternative is the situation of the Hispanic press in Florida. In its most important representatives, it is not about ignoring a reality but fighting to strangle Cuba. Continuing with Alfredo Prieto:

If an obvious degree of diversity with respect to formulas and ways of treating the Cuban question is caught sight of in the

---

[48] Alfredo Prieto González: "Cuba en los medios de difusión norteamericanos". Temas Magazine, N° 2, Havana, 1995, p. 17.

English-speaking mainstream press, this tendency is much less obvious in Southern Florida's Hispanic press. This subsystem is controlled by power groups who have made anti-communism a cultural industry of important dividends and a functional way of life for conservative sectors that control public spaces in Miami.

He adds, specifically referring to the Opinion Section of El Nuevo Herald, a supplement of the Miami Herald:

Its columnists and reporter often have an organic affiliation to counterrevolutionary organizations and in Cuba were "well known dissidents", writers who left the country or conservative intellectuals who work as professors [...]. In general, objectivity gives way to an interpretive scheme that leave little space for more moderate positions, such that it converges with the hard line of the community's policy which is a recurrent trend in that section of the paper [...].

He concludes that:

The most common platform asks the government for a strengthening of the blockade [...] as an instrument of pressure to obtain political changes in Cuba, in a word, support for the pressure cooker policy, characteristic of CANF and the Congressional right wing of Cuban origin [...] it supports any harshening of the policy, including a reduction of the number of flights and the suppression of family remittances [...].[49]

Embargo or Blockade?

In previous pages we spoke of the semantic juggling practiced by the U.S. government to deceive and confuse as regards its true intentions towards the Cuban Revolution, as a subversive strategy in the field of ideas. Possibly one of the best examples we can invoke to define the most important U.S. measure against the Cuban economy is the substitution of the word "blockade" with "embargo".

[49] Ibid., p. 19.

196

The president of the National Assembly of the People's Power describes it as a "linguistic falsification". Referring to the economic war as a whole, he expresses: "Official propaganda refers to it simply as an 'embargo', a hypocritical and false word, deliberately used to cover up the truth, an irrefutable institutionalized lie, deliberately and carefully employed by a government with the clear intention of inducing error, which is repeated by no few journalists, academicians and politicians."[50]

The fact is that, since the establishment of the blockade on Cuba in the early 1960s, a strategy of disinformation also began: according to the U.S. government and its propagandists, what were established were restrictions on bilateral trade within existing legal frameworks, in nothing opposed to international law.

For forty years, the United Sates has followed a strictly Goebbelsian formula in this matter, constantly repeating the lie that "it is only an embargo", to make people believe the blockade does not exist, and consequently, the economic war also does not exist. It thus trumps up an additional argument against the Revolution: the problems faced by the Cuban economy stem, if anything, from the inefficiency of the state administrative apparatus and the solution can only be found in a return to capitalism.

This subject has been extensively analyzed in our country.

A group of authors from the Center for United States Studies (CESEU) of Havana, Cuba, addressed this issue in the article "Blockade, not embargo"[51], expressing that: "One of the reasons why U.S. representatives do not use the word blockade for their actions, is the legal consistency of the concept of 'embargo, which reduces the problem, in one fell swoop, to a 'bilateral dispute'".

These authors demonstrate the extraterritoriality of the U.S. measures and how they harass Cuban economic, trade and financial

[51] Carlos A. Batista Odio, Graciela Chailloux Laffita, Esteban Morales Domínguez and Jorge Mario Sánchez Egozcue: "Bloqueo, no embargo", in Colectivo de Autores: pp. 38-48.

[50] Ricardo Alarcón de Quesada: "El embuste: arma inseparable de la agresión imperialista" («The tall story: an indispensable weapon of imperialist agression"). Speech for the 2nd World Meeting of Friendship and Solidarity with Cuba, November 10, 2000. Appears in Ricardo Alarcón de Quesada and Miguel Álvarez Sánchez: *Guerra económica de Estados Unidos contra Cuba (The United States' economic war against Cuba)*. Editora Política, La Habana, pp. 40-65.

relations around the world, in actions that go beyond the bilateral dispute invoked.[52]

A profound legal analysis of the issue was conducted for the proceedings of the First Civil and Administrative court of the People's Provincial Court of Havana, on May 5, 2000, following the conclusion of hearings in the suit brought against the United States Government for economic damages. It demonstrated that, according to the most advanced legal doctrine, the word embargo[53] cannot be invoked by the United States in its relations with Cuba; the U.S. presidential decree of February, 1962, has no doctrinal support and this figure of speech has no legal basis. What the United States has imposed on Cuba, rather, is a blockade[54], in pursuit of a political end: to destroy the Revolution.

Another facet of this same phenomenon was revealed during the sessions of the proceedings.

The chairman of the Standing Commission for Economic Affairs of the National Assembly of the People's Power Dr. Osvaldo Martinez told the court that: "The most recent economic warfare action has been a propaganda and disinformation maneuver, in response to the solid international repudiation of the blockade, to spread the idea that it has been lightly softened through illusory promises to grand licenses that permit trade relations, not with institutions that are actually involved in the purchase of food products, but with the

[52] When Cuba presented the proposed Resolution condemning the blockade before the UN for the first time, the U.S. Department of State responded by claiming it was an embargo because it only affected bilateral relations and acknowledged that the United States would be enforcing a blockade "if it was to carry out actions to prevent other countries from trading with Cuba" which, according to them, "is not the case". Here we can see that, with a confession in hand, proof is not needed. See Michael Krinsky and David Golove: p. 20. Also Carlos A. Batista Odio, Graciela Chailloux Laffita, Esteban Morales Domínguez and Jorge Mario Sánchez Egozcue: p. 42.
Álvarez Sánchez: Guerra económica de Estados Unidos contra Cuba. Editora Política, Havana, pp. 40-65.

[53] Defined as a "legal concept linked to General Proceedings Theory [...] (and that) [...] it is a cautionary measure, be it preventive or executed, always decreed by the legal organs of one part, to prevent or hamper the free disposition of goods of a certain person and thereby guarantee compliance with an obligation".

[54] Meaning "to shut off, cut off, isolate from abroad, asphyxiate, enclose, trap, besiege".

private sector they wish to develop in Cuba to use it as in internal destabilization instrument".[55]

Propaganda and disinformation are classic examples of political and ideological subversion and are presented here, in the expert testimony of Osvaldo Martínez, as a unique form of economic war, aimed at deceiving the international community which, for the most part, is opposed to the blockade.[56]

There is another highly interesting aspect of this quotation that we should emphasize: another instrument used in the economic war is the stimulation of economic actors with no links to the State, with a view to having them gain in strength and then demand political participation. An expression of imperialist stubbornness, this strategy aims to organize counterrevolutionary forces in Cuba according to the erosion of socialism from within scheme.

The bolstering of a predominantly terrorist counterrevolutionary opposition was secretly carried out by the CIA until the early 1980s. With the Reagan Administration, it began to be done openly and publicly.

Funds that previously came from the CIA were now given openly by the National Endowment for Democracy, NED, or directly by the U.S. government, which including them in the official budget, as was the case of the 1999 budget, where 2 million dollars were set aside for subversive work in Cuba.

The importance given acts of subversion and ideological influence in the Torricelli and Helms-Burton Acts are extremely significant, acknowledging the link between the enemy club and (poisoned) carrot: through the blockade, they produce feelings of despair and

---

[55] Osvaldo Martínez: "El bloqueo económico impuesto a Cuba por el Gobierno de Estados Unidos". Expert report for the public hearing of the Provincial Court of Havana in the sessions of the Suit of the Cuban People brought against the United States Government for economic damages to Cuba, March, 2000.

[56] Among the propaganda campaigns characteristic of political and ideological subversive strategies used in the economic war are those which attempt to imply that the blockade is being softened, as a variant of this, that medicines have been allowed to be freely purchased in recent years; that the sale of medicines is one of the benefits of the Torricelli Act; that Cuba's problems have nothing to do with the blockade but rather the Revolution's poor economic management; those that claim that Cuba had a higher degree of economic development in 1959 than what it actually had, to speak of regression rather than progress under the Revolution; those that claim that most donations received by the country during the special period have come from the United States, and others.

defeat in Cubans, to present a return to capitalism as the solution to those problems. This is evident in article g (Aid to support democracy in Cuba), section 1705, "Support for the Cuban people" of the Torricelli Act, which lays the foundation for what has become known as Track II of this act, which establishes that "the Government of the United States can offer aid, through the proper non governmental organizations, to individuals and organizations that promote peaceful changes towards democracy in Cuba". Next to the club, the "carrot". In section 1707, "Policy towards a transition government in Cuba", that is, after the expected defeat of the Revolution, we find that "[...] food, medicines and medical supplies [...] will be available for humanitarian purposes [...]".

Referring to political and ideological subversion carried out against Cuba by the United States since the very beginning of the Revolution and evaluating the role of the Torricelli Act, experts who participated in the televised Round Table on the economic war against Cuba, aired on July 10, 2000, expressed: "[...] from the very beginning there has been a policy aimed at creating, organizing and financing an opposition. And if there was anything new to find in the Torricelli Act is that for the first time, it is openly expressed as a U.S. Law, as a State policy".[57]

An interesting methodological conclusion can be arrived at: there are no empty spaces within the anti-Cuban activities prepared and directed from the United States. There is a causal link between economic measures and the results expected from this, as regards the fostering of counterrevolutionary stances within the populace and reaching "[...] the aims traced in the famous Track II: complement the blockade with subversion".[58]

There are differences in the actions against Cuba's economic infrastructure and subtleties that would be convenient to note to correctly evaluate current enemy actions against economic sectors. In essence it is, on the one hand, a total war against anything that can imply a strengthening of the state economy, either through state companies, state companies with a private component or any form of cooperative effort involving foreign capital. On the other hand, it

---

[57] Miguel Álvarez: Remarks for Round Table discussion aired on July 10, 2000. Special Newspaper Supplement N° 18, p. 15.

[58] Idem. Miguel Álvarez substantiates this through Richard Nuccio's declarations for the Washington Times, July 30, 1995, where he expressed that Track II was not an alternative to the embargo but a complement to make it more effective.

entails support and encouragement for those in that business environment, such that these will abjure any attempts at supporting socialist production schemes and gradually introduce capitalist means of production, which will be reflected in the minds of the participants.

Never before in the history of enemy aggressions have economic sectors been the object of such sustained subversive efforts in the field of ideas: never before did conditions exist for these actions to meet with success.

It is within this context that we should seek to understand foreign interests to boost and promote the advantages of private small and medium-size companies, to increase individual participation in the business sector and thereby stimulate the creation of a national bourgeoisie; to try to have a bearing on farming sectors and similar actions, in which some foreign organizations are set on expressing their willingness to "help" Cuba confront the challenges it faces after the disappearance of the socialist block.

It is in this light that we must understand the ends pursued by the United States government in this field. During the early part of 1999, then U.S. Secretary of State Madeleine Albright expressed: "we are using intelligent weapons aimed at the target we want. We wish to help create an independent market economy and try to continue expanding it and have it be completely separate from the State."[59]

These actions are directed by the state according to the Track II policy and openly and publicly developed, using official resources such as the United States Information Agency (USIA) and official funds received from the NED which, through these means, are channeled to universities, non governmental organizations and other recipients.

If the blockade is aimed, fundamentally, at Cuba's economy, trade and finances, what this unique form of economic war seeks to achieve is to change the way the Cuban people think: a vain attempt, by other means, to have them abjure their ideas and promote, as it has already achieved in other regions of the world, a return to capitalism.

---

[59] Quoted by Ricardo Alarcón de Quesada, President of the National Assembly of the People's Power during the closing of the Extraordinary Session of the 5th Legislature of the National Assembly of the People's Power, February 16, 1999. Granma newspaper, Friday, February 19, 1999, p. 4.

CHAPTER VI The battle at the United Nations and the economic war against Cuba in light of Cuban laws

Cuba has systematically unmasked, before national and international public opinion, the brutal economic pressures it has suffered at the hands of the U.S. government and has justly insisted on the elimination of the blockade and subversive actions against its economy as the first of measures required to normalize relations with its powerful neighbor of the North.

Two important events inscribe themselves within Cuban measures in that direction, one within the framework of international relations and the other as a legal response within the framework of its own laws. We are referring to the discussion and approval by the General Assembly of the United Nations, invariably since 1992, of a proposed resolution condemning the U.S. economic blockade against Cuba and the suit, brought before the People's Provincial Court of Havana in 2000 by Cuban grassroots organizations, against the U.S. government, holding it liable for economic damages to Cuba.

The international community is opposed to the economic war that Cuba is subjected to: the battle at the UN

The brutal economic war the United States wages against the Cuban people has been described in previous chapters and has met with the repudiation of the international community in the United Nations' most representative institution: the General Assembly.

Since 1992, when, at Cuba's instance, this body began to analyze the proposal titled "The need to put an end to the economic, trade and financial blockade imposed by the United States of America on Cuba", the number of votes supporting the motion has increased from 59 in favor, 3 against and 71 abstentions (in the 1992 vote) to 183 in favor, 4 against and 1 abstentions in 2006.

The Resolutions basically maintain the same structure, language and reach.[1] Let us take the first, the 47/19, presented at the forty-seventh period of sessions of the General Assembly on November 24, 1992, whose content has not changed since then. In the four-paragraph preamble, it expresses the decision to promote strict respect for the purposes and principles of the United Nations Charter, reaffirming, among other principles, the sovereign equality of States, non-interference in their internal affairs and freedom of trade and navigation, enshrined in numerous international legal instruments; it expresses concern over the promulgation and application, by member States, of laws and regulations whose extraterritorial nature encroach upon the sovereignty of other States and the legitimate interests of entities or persons under its jurisdiction as well as freedom of trade and navigation, pointing to the recent promulgation of these kinds of measures aimed at strengthening and broadening the economic, trade and financial blockade against Cuba.

In its resolution, it calls on all States to abstain from promulgating and applying laws and measures of the kind mentioned in the preamble in fulfillment of their obligation to comply with the United Nations Charter and International Law as well as the commitments they freely contracted upon signing legal international instruments that, among other things, enshrine freedom of trade and navigation. The second called on the States where these laws or measures exist, in the briefest time possible and in accordance with their legal structures, to take the necessary measures to eliminate them or annul their effect. The third point asked the Secretary General to make a report on the fulfillment of the Resolution, which was to be presented to the General Assembly in its forty eighth period of sessions, in the

---

[1] These Resolutions were, since 1992 and until 2006, 47/19, 48/16, 49/9, 50/10, 51/17, 52/10, 53/4, 54/21, 55/20, 56/9, 57/11, 58/7, 59/11, 60/12, 61/11. United Nations web site http:www.un.org.

year 1993; the last point decided to include the subject in the provisional agenda for the next period of sessions.

This format has been maintained since then, with slight modifications which update the contents in some aspects. Later Resolutions deplored not only the promulgation and application of extraterritorial regulations but also pointed to their continued promulgation and application, adding a new paragraph, in 1993, referring to the fact that, after the approval of Resolution 47/19, new measures were passed to strengthen and broaden the blockade, with negative effects on the Cuban population (expressly mentioning the approval of the Helms-Burton Act as an example, in all resolutions since 1996). The 1993 resolution began by recalling that other forums called for the elimination of the unilateral application by any State, in pursuit of political ends, of measures of an economic and commercial nature against other States (particularly the Ibero-American Summit since its third meeting on July 15 and 16 in San Salvador, Brazil) and in the meetings of the Economic Commission for Latin America and the Caribbean, ECLAC, that also called for the lifting of the economic, trade and financial blockade against Cuba. A later reformulation of this point expressed that it took note of declarations and resolutions by different intergovernmental forums, bodies and governments that manifested the international community's and public opinion's opposition to the promulgation and application of these kinds of measures.

The United Nations has had, since the matter began to be analyzed by the General Assembly in 1992, invaluable, valid and confidential resources to keep informed of the economic war against Cuba and, on that basis, resolutely condemn it in the report of the General Secretary, which began to be drafted in 1993, in fulfillment of point 3 of Resolution 47/19,where Cuba has supplied abundant information, from international institutions or other bodies, on the systematic strengthening of the blockade each year. The Cuban delegation has also presented the proposed Resolution to the General Assembly before each voting session. Other documents supplied by Cuba and circulated as official General Assembly documents have contributed to international awareness and rejection of the United States' genocidal policy.

A rapid evaluation of some of the most important points gathered by Cuba for the reports to the General Secretary, in presenting the re-solution before the General Assembly or other documents circulated in that institution, affords us the possibility of assessing in its just measure, how Cuba has availed itself of this important forum, the most representative and democratic of the entire United Nations system.

A recurrent point in all these texts is the denouncement of the United States' systematic violation of the resolutions approved since 1992. In fact, what is denounced in all cases is a strengthening, broadening and deepening of these violations through legal, covert and slanderous measures that sometimes include the use of pressures and blackmail upon third countries, a policy which "[...] not only demonstrates a deep disregard for the universal principles and norms of coexistence that it claims to respect but also rides roughshod with premeditated inhumanity over the dignity and fundamental rights of the Cuban people, such as independence, sovereignty, self determination, right to development, health, food, employment and life itself"[2]. Its illegality has also been revealed, an affirmation made according to section c of article II of the Convention for the Prevention and Sanction of the Crime of Genocide, of December 9, 1948, by virtue of which anti-Cuban economic pressures by the Government of the United States can be characterized as a violation of International Law.[3] It has also been shown that the United States violates resolutions 38/197 of December 17, 1983; 39/210 of December 18, 1984; 40/185 of December 17, 1985; 41/165 of December 4, 1986; 42/173 of December 11, 1987; 44/215 of December 22, 1989 and 46/210 of December 20 1991 of the same institution, where the Assembly has deplored the adoption of economic measures to apply coercion on the sovereign decisions of developing countries. [4]

The objectives of the United States have been denounced with crystal clarity in the Report of the Secretary General that, in 1993, qualifies these actions as "[...] aggression through economic means

[2] UN General Assembly, forty ninth period of sessions: Report by the General Secretary (A/49/398). United Nations Web site http:www.un.org. September 20, 1994, response of the Cuban government, paragraph 122.

[3] United Nations General Assembly, fifty seventh period of sessions: Report of the Secretary General (A/57/150), United Nations Web site http:www.un.org. July 26, 2002, response of the Cuban Government, paragraph 3.

[4] United Nations General Assembly, forty eigth period of sessions: Report of the Secretary General (A/48/448), United Nations Web site http:www.un.org. September 28, 1993, response of the Cuban Government, paragraph 5.

to create economic difficulties for Cuba and affect the health, well-being, peace and life of the population, pursuing the declared objective of overthrowing the political, economic and social system that the Cuban people have freely chosen".[5] The following year, it expressed that the anti-Cuban measures aimed to create "[…] additional difficulties to promote unrest in the Cuban government and repudiation of its Government […]" and that these measures, in the words of a U.S. Congressman, were "necessary" because they impelled "[…] a corrosive process from below to make the people ungovernable".[6]

In 1995, the Report of the Secretary General emphasized that in her letter of April 28 to Benjamin Gilman, President of the Foreign Affairs Committee of the House of Representatives, Wendy Sherman, Assistant Secretary for Legal Affairs of the State Department, pointed out: "We [the United States] will continue with our embargo as a lever to pressure the regime to adopt reforms."[7] Referring to the economic, trade and financial blockade, in 1996, the year the United States approved the Helms-Burton Act, the Report expressed: "Its effect […] is cumulative and debilitating and is felt in all and each of the spheres of Cuban life. Its objective continues to be the same, to bring about a total economic collapse in the country that would lead the population to put an end the revolutionary process."[8] In 1999 it expressed: "The intentions are obvious: to economically asphyxiate the country and lead the population towards a situation of extreme deprivation, with the aim of having them renounce their independence and self-determination, to submit to the dictates of United States policy."[9] In 2002 it noted that: "The decision to cause hunger, disease and the desperation of the Cuban people, as a tool to achieve the goal of political domination, has not only been maintained but has been strengthened […]".[10]

[5] Ibid., paragraph 13.

[6] United Nations General Assembly, forty ninth perioed of sessions: paragraphs 28 and 29.

[7] United Nations General Assembly, fiftieth period of sessions: Report of the Secretary General (A/50/401), United Nations Web site http:www.un.org. September 1, 1995, response of the Cuban Government, paragraph 68.

[8] United Nations General Assembly, fifty first period of sessions: Report of the Secretary General (A/51/355),United Nations Web site http:www.un.org. September 13, 1996, response of the Cuban Government, paragraph 73.

[9] United Nations General Assembly, fifty fourth period of sessions: Report of the Secretary General (A/54/259),United Nations Web site http:www.un.org. August 18, 1999, response of the Cuban Government, paragraph 14.

[10] United Nations General Assembly, fifty fourth period of sessions: paragraph 9.

Each new escalade has been promptly denounced and exposed in the United Nations. The same occurred with the Torricelli Act, which, among other things — as the representative that gave it its name boasted of— had meant a 15% increase in the cost of foreign economic relations;[11] Cuba exposed the United States' attempt to fool international public opinion by noting the fraudulent humanitarian character of this Act, which refers to the authorization of food donations in one of its sections, entitled Aid for the Cuban People, "while the Law established the prohibition of granting licenses to company branches in third countries to trade with Cuba,"[12] trade that, at the time the act was passed, was mostly in food and medicines, trade that, in a short period of time, was reduced to naught. Boasting of the flexibilization of licenses for medical exports to Cuba, the act forbids the export of raw materials and intermediary products for the pharmaceutical industry and Cuban medical equipment to the country. These alleged flexibilities are limited to finished products, but they entail many conditions that are impossible to comply with or to accept.[13] The obvious extraterritoriality of this act was also revealed, although it was noted that this extraterritoriality has been an obvious component of U.S. foreign policy since the early 1960s.[14]

The United Nations General Assembly was also an adequate forum to expose the Helms-Burton Act, even before it was approved. In the memorandum titled "The so-called 1995 Cuban Liberty and Democratic Solidarity Act" of May 1995, circulated as an official document,[15] Cuba called on the international community to note U.S. intentions of taking Cuba back to a colonial system and seven essential provisions "aimed, in a most flagrant manner, at third countries and against the citizens of those countries."[16] Another

---

[11] United Nations General Assembly, fourty eighth period of sessions: paragraph 8 of the Annex. Taken from the Foreign Affairs journal, p. 219, summer of 1993.

[12] United Nations General Assembly, forty ninth period of sessions: paragraphs 09 and 99.

[13] Ibid., paragraph 103.

[14] United Nations General Assembly, forty eighth period of sessions: paragraph 6.

[15] Memorandum of the Cuban Foreign Affairs Ministry circulated as an official document in the General Assembly (A/50/172, annexo) on May 4, 1995.

[16] The seven points of the bill that were highlighted for their contempt towards International Law were: exclusion of sugar imports from countries buying sugar from Cuba; trials in United States courts against nationals of third countries for having trade relations with Cuba or investing in the country; prohibition of credit concessions by companies of third countries that have trade relations with Cuba

document issued the following month by Cuba's Foreign Ministry, entitled "New attempts at strengthening the U.S. economic blockade against Cuba and the truth about Cuban nationalizations",[17] underscored three points: the reasons why the United States could not justify its blockade policy; the legitimacy of the nationalization process undertaken by Cuba as early as 1960, executed within the framework of International Law and justified by the national interest of a State that undertook the radical transformation of society and, finally, Cuba's reaffirmation that it cannot submit to any State under economic, political or other forms of coercion in the exercise of its right to nationalize properties in its own territory following a sovereign decision. The Report of the Secretary General that year noted six aspects of the bill being discussed by the U.S. Congress and, recognizing its extraterritoriality, considered it "[...] absurd from the legal, economic and political points of view."[18]

A detailed dissection of these absurdities was made in the Report of the Secretary General in 1996, the year the Helms-Burton Law was approved.[19] With respect to Title I, it noted the ridiculous pretensions of the United States to internationalize the blockade as an agreement of the UN Security Council.[20] Regarding the freezing of payments to international financial institutions that had granted Cuba credits, it considered this policy of financial blackmail a violation of articles 8 and 9 of the IMF and articles 6 and 10 of the World Bank Agreement, article 8 of the Agreement of the Intenational Development Association, articles 2,3 and 6 of the Agreement of International Financial Corporation; article 34

---

or have investments in the country; additional reprisal measures against companies of third countries for investing in Cuba or trading with the country; interference in the work of international financial institutions; attempts at coercing independent States of the former Soviet Union and other reprisal measures against third countries for trading with Cuba or investing in the country.

[17] Circulated as an official document of the General Assembly (A/50/211, annex) on June 7, 1995.

[18] United Nations General Assembly, fiftieth period of sessions: paragraph 67.

[19] United Nations General Assembly, fifty first period of sessions: paragraphs 7 to 51.

[20] The absence of all logic is taken by this piece of legislation to ridiculous heights. When the act was drafted and approved, the United States was, as it continues to be, increasingly, with each day that passes, the country being questioned by the General Assembly for maintaining an illegal blockade on Cuba.

of the Convention for Establishing a Guarantee Agency of Multilateral Investment and articles 2 and 11 of the Convention for the Establishment of the Inter American Development Bank, all of which prohibit restrictions, regulations, controls or moratoria of any kind against their shares or properties.[21] Another violation noted is the prohibition of indirect finances for Cuba by U.S. entities and their branches, which infringes upon international principles that acknowledge freedom of financing and investments and the subordination of branch companies to the laws of the resident country.[22]

It qualifies Title II as completely extraterritorial, intent on empowering the United States of America to decide Cuba's political, economic and institutional future. It expresses that, beyond this, it makes the lifting of the blockade and the establishment of normal relations with Cuba conditional on a series of requirements that entail political transformations, a change of economic system and, especially, the unconditional return of all properties legally nationalized by the Cuban government since January 1, 1959.[23]

Title III of the Act, with the apparent pretext of demanding compensation or allowing claims for "U.S."[24] properties nationalized in Cuba, is in fact aimed against foreign investment, sought as a means of confronting the loss of Cuba's main trade partners and the disappearance of the USSR and European socialist community, in violation of internationally acknowledged principles and concepts, including: those that establish that the settlement of international claims be made through bilateral agreements between the interested countries, that the ownership of a property is determined on the basis of the laws of the country where they are found; that confiscation by a country of the properties of nationals is not a violation of international law or be considered by courts in a different jurisdiction. The title also violates a principle of International Law (the State Act Doctrine) and thereby does not acknowledge practices and decisions by prior rulings of U.S. courts.[25]

---

[21] United Nations General Assembly fifty first period of session: paragraph 17
[22] Ibidem, paragraph 20.
[23] Ibid., paragraph 23.
[24] We place the word between quotation marks to indicate that the United States demands that persons who were Cuban citizens at the time be recognized as nationals of that country.
[25] United Nations General Assembly, fifty first period of sessions: paragraphs 24-26.

Referring to the refusal to grant entry to the United States to and the expulsion of those who "traffic" in nationalized properties in Cuba, the intimidation and blackmail components of Title IV are underscored. These, as such, constitute a violation of principles enshrined in the United Nations Charter, the Declaration of Marrakech and the Agreement by virtue of which the World Trade Organization was established as the successor of the General Agreement on Tariffs and Trade (GATT), of which both the United States and Cuba have been members since its creation. It also points out that it violates, among others, chapters XI, XVI and article 1110 of the North American Free Trade Agreement (NAFTA) with respect to relations between Cuba and Mexican and Canadian investors. The measures of this Title, in effect demonstrative, began to be applied immediately against the companies Sherrit Gordon, Domos and Stet from Canada, Mexico and Italy, respectively.[26]

Though extraterritorial provisions have been a part of economic actions against Cuba since 1959, the Helms-Burton Act took these to a higher plane. The text circulated by Cuba in the General Assembly that year exposed the foundation of that extraterritoriality: a "selective and discriminatory interpretation of the concept of the sovereignty of States" that, since the 18th century, has been everywhere accepted as: "the authority of a State to decide its internal and external affairs that entails, at the same time, respect for the sovereignty of other States".[27] The fact that the Helms-Burton Act grants the United States the right to decide the political future of the Cuban people, that it establishes sanctions against businesspersons in third countries and their families for maintaining trade relations with Cuba or that it establishes prohibitions applicable to branches of U.S. companies in third countries, subject to the laws of those countries, are examples of that aberrant interpretation of sovereignty.

The Report of the Secretary General for 1998 noted the pleasure of the head of the State Department Office for Cuban Affairs Michael Ranneberg, on referring to the Helms-Burton Act and the fact it had had "[...] an important and significant impact on the Cuban economy", increasing "[...] penalties on those who violated the embargo", and also because "[...] the Cuban Government has

---

[26] Ibid., paragraphs 28-50.
[27] United Nations General Assemby, fifty seventh period of sessions: paragraph 37.

encountered greater difficulties in securing financing and potential investors."[28]

This sense of satisfaction can only be described as inhuman and immoral. Examples of the blockade on the import of medicines, of raw materials to produce them, medical equipment and some of their components or, in general, any goods needed in this sphere, which have been divulged to the international community since the United Nations began to analyze the necessity to put an end to the U.S. blockade on Cuba in 1992, are proof of this. After 1996, with the approval of the Helms-Burton Act, this situation worsened.

In 1992 and 1993, in compliance with the precepts of the Torricelli Act, a constant of the U.S. policy of harassment was the neutralization of new agreements that involved granting Cuba special credits to facilitate the purchase of medicines or Cuban sales of pharmaceutical and biotechnological products, which were more common in Latin America. Pressures were brought to bear on several governments in order to hinder the sale of these medical products in those countries. The U.S. government also prevented Cuba from purchasing medicines that were scarce in the country, such as plasma, thyroid hormones, penicillin, antibiotics, alkaloids and cortisone. The U.S. government prevented the sale of respiratory valves, connections, pressure boxes, nebulizers, micronebulizer flasks and other components, all spare parts for the Bird respirator, widely used in Cuba in intensive and medium post operating wards, wards for asthmatics and urgency services. In this period, executives of the Canadian medical company Eli Lilly Canada Inc., a subsidiary of the U.S. Eli Lilly and Co., a leading producer of insulin in the world, reported that under U.S. law they were not allowed to sale their products to Cuba, even though their exports consisted of medicines for such common diseases as vascular, pulmonary, cancer-related disorders and others.[29]

In 1994, it was reported that Cuba had seen a dramatic reduction in its supply of pacemakers for persons with heart conditions because the Australian company Telectronics had been forbidden to sell them to Cuba because they had components manufactured in the United

---

[28] United Nations General Assemby, fifty third period of sessions: Report of the Secretary General (A/53/320). United Nations Web site, http.www.un.org. September 3, 1998, response of the Cuban Government, paragraphs 37 and 38.
[29] United Nations General Assemby, forty eighth period of sessions:, paragraphs 29-32.

States. Shortly after, the Swedish company Siemens Eleina Ab was bought over by a U.S. company that immediately stopped the sales. The same occurred with the British company JBIW.[30]

In 1995, a scarcity of lavatory, hygiene and vector control articles threatened the country with the deterioration of hygienic and health conditions and with the emergence and spread of diseases. It was also reported that important pharmaceutical companies and suppliers of medical equipment and spare parts in third countries saw themselves obliged to discontinue their long-standing trade relations with Cuba, after being notified of the prohibition, enforced by U.S. federal agencies, of using U.S. materials or technological licenses. These included the Diagnostic Division of Wellcome and the sale of pulmonary respirators and Ohmde anesthesia machines, both from Great Britain and Northern Ireland, as well as the Danish Suber Seals, specialized in rubber stoppers for medical use. The German company Hospal was approached for dialysis and plasmapherisis equipment and reported their sale was prohibited under U.S. regulations. Similarly, the Belgian company Janssen reported that, in order to sell medicines to Cuba, it needed to request an export license from the United States, a request that took six months to process. For similar reasons the Italian firm Miramed, specialized in medical and instrumental material used in the care of patients with kidney deficiencies, denied Cuba the sale of its products.[31]

In the 1996 report, it was pointed out that a Cuban import company had been denied the possibility of negotiating the purchase of catheters for peritoneal dialysis. Another company expressed that due to the U.S. "embargo" it could not offer Cuba pumps or compressors for medical equipment. That year, an estimated 2 700 000 dollars in the air and maritime transportation of supplies for the health sector were paid over and above what would have been paid had the same supplies been bought from the United States or from subsidiaries of U.S. companies in the region. It was also reported that, on three occasions, the sale of equipment for health services, laboratory supplies for immunological tests and diagnostic supplies was suspended due to mergers and associations of suppliers in third countries with U.S. companies.[32]

---

[30] United Nations General Assembly, forty ninth period of sessions: paragraphs 81 and 82.

[31] United Nations General Assembly, fiftieth period of sessions: paragraphs 52-53.

[32] United Nations General Assembly, fifty first period of sessions: paragraphs 47-57.

The 1997 report expressed that since the patents for U.S. medicines, their technology and equipment are valid for seventeen years, Cuban citizens were deprived of access to medicines patented in 1979. These included third generation antibiotics and several products used for the treatment of AIDS. It noted that the inexorable mergers of companies, characteristic of the process of economic globalization, in which U.S. companies are at the fore, had led to the increased loss of traditional suppliers of medical equipment, medicines and supplies. This report referred to a publication of March 1977, which reported on the trip to Cuba of a well-known health organization based in Washington —the American Association of World Health— which conducted a thorough analysis of the damages caused by the blockade in the health and nutrition of the Cuban people.[33] In answer to declarations by U.S. government spokespersons that the export of medicines to Cuba is not forbidden and that a mechanism exists for granting licenses permitting their sale, the report of the Secretary General pointed out that officials of the Departments of Commerce and Treasury ignored, misinformed or discouraged suppliers interested in requesting these licenses, and that they systematically delayed their replies. The conditions for the granting of licenses, which include in situ inspections of the destination site of the sold products and other requirements, are not only unacceptable, they noted, but also impracticable. Licenses for the supply of some medicines, issued through the International Red Cross and some diplomatic offices, involved such a complex and slow process, with an average of six months wait, that they dampened the initiative of some organizations to donate materials to Cuban hospital institutions.[34]

Among other points of interest, the report of the Secretary General in 1998 referred to the study of an organization that provides

[33] The report of this study was circulated in the General Assembly as an official UN document. Some parts expressed that: "The U.S. embargo has significantly increased suffering in Cuba [...]. We visited patients who did not have the necessary medicines and must resort to procedures without the proper equipment [...]. The reduction in available food, medicines and basic medical suppliles [...] is having a high human cost [...]. Few embargos in recent history have totally forbidden the sale of foods. Few embargos have restricted with such determination the sale of medical products and have reached such extremes as denying access to medicines to save lives [...]."

[34] United Nations General Assembly, fifty second period of sessions: Report of the Secretary General (A/52/342). United Nations Web site http:www.un.orgm September 15, 1997, response of the Cuban government, paragraphs 43-52.

information to U.S. Congresspersons on specific subjects, the Congressional Research Service of April 28, 1998, that demonstrated the incongruence and irregularities in information, offered by the United States Departments of State, Treasury and Commerce, regarding the alleged granting of licenses for the sale of medicines to Cuba, information that, in many cases, was proven to be false. Reference was also made to a study, conducted in 1997 by the American Association for World Health, which reported that the sector most affected by the U.S. economic blockade were women, children and the elderly, and expressed that Cuban children with cancer were unable to receive treatment with several drugs manufactured in the United States, medicines that could have prolonged their life expectancy. Also unavailable were special arterial catheters that would help avoid unnecessary pain. Cuba has received donations of dialysis units or neonate respirators for children with low weight at birth or which experienced difficulties at birth. The sale of spare parts for these units was denied.

The extraterritoriality of the blockade policy hurts companies in third countries and deprives them of the benefits they could obtain through relations with Cuban companies, making it more difficult for the people of the United States and those of other parts of the world from accessing Cuban scientific achievements. This is clearly illustrated by the difficulties the British company SmithKline Beecham Pharmaceuticals faced in order to obtain a government license to test the efficacy of the Cuban meningitis B vaccine in one of its laboratories in Belgium, a subsidiary of a United States company. According to the World Health Organization and the Pan-American Health Organization, respectively, this Cuban vaccine offers the best results obtained in the prevention of the disease.[35] In spite of the measures announced in March 28, 1998, the simplification of license procedures for the export of medicines never materialized. On April 28, 1999, the U.S. government changed part of the political sanctions it uses as a foreign policy instrument and authorized penalized countries to purchase medicines and food, but not Cuba, the only country in the world forbidden to do so.[36]

The Secretary General Report of 2000 refers to the alleged flexibility of the U.S. government in the granting of licenses for the

---

[35] United Nations General Assembly, fifty third period of sessions: paragraphs 26-27; 31-33 and 41-43.

[36] United Nations General Assembly, fifty fourth period of sessions: paragraph 28.

214

sale of medicines and other products. Begun in March of 1998, and in fact inoperative, these measures were an attempt to silence and halt a growing movement, gaining in strength, against the use of unilateral economic sanctions as a foreign policy instrument. In January 2000, the U.S. Medical Products and Medical Equipment Exhibition was held in Havana. The U.S. government denied the contracts negotiated a license. The report also referred to an international study on the impact of economic sanctions on the health and well-being of the population, which corroborates that political sanctions cause macroeconomic disruptions and economic and social effects of such magnitudes that they cannot be remedied through humanitarian aid, and that the consequences of these harm more than the health of populations, victims of these policies.[37]

The Report of the Secretary General for 2002 is extensive in its denouncements. It begins by referring to the legal proceedings instituted against Canadian citizen James Sabzali and U.S. citizens Donald E. and Stefan E. Brodie, who could face up to 205 years imprisonment for the simple crime of having sold Cuba materials used to purify drinking water supplied to the population for direct consumption. James Sabzali was sentenced on 21 charges of violating the blockade on Cuba.[38] After agreeing to plead guilty, he was sentenced to conditional prison and fined 10 thousand dollars. The Report of the Secretary General for 2002 also refers to the "balloon catheter" used in pediatric procedures of great complexity, in a process named fetostomy, that is sold by the U.S. Rashkind company and that must be purchased in Canada, not at the original price of 110 dollars per unit but at 185, a price which does not include the cost of transportation. State of the art technology controlled by the United States such as peritoneal dialysis, out patient treatment and modern immunosuppressors such as FK506, Micophenilate Mophethil and synthetic dialysis membranes, among many others, cannot be purchased by Cuba. The most useful kit for HLA typing (histocompatibility lymphocyte antigen) required to test kidney donors for transplants cannot be purchased by Cuba because

---

[37] United Nations General Assembly, fifty fifth period of sessions: Report of the Secretary General (A/55/172). United Nations Web site, http:www.un.org. July 24, 2000, response of the Cuban government, paragraphs 7-11.

[38] United Nations General Assembly, fifty ninth period of sessions: Report of the Secretary General. United Nations Web site, http:www.un.org. 2004, response of the Cuban government.

it is produced by the U.S. company One-Lambda, and forbidden by blockade laws. A contract with the Vitamin Division of Roche had to be canceled in April, 2001, because the U.S. government denied permission. The same thing happened with Amagquin, a supplier of glue used in the labeling of hemoderivative flasks.

In the first years of the current millennium, existing limitations which affected the treatment of hepatitis, gastrointestinal complications and dengue fever recalled the United States' refusal to sell Cuba products and equipment, in 1981, to combat the *Aedes agypti* mosquito during an epidemic introduced as part of the U.S. biological war against Cuba which cost the lives of 158 persons, 101 of whom were children. Considering the alleged flexibility in the granting of licenses for the export of medicines, it was reported that the Cuban import company Medicuba contacted 17 U.S. companies to request medicines urgently needed to restore the reserves consumed when and after hurricane Michelle lashed the island. Of these, 8 did not respond, 4 showed interest but did not make an offer, one answered that it could make no offer without first receiving instructions from its government (Pharmacia-Upjohn) and the remaining 4 made offers but the operations could not be carried through for different reasons.[39]

One example included in the 2001 Report suffices to summarize this drama: the suffering of the parents of eight-month-old Johnatan Guerra Blanco would have been less had it been possible to purchase a device known as *stent* , whose sale was forbidden by Johnson & Johnson.[40]

The 2003 Secretary General report described the difficulties faced by the Pedro Kourí Tropical Medicine Institute in trying to obtain the VITRO GEN kit, used in the detection of the coronaviurs that causes Atypical Pneumonia (SARS), as a result of existing restrictions. The same difficulties arose in efforts to purchase reagents for diagnostic procedures from the Beckman-Coulter, Dade-Behring, Abbot and Bayer companies. Cuba was unable to purchase Ir-I92

[39] United Nations General Assembly, fifty seventh period of sessions: op. cit., paragraphs 55-71.

[40] United Nations General Assembly, fifty sixth period of sessions: Report of the Secretary General (A/56/276), United Nations Web site, http:un.org. 2001. Response of the Cuban government, paragraphs 53-62.

radioisotopes for the eradication of cancerous tumors because the Canadian MDS Nordion's company specializing in brachiotherapy equipment was bought over by the U.S. company Variahn Medical Systems. Following negotiations with the Dutch company Nucletron, the latter's manager informed Cuba that they could not deliver the accompanying computer since this piece of equipment was manufactured in the United States.

Health programs for children who require transplants also suffered because the adequate technology could not be purchased. The quality of medical attention for children with disabilities has been limited due to the scarcity of cortico-steroids, third generation antibiotics, anti-oxidants and infant urinary bags. The cost of purchasing spare parts for water chlorination equipment from the U.S. companies Wallace & Tiernan and Capital rose by 60 thousand dollars due to the impossibility of acquiring these pieces in the United States. The non governmental organization "Disarm Education Fund" was told it could not offer Cuba a donation of medicines if the antibiotics CIPRO and DOXYCYCLIN, used for treating anthrax patients, were not excluded from the donation. The United States government invoked (?) "national security reasons". In April 2003, the Department of Commerce denied an export license to the non governmental humanitarian organization USA/Cuba InfoMed, which was preparing to donate 423 computers to Cuba's Nephrology Institute and national network for kidney treatment; the "William Soler" Pediatric Heart Center, the national pediatric heart network and the Latin American School of Medical Sciences, where more than 7 thousand young people of humble backgrounds from Latin America, the Caribbean, United States and Africa study. The United States argued that the Departments of Commerce, State and Defense considered that this export would be detrimental to U.S. foreign policy interests, something inconceivable given its humanitarian nature.[41]

---

[41] United Nations General Assembly, fifty eighth period of sessions: Secretary General Report. United Nations Web site. http:www.un.org. 2003. Answer of the Cuban government, paragraphs 77-97. Also Cuban Foreign Affairs Ministry: Cuban report to the Secretary General concerning Resolution 57/11 of the United National General Assembly. Granma newspaper, Havana, special supplement, July 8, 2003, p.4

The 2004 report noted Cuba's difficulties in acquiring the I-125 isotope, used in the treatment of children with eye cancer, who are often sent abroad for treatment by Cuba's health system, to undergo costly procedures. Children with cancer are also affected by the scarcity of bone endo-prostheses for amputations that would alleviate the emotional and psychological distress that these amputations cause, especially in adolescence. Due to these restrictions, new inhalers for children with asthma cannot be purchased. In 2004, it was reported that it was impossible to get certain pieces of medical equipment manufactured in the United States running again because of a lack of spare parts, as was the case with a number of X Ray machines missing essential parts. The U.S. Department of Commerce prohibited the Canadian branch of Picker International to sell these parts to Cuba because 27% of the components were of U.S. manufacture. Costs continue to be high due to the need to import clinical laboratory and microbiology reagents and other similar items from Europe, in view of the high percentage (70 %) of U.S. companies that produce the diagnostic equipment and reagents. Veckman-Coulter, Dade-Behring, Abbot and Bayer are not allowed to sell their technologies to Cuba, some of which are unique in the world.

That same year, the diagnosis of new and dangerous diseases is hindered by the blockade measures. The "Pedro Kourí" Tropical Medicine Institute was unable to purchase the TermoScript RT-PCR kit from the U.S. company Invitrogen, for the detection of the corona virus that causes Severe Acute Respiratory Syndrome (SARS).

In addition to this, limitations imposed by the U.S. Center for Disease Control (CDC) in Atlanta, coupled with the refusal of the laboratories of U.S. companies Focus Technology and Panbio, producers of IgG and IgM kits, to sell their products, have created difficulties in the detection of encephalitis, caused by the Western Nile virus and bird influenza. U.S. scientific publications, (some as renowned as Current Contents and Annals of Tropical Medicine and Parasitology) must be purchased from third countries at an annual subscription rate hundreds of dollars higher than the regular. The U.S. government did not authorize the non-governmental organization "Disarm Education Fund" from offering lectures and training to Cuban pediatricians, saying the people would not directly benefit from these and that it constitutes an export of services to our country.

A program of cooperation with Cuba financed by the United Nations World Fund to fight AIDS, Tuberculosis and Malaria was unable to purchase anti-retroviral medicines (Ritonavir and

218

Lopinavir+Ritonavir) in the United States for patients with HIV/AIDS when Abbot refused to sell these because of blockade restrictions. These medications were eventually purchased in other markets at six times their cost in the United States.

Dr. Maria Alfonso Valdes was not allowed to participate in a training course organized by the Pan American Health Organization on Safe Blood, held in El Paso, Texas in the first half of 2004, because the U.S. government denies visas to Cubans seeking training in the United States. The blockade has also prevented the participation of U.S. scientists in events held in Cuba. The 3rd International Symposium on Coma and Death was held in Cuba from March 9 to 13, 2004 and the U.S. delegation, which accounted for 40% of participants and included 70 scientists, was denied permission to travel to Cuba by the U.S. government.[42]

We qualified as inhuman and immoral the United States' delight over the increased hardships imposed on the Cuban people through the blockade. Cuba's denunciations before the United Nations General Assembly so prove it.

For lack of space, we cannot detail the effects on all and each of the sectors of Cuba's economic and social life had by this criminal policy. We will thus limit ourselves to describing the most important repercussions in each of these sectors.

Food

The blockade's negative impact on the food sector, exacerbated by its impact on the sphere of medicine, designed to exhaust the Cuban people through hunger and disease, is a clear example of the crime of genocide according to the Convention for the Prevention and Sanction of the Crime of Genocide of December 1948, referred to above. The factors that make it difficult for Cuba to purchase processed and semi-processed foods or raw materials for subsequent use are varied. They include differences in costs, for items that could be purchased in the United States or branches of that country in our geographic vicinity, as well as the added cost of importing these products from distant markets.

[42] United Nations General Assembly, fifty ninth period of session: Report of the Secretary General (A/59/150). United Nations Web site htt[:www.un.org. 2004. Anwer of the Cuban government.

The additional cost of purchasing the most heavily imported food products (wheat, powdered milk, soy flour and corn) from sources other than the U.S. market was calculated for 1996 at 43,8 million dollars;[43] for 1997, additional costs were of 48 million;[44] for 1998, 30 million (had this not been the case, an additional 15 thousand metric tons of powdered milk could have been purchased);[45] and for the year 2000, an additional 38 million were paid (enough to purchase 100 thousand extra metric tons of baking flour, 20 thousand of wheat, 40 thousand of rice, 5 thousand of powdered milk and 1 000 of chicken meat).[46] For 2001, the additional cost of purchasing these products from markets other than that of the United States was calculated at 38 million dollars.[47]

The increased costs of transporting the main food imports is also significant. For 1996, and only for three products (wheat, corn and flour) the total amount in duty payments was 13,4 million U.S. dollars, much higher than what thy would have been had the purchase been done in the U.S. markets or in the same geographic region.[48] For 1997 the additional cost was 21 million,[49] and for 1998 it was 21.5 million (enough to purchase 130 thousand metric tones of wheat).50 In 2000, importing 63% of the total amount of food required cost [50] million dollars. Under normal conditions, it would have cost only 19 million.[51]

The 2002 report pointed out that, because of the enormous distances, transportation costs in 2001 reached the figure of 30 million, noting that an additional 35 million in operational costs, increased considerably by the blockade, were spent. The report that year introduced novel elements since specific purchases of food, medicine and raw materials had been made with a view to producing these products under licenses,[52] to recover the reserves employed in

[43] United Nations General Assembly, fifty second period of session: paragraph 28.
[44] United Nations General Assembly, fifty third period of session: paragraph 21.
[45] United Nations General Assembly, fifty fourth period of session: paragraph 8.
[46] United Nations General Assembly, fifty sixth period of session: paragraphs 40-41.
[47] United Nations General Assembly, fifty seventh period of session: paragraph 74.
[48] United Nations General Assembly, fifty second period of session: paragraph 26.
[49] United Nations General Assembly, fifty third period of session: paragraph 18.
[50] United Nations General Assembly, fifty fourth period of session: paragraph 9.
[51] United Nations General Assembly, fifty sixth period of session: paragraph 42.
[52] This cannot be seen, not remotely, as the disappearance of blockade conditions. On May 20, 2002, President Bush stated: "The United States will continue to enforce economic sanctions against Cuba" (United Nations General Assembly,

attending to the victims of hurricane Michelle, a gesture the Cuban government considered generous. However, these transactions were only allowed in one direction, as the sale of Cuban products continued to be prohibited. This caused substantial losses, since ships could not return with Cuban cargo to that country, something which would have resulted in savings of about 36% in bulk cargo transportation costs. Additionally, licenses issued by the Treasury department, authorizing ships under any flag to transport food to Cuba, explicitly prohibit the loading of any product in Cuban ports, be the product bound for U.S. market or any other destination. Additional expenditures resulting from the impact of the blockade on imports of food fluctuate between 20 and 25% their value, money that under other circumstances could be used to purchase a greater quantity of these products. If trade with the United States could be conducted under normal conditions (with financing possibilities, transportation conditions, no license requirements) the purchase of food from U.S. farmers could increase to over 500 million dollars above the sum in purchases made during the same period under licenses granted.[53]

At the time this book was being completed and following Cuba's request for the exceptional sale of certain medicines and food products to re-supply reserves used for victims of hurricane Michelle, "the broadest representation of civil society and business organizations have called for the elimination of the blockade and normalization of all economic ties with Cuba". "Farmers, their organizations and their main production and exporting companies have been especially active in this connection. Thanks to their efforts, it has been possible to take some steps towards significant changes in current policy". The result is that "for the first time in four decades it was possible for some U.S. farmers to sell their products to Cuba and conclude the necessary operations in spite of severe obstacles and the discriminatory practices they had to confront."[54]

---

fifty seventh period of sessions: paragraph 5). Subsequent actions have demonstrated it.

[53] United Nations General Assembly, fifty seventh period of sessions: paragraphs 74-80.

[54] Ricardo Alarcon de Quesada: presentation of the resolution project A/57/L.5 before the United Nations General Assembly, fifty seventh period of sessions, November 12, 2002. United Nations Web site http:www.un.org.

The 2003 Report pointed out that the commercial disparities recognized by the Trade Sanction Reforms for the Increase of United States Exports Act of October 2000, while allowing, to a certain extent, the controlled sale of food products to Cuba, was proof of the continued enforcement of the blockade. Prohibitions imposed on the export of food to the United States prevent two-way trade and represented a loss of 114 million dollars for Cuba during 2002.[55]

The data taken before the General Assembly, a mere reflection of the criminal policy of the United States against Cuba in this sphere, show that the consumption and export-aimed food production sector was, without a doubt, the most severely affected during the 1990s, the decade of the Torricelli and Helms-Burton acts, not only as a result of the fall of the European Socialist block and the USSR but, above all, due to the intensification of the blockade and bacteriological war waged by the United States against Cuba.[56]

Finances

The intensification of existing difficulties due to a deprivation of sources of foreign financing became a constant since the beginning of the 1990s. The pressures that the United States brings to bear on financial institutions prevent any kind of assistance to Cuba, or that preferential treatment be given it in the granting of credit. Cuba has had to accept less favourable financing conditions in face of the urgent need to secure supplies and has had to offer discounts on its export goods in terms of surcharges for the risks faced by those who ignore US pressures and have business dealings with the island[57], what has come to be known as the "Cuba risk". It was calculated that, in 1998, the rise in the cost of transactions between Cuban and foreign companies was between 3 to 5% of their total value, reaching higher levels at times.[58]

The 1996 Secretary General Report expressed that the high financial costs associated to the credits received to cover basic import

---

55 United Nations General Assembly, fifty eighth period of sessions: paragraphs 41-44, 100 and following. Also in Cuban Ministry of Foreign Affairs: pp. 3-5.
56 United Nations General Assembly, fifty sixth period of sessions: paragraph 49.
57 United Nations General Assembly, forty ninth period of sessions: paragraphs 30 and 32-33.
58 United Nations General Assembly, fifty first period of sessions: paragraph 14.

necessities during 1995 were, on average, 13% of the credit values, and rose, at times, to 20%, following an upward trend in correspondence with the intensification of the blockade. The need Cuba and its partners have of dealing in the exchange market, owed to Cuba's inability to carry out transactions in U.S. dollars, results in additional expenditures in bank operations and has an added element of risk.[59] In 1999, losses due to variations in currency exchange were of 127,3 million dollars.[60] In 1997 losses in export costs were 3.5% of the charge value.[61] In addition to this, transferences made in Cuba have to go through third parties and, at times, involve more than three banks to reach their destination. Consequently, payment by any Cuban entity often has a date-value that does not correspond to international practice. The long delay involved in the reception of funds by the final beneficiary implies greater expenditures.[62] The prohibition barring Cuba from using the U.S. dollar in transactions and bank transferences also prevents the use of credit cards, creating additional difficulties for tourists and raising costs.[63]

In 1997 the Helms-Burton Act increased the cost of financing and deferred the granting of credits, discontinuing financing for the sugar harvest, something which continued to limit access to medium range credits since, because of the "Cuba risk", insurers demanded higher interest rates and limited Cuba's possibility of assuming those commitments. As a direct result of the approval of the Helms-Burton Act, financial flows for the purchase of food and fuel were interrupted, causing additional damage to the economy.[64] Not only are credits not granted to Cuba because of U.S. pressures, those finally obtained for Cuban companies entail terms and conditions that are far more onerous than those established in international practice, with shorter repayment periods and higher interest rates, sometimes double the standard.[65] The 2003 report places the total in damages in this sector at 121,7 million dollars.

[59] United Nations General Assembly, fifty first period of sessions: paragraphs 67 and 72.
[60] United Nations General Assembly, fifty fifth period of sessions: paragraph 30.
[61] United Nations General Assembly, fifty second period of sessions: paragraph 33.
[62] United Nations General Assembly, fifty third period of sessions: paragraph 16.
[63] United Nations General Assembly, fifty sixth period of sessions: paragraph 96.
[64] United Nations General Assembly, fifty second period of sessions: paragraphs 34-36.
[65] United Nations General Assembly, fifty third period of sessions: paragraph 17.

The Secretary General Report of 2001 noted an interesting fact: Had Cuba had access to financial funds from international and regional institutions which were set aside for Latin America and the Caribbean during the 1997-2000 period, a total of 53 billion dollars, it would have had access to 1,2 billion dollars over those four years, at market rates and long terms, which would have allowed it to build 100 000 homes and four hospitals with 600 beds each.[66] In 2001 alone, of the 13,256.9 million dollars set aside for Latin America by the World Bank and the Inter-American Development Bank, Cuba would have had access to 250 million.[67] In 2002 and because of the "Cuba risk", the few development loans received had interest rates between 11 and 18%, a significant increase in expenditures in comparison to the credits it could have received from development institutions if U.S. restrictions did not exist.[68]

In 2002, because of unfavorable financing conditions alone, the country lost 62,3 million dollars, 41,8 million dollars more than it did in 2001.[69] During the fiscal year, the World Bank and Inter American Development Bank approved 4.365 billion and 4.548 billion dollars, respectively, in loans for Latin America. If Cuba had had access to these loans in 2002, it would have secured 200 million dollars that would have allowed it to revitalize many public health facilities, constructively and technologically.[70] The 2004 report pointed out that if Cuba had received merely 1% of the credits granted the previous year by the Inter American Development Bank, which described itself "as the main source of multilateral financing for development in the region for the tenth consecutive year", it could have undertaken important social and infrastructure projects in the country. If Cuba had been granted a credit similar to the one the World Bank and the Andean Cooperation Fund granted Bolivia for the construction of highways —of approximately 558,3 million dollars— it could have financed the foreign currency component of the project to repair and maintain the National Central Highway and the North

[66] United Nations General Assembly, fifty sixth period of sessions: paragraph 132.
[67] United Nations General Assembly, fifty seventh period of sessions: paragraph 137.
[68] Ibid., paragraph 138.
[69] United Nations General Assembly, fifty eighth period of sessions: paragraphs 152-153, Also in Cuban Foreign Affairs Ministry; p. 6.
[70] United Nations General Assembly, fifty eighth period of sessions: paragraph 210, Also Cuban Foreign Affairs Ministry; p. 8.

and Central circuits. In addition to this, the capital could have repaired the network of streets and buildings in the tunnels of Bahia, Linea and Quinta Avenida.[71]

Cuban insurance and reinsurance transactions for operations continued to be hindered by the predominance of U.S. capital in the financial market, restricting these and increasing their cost through the "Cuba risk". The Report stressed that 90% of Lloyds' market, the largest and most important international insurance company, is concentrated in U.S. corporate capital and, consequently, cannot operate with Cuba, implying a substantial restriction in the markets available to the country and, therefore, non competitive prices. The re-insurance operations of agencies offering insurance for export credit, which are 30 % more expensive than average, behave similarly because the market is controlled by U.S. companies. Therefore, Cuba is forced to pay more for its insurance.[72]

Energy Sector

When Cuba lost its main market supplier of oil in the early 1990s, the Government of the United States worked hard to identify potential alternative markets Cuba was exploring to satisfy its most basic needs and prevent such purchases. To this effect, it launched an offensive through its embassies in oil-producing countries in the Caribbean, Latin America, Africa, Asia and the Middle East. Some of these countries were warned that sales to Cuba could have a negative impact on their relations with the United States and could potentially obstruct the granting of credits by the International Monetary Fund and the World Bank. The more specific message conveyed to African countries pointed out that funds for existing programs to combat drought could be endangered.

These pressures became stronger in the course of the decade as they came to bear upon several foreign companies that negotiated with Cuba the prospecting of oil in the country. One of the first companies to be the object of U.S. pressures was the French Total, which was threatened with lawsuits by U.S. government emissaries, in line with the arguments that were in vogue in the 1990s,

[71] United Nations General Assembly, forty ninth period of sessions.
[72] United Nations General Assembly, fifty eighth period of sessions: paragraphs 221-222 Also in Cuban Foreign Affairs Ministry; p. 8.

who insisted the areas offered by Cuba for prospecting and exploitation had been legally registered before 1959.[73] From 1996 to 1998, unsuccessful efforts were undertaken to sign contracts with European companies to create and economic association in the oil industry and for risk drilling. These did not come to fruition because of new conditions established by the Helms-Burton Act and pressure applied by the United States to have them withdraw from Cuba.[74]

The 2003 Report of the Secretary General noted that oil companies that have contracts to drill in Cuba, owing to the innumerable existing restrictions, are forced to contract products and services at costs 25% above market value. In 2002 and 2003, this mean excess payments of 187,5 million dollars.[75]

Sugar sector

U.S. measures against Cuban sugar production and imports have been systematically exposed before the General Assembly. The United States imported from Cuba about 58,2% of its total sugar imports, a figure which was reduced to zero in the brief period of 1960-1961. Through variations in the quota system established by the Department of Agriculture in May of 1982, 40 sugar-producing countries benefit from a market that guaranteed them prices of 21 cents a pound, four times more than those of the world market, which is increasingly a residual market and is where Cuba must sell its production. For Cuba, the impossibility of accessing the U.S. market, in 2001 alone, meant losses of 177,3 million dollars. The blockade also blocks Cuban sugar access to the New York Coffee, Sugar and Cocoa Stock Exchange, which sets the reference price for exports of raw sugar in the world. This translates into an economic loss and loss of competitiveness which, during the period of 2001-2002, caused economic losses calculated at 193,9 million dollars.[76]

Other examples which help us appreciate the virulence of actions against this sector have been given before the General Assembly.

---

[73] United Nations General Assembly, forty eighth period of sessions: paragraphs 18-20.
[74] United Nations General Assembly, fifty sixth period of sessions: paragraph 122.
[75] United Nations General Assembly, fifty eigth period of sessions: paragraph 159.
[76] United States General Assembly, fifty sixth period of sessions: paragraphs 100-103.

After the dramatic changes in the former USSR, Cuban sugar's main market, the United States sought alternate sources of sugar from member States of the Community of Independent States in an attempt to divert exports of Cuban sugar and deprive Cuba of those incomes.[77] The United States also brought pressures to bear on the British sugar company Tate and Lyle, to force it to sever its economic ties with Cuba, after company representatives participated in the sugar fair held in Cuba in May 1992.[78]

Since 1995, the information provided to the General Assembly stressed that the progressive deterioration of sugar crops was caused, to a significant extent, by the lack of chemical products (fertilizers, pesticides, herbicides) that this crop requires and fuel to maintain the high level of mechanization reached in the sector.[79] An illustrative example of U.S. measures against Cuba in this direction was what occurred, towards the end of 1997, when the U.S. company Dow Chemical purchased all of the South African Sentrachen group's shares. The United States suspended the sale of pesticides to Cuba, which, between 1992 and 1997, had bought these for a total value of 82 million dollars. In spite of the good faith of South African authorities, the U.S. State Department did not authorize the continuation of business relations with the island and even denied the granting of a license to cover the shipments that were already in transit. Important supplies which had already been purchased were unable to reach their destination, affecting the sugar production and supply of food.[80] In the case of fertilizers, the blockade has forced the country to pay up to 47 additional dollars per metric ton above market prices, for an additional expenditure of 2,3 million dollars.[81]

Damages to Cuban exports of crude sugar in 2002 have been calculated at 182,9 million dollars, 179,3 of which resulted from the impossibility of accessing the U.S. market, in which Cuba could have been able to sell 800 000 metric tons of sugar at preferential prices, according to the Quota System set up by the U.S. Department of Agriculture in 1982 and from which the island was

[77] United Nations General Assembly, forty eighth period of sessions: paragraphs 24-28.
[78] Ibid., paragraph 32
[79] United Nations General Assembly, fiftieth period of sessions: paragraph 23.
[80] United Nations General Assembly, fifty third period of sessions: paragraph 22-25.
[81] United Nations General Assembly, fifty seventh period of sessions: paragraph 106.

227

excluded.[82] Losses for the 2002-2003 period were of 196,25 million dollars.[83]

Maritime transportation

Damaging maritime transportation of products from and to Cuba was one of the basic objectives of the Torricelli Act of 1992. This reached extreme levels in 1993 due to U.S. pressures on ship owners around the world, who were forced, under threat of facing different sanctions, to avoid Cuban ports in their voyages.[84] Coupled with the added costs which the comparatively longer voyages entail (in 1995, the extra costs of transporting goods from Europe and Asia were calculated at 215, 800 and 516, 700 respectively), transportation costs are artificially raised because many transport companies demand greater payments as a result of the immense pressures that are applied by U.S. authorities. Although it may seem unbelievable, for port operations in the State of Virginia on the Eastern coast of the United States, authorities require, as official documentation from ships, a declaration stating the have not touched a Cuban port in the 180 days prior to their arrival.[85] All these measures result in the low availability of ships willing to transport cargo to Cuba, resulting in higher costs and making the operations more difficult. For 2000, reported losses were of 12 million dollars in imports and 1,8 million in exports because of added freight costs alone.[86]

In 2002, the costs of maritime transportation were among the factors that most severely affected Cuban exports. The same situation was observed in terms of imports, with losses in the vicinity of a million dollars because of increased freight costs in the import of oil that year. Cuba's Ministry of Transportation reported damages of 96 million dollars resulting from the prohibition barring ships which dock in Cuban ports from touching U.S. ports; the impossibility of using the U.S. dollar as currency in transactions, the increased costs of equipment and other limitations and prohibitions imposed by the

[82] United Nations General Assembly, fifty eighth period of sessions: paragraph 157. Also Cuban Foreign Affairs Ministry: 6
[83] United Nations General Assembly, fifty ninth period of sessions.
[84] United Nations General Assembly, forty eighth period of sessions: paragraph 37.
[85] United Nations General Assembly, fiftieth period of sessions: paragraphs 16-18.
[86] United Nations General Assembly, fifty sixth period of sessions: paragraph 119.

blockade.[87] The 2004 report reported losses of more than 53,6 million dollars resulting from inhibitions as regards transporting cargo to Cuba in view of the prohibition to touch U.S. ports for a subsequent period of six months. Ship owners willing to enter Cuba have ships which have been in use for 15-20 years and do not fulfill the requirements to dock in U.S. ports. This increases the risk of accidents and possible damage to the cargo and, therefore, transportation and insurance costs. For the transportation of ammonium alone, there was an additional expenditure of 648 thousand dollars in 2004. The development of port infrastructure of two of the most important ports in the country, for unloading containers and moving them to the main markets in the region, required an investment of between 100 and 200 million dollars and, consequently, have had to be postponed due to Torricelli Act prohibitions.[88]

Tourism, travel by U.S. citizens to Cuba

Prohibitions on travel to Cuba by U.S. citizens and the severe sanctions applied to those who do not comply with existing regulations have been systematically denounced before the United Nations General Assembly. Before the establishment of the blockade, 80 % of U.S. citizens who traveled to the Caribbean visited Cuba. After its establishment, our country was deprived of the benefits derived from the expansion of that sector. Had these prohibitions not existed, no less than 25 million U.S. citizens would have visited Cuba, providing Cuba with incomes of more than 16 billion dollars. For the year 2000 alone, the number of U.S. tourists who would have visited Cuba was calculated at 1,45 million persons, with an approximate expenditure of 800 and 900 million dollars. According to the president of the American Society of Travel Agents, in declarations made in April of 2002, if existing prohibitions were lifted, a million U.S. tourists would visit Cuba during that first year and 5 million would visit the island on the fifth year.

On March 24, 2003 the Treasury Department's Office of Foreign Assets Control (OFAC) issued new regulations limiting travel by U.S. citizens to Cuba even more and totally eliminating licenses for

---

[87] United Nations General Assembly, fifty eighth period of sessions: paragraphs 155, 158 and 217. Also Cuban Foreign Affairs Ministry, p. 8.
[88] United Nations General Assembly, fifty ninth period of sessions.

people-to-people educational exchanges, although travel facilities where offered visitors to Cuba whose aim was to encourage illegal activities against the established order. The case of the elderly woman Joan Slote was widely covered by the media. She was a retired health worker who had visited Cuba two years before and had traveled around the island on bicycle. For this activity, she was fined 8 500 dollars.[89]

Cuba continues to be the only country that U.S. citizens are forbidden to visit. In 2003, on the basis of studies by Denver's Colorado University and the consulting firm "The Brattle Group", it was reported that if prohibitions were lifted the Cuban tourist sector would take in close to 576 million dollars in the first year alone.[90] 2004 estimates for the past five years reported that about 6,5 million U.S. citizens had been unable to travel to Cuba because of existing restrictions, meaning losses for Cuba of close to 4.225 billion dollars.[91]

Significant pressures have also been brought to bear against entrepreneurs of other nationalities who had intentions of investing in this sphere. Already in 1994, U.S. actions aimed at identifying Mexican businesspersons interested in investing in the Cuban tourism sector, to offer greater benefits to these if they invested in Puerto Rico instead, had been denounced. That year, private conversations of the Governor of that U.S. colonial enclave were made public. They revealed that the Government of the United States was especially interested in strengthening Puerto Rico's economic relations with Mexico and the Caribbean to prevent a rapprochement between those countries and Cuba.[92] Other examples since 2000 include the failure of an investment by a Spanish transnational to build 12 and 14 thousand rooms in Cayo Coco, in Ciego de Avila province; the withdrawal of another financial firm which was to invest about 100 million dollars to integrally develop the region of Paredon Grande and Romano Keys; and the halting of the construction of a hotel being built in Varadero and another in Cayo Coco by a Latin American corporation. Another significant examples is: the Hilton

[89] United Nations General Assembly, fifty eighth period of sessions: paragraphs 38-39. Also Cuban Foreign Affairs Ministry, p. 3.
[90] United Nations General Assembly, fifty eighth period of sessions: paragraphs 174. Also Cuban Foreign Affairs Ministry, p. 7.
[91] United Nations General Assembly, fifty ninth period of sessions.
[92] United Nations General Assembly, forty ninth period of sessions: paragraph 94-96.

International Group, with head offices in England, had to abandon negotiations, well underway, to run two hotels of the joint venture company Quinta del Rey in Cayo Coco and Havana, since operations had to be managed through the Hilton International Corporation, a U.S. company subsidiary. Losses for the following 25 years are calculated at 107.2 million dollars.

Another negative impact on the Cuban economy results from pressures brought to bear on cruise ship companies, to prevent Cuba from obtaining benefits from their stopovers in the island. One example is telling: the Cuba Project of the European cruise ship company Costa Crucierre had to be aborted after the company was bought over by the U.S. Carnival Corporation. Losses were around 62.2 million dollars, an amount that included the remodeling of the Sierra Maestra docks at Havana's port.

An example described in the 2003 Report refers to the loss, from January 2002 to April 2003, of 1,4 million dollars by hotels of the tourist company Cubanacan, due to a decrease in services rendered and the termination of contracts with170 Utell International — in charge of a general reserves system that had maintained relations with Cuba since 1993—after having been bought over by the U.S. company Pegasus Solution.[93]

Denunciations of terrorist actions against Cuban tourism at the end of the 1990s were brought before the United Nations General Assembly. These actions were mostly aimed at hotels in the capital and Varadero Sea Resort to frighten potential tourists and deter them from traveling to Cuba. In the following three years alone, calculated losses were in the region of 350 million dollars.[94] One of the harshest blows dealt U.S. citizens who travel to Cuba occurred when the Republican leadership and Cuban American congress persons openly ignored the Dorgan-Gordon amendment approved by the Senate on July 20, 2000, an amendment that would have allowed U.S. citizens to travel freely to Cuba. The resultant aberration, instead of softening, tightened the blockade and, for the first time since October 28 of that year, the prohibition of trips to Cuba by U.S. citizens

---

[93] United Nations General Assembly, fifty eighth period of sessions: paragraphs 170-171. Also Cuban Foreign Affairs Ministry, p 6-7.

[94] United Nations General Assembly, fifty sixth period of sessions: paragraphs 93-99; fifty seventh period of sessions: paragraphs 108-117.

reached the category of law. In reference to this action, Cuban American congresswoman Ileana Ros-Lehtinen said: "We have obtained a great victory by freezing the prohibition that prevents U.S. citizens from going to Cuba."[95] This resulted in a worsening of fines and other sanctions against those who defy the prohibition. In 2001 alone, the Treasury Department Division that investigates trips to Cuba applied 198 fines to U.S. citizens for a value of 7 500 dollars each, 520 more than in the previous year.[96]

Air transportation

The civilian aviation sector is intimately linked to tourism. In 1996, in denunciations brought before the General Assembly, it was reported that the costs of operating Cuban planes was increasing because of the prohibition of using international air routes over U.S. territory in flights to Canada.[97]

The United States violates the International Civilian Aviation Convention (Chicago Convention) of which both countries are signatories. U.S. regulations prohibit Cuban commercial flights to that country. Cuban airlines cannot access ticket sale services offered by travel agencies belonging to the International Air Transportation Association, according to what has been universally established by the Bank Settlement Plan, since it uses U.S. bank branches in certain locations. Cuban airlines cannot be serviced U.S. airplane fuel in any region of the world, preventing transit through airports where U.S. companies have a monopoly. Cuba is also prevented from hiring or renting efficient high technology planes from European plane builders because these planes may have U.S. components. Cuban airlines are thus compelled to use planes that consume more fuel and have less passenger and cargo capacity, reducing its competitiveness and efficiency.

Cuba does not have access to new communication, navigation-aiding and radio-localization technologies developed in the United

[95] Felipe Perez Roque: presentation of the draft resolution A/55/L7 before the United Nations General Assembly, November 9, 2000. United Nations Web site http:www.un.org.

[96] United Nations General Assembly, fifty seventh period of sessions: paragraph 116.

[97] United Nations General Assembly, fifty first period of sessions: paragraph 69.

States. Since the United States is responsible for the distribution of this equipment, as per agreements of the International Organization of Civilian Aviation and the World Meteorology Organization, our country is marginalized in this important activity. When, through third parties, Cuba receives this equipment, the costs are extremely high. The United States' violation of the Conduct Code of Air Reserve Computerized Systems implies that the distribution systems Sabre, Galileo and Worldspan, based in that country, do not accept requests from the Cubana de Aviacion company. In 2000, this limited the airline's access to 65,7% of the reserve locales then available. Cuban denounced the loss of 153,6 million dollars before the United Nations General Assembly. [98]

For the same reasons, the 2003 Report noted the loss of 142.6 million dollars,[99] that, in the 2004 Report, reportedly increased to a little over 163 million.[100] That year, it was reported that even though more than 60 U.S. charter flights to and from Cuba were operated a week, and the Cuban state received every facility in this connection, the United States government did not authorize Cuban airlines to fly to their territory on the basis of section 515.201 (a) of the "Cuban Assets Control Regulation", 31 C.F.R. Part 515, which states that it could constitute a violation for a Cubana de Aviacion airliner to land in Miami without a specific license, and that said plane could be confiscated. In addition to not having access to any kind of aeronautical technology developed by the United States, the fact Cuban airlines cannot even purchase, in third countries, spare parts for 97 HS explosive detectors employed by security personnel in flights, illustrates the lack of commitment and double standards of the U.S. administration in their fight against terrorism. This product was purchased from the British firm, Ion Track Instruments, shortly before it was bought over by U.S. capital. With these measures, the United States violates principles set down in the Preamble to the Chicago Convention, which states that "international civilian aviation can develop in a sure and orderly fashion and that international air transportation services can be established on a basis of equal opportunity and be carried out in a safe and economic manner".

[98] United Nations General Assembly, fifty sixth period of sessions: paragraphs 100-110; fifty seventh period of sessions, paragraphs 118-119.
[99] United Nations General Assembly, fifty eighth period of sessions.
[100] United Nations General Assembly, fifty ninth period of sessions.

Similarly, it violates established norms and precepts of the Chicago Convention and, particularly, those referred to in its Article 44, clauses a), c), d), f), g), h) and I), which set down the purposes and objectives of the ICAO: promoting the development of international air transportation; satisfying the needs of the peoples of the world in this matter, assuring that the rights of the Signing States are fully respected and preventing discrimination among them, and, in general, promoting the development of international civilian aeronautics in all its aspects.

Also, the 2004 report noted that the hiring of an Airbus-320 cost the Cuban airline company 9,2 million dollars, 2.1 million more than any other airline from any country would have paid. When the plane rented was an Airbus-330, the additional cost was over 3.3 million.[101]

As mentioned above, it is impossible for this book to give an exhaustive account of all Cuban denunciations made before the General Assembly with respect to the genocidal measures the U.S. blockade on Cuba. The readers can access this information at the UN General Assembly Web site, verifying for themselves this aberrant injustice and partially contributing to mitigate the effects of such an impossibility.

In what we have addressed so far, we have neglected to touch on aspects related to the extraterritoriality of the economic measures against Cuba; missing in this work are measures in sectors such as telecommunications, mining (export of nickel and cobalt) and the iron and steel industry, construction, nuclear energy and advanced technologies, production and exportation of tobacco and cigarettes, services to the population and others; no reference has been made to damages in the field of sports, in academic and scientific exchanges between the Cuban people and the people of the United States, education and culture.

We will close this section with reference to the unbelievable measures implemented in the last sector mentioned. These measures would be a laughing matter if they did not involve such an outrageous way of curtailing all kinds of exchanges between our two peoples and discouraging the promotion of Cuban artists in the U.S. cultural scene. In addition to denying visas to about fifty artists, 210 genuine representatives of Cuban culture —including the internationally

[101] United Nations General Assembly, fifty ninth period of sessions.

renowned Ibrahim Ferrer and Manuel Galban, writers such as Miguel Barnet and Eduardo Heras Leon, filmmakers such as Lisette Vila and Gerardo Chijona and an actress like Veronica Lynn— did not receive visas to participate in presentations and events in the United States under an unbelievable and false argument, contained in clause 212-F: the United States considers them a danger to the interests of the nation.[102]

New legislation

The degree of aberration that anti-Cuban legislation reached in the United States with the Torricelli and Helms-Burton acts did not disappear with the passing of the latter in 1996. New and more absurd projects have been presented to the U.S. Congress in flagrant violation of Cuban sovereignty and the right to life of its people, measures that have been unyieldingly denounced by Cuba before the United Nations General Assembly. In April of 1998, Congress approved several amendments to strengthen the blockade and its extraterritorial effect, in compliance with the provisions set down by the Helms-Burton Act. It is within this context that new projects, cloaked as humanitarian endeavors, were hatched to grant decisive support to a counterrevolutionary opposition inside the country, to produce social and political changes.[103] The Omnibus Law of Budget Assignations for the fiscal year of 1999 included 12 amendments that extended and worsened the blockade, secretly negotiated by a small group of legislators and government officials. Sections 2225 and 2802 strengthen sanctions imposed by Title IV of the Helms-Burton Act and makes them extensive to the rest of the world. It extends the blockade to funds of international credit institutions for any assistance or repairs to Cuba. Its Section 211[104] prohibits transactions or payment in the United States related to a confiscated label or commercial name, unless authorized by the original owner or heir, a provision that is also valid for the prohibition of recognition

[102] United Nations General Assembly, fifty third period of sessions.

[103] United Nations General Assembly, fifty third period of sessions: paragraphs 49-50.

[104] Attached to the application of part 515 of title 31 of the Code of Federal Regulations in force on September, 1998, applied by the Treasury Department regarding Cuba through the Office for Control of Foreign goods.

and validation of these labels or commercial names by United States courts. This is in violation of articles of the Agreement on International Property related to Trade of the World Trade Organization. This section served as the basis of a court decision in New York on April 24, 1999, to the detriment of the common interests of the Havana Club Holding Company (a joint venture company formed by the French Pernod Ricard and a Cuban company) and Havana Club International (a share-holding company based in Cuba), stripping it of its rights to register and eventually market the Cuban rum Havana Club, in the United States, and illegally benefiting Bacardi.[105]

Cuba's denunciation of these dealings, unprecedented in the history of intellectual property, has exposed the true intentions of the legislators: to create obstacles to foreign investments in Cuba that are associated to the international sale of prestigious Cuban products. In January 2002, the Appellate Institution of the World Trade Organization acknowledge that Section 2211 violates the basic principles of the WTO, such as national treatment and most favored nation treatment, opining that it should be modified or repealed.[106]

Another turn of the screws in blockade policy, in 2000, abolished proposals in favor of the sale of food and medicines (Ashcroft amendment approved by consensus in the Senate Foreign Affairs Committee on March 23; the Nethercut Amendment, in the House Assignation Committee on May 10, the Dorgan-Corton Amendment in the Senate on July 20) and free travel to Cuba by U.S. citizens (Stanford Amendment approved by the House on July 20). The Republican leadership and Cuban-American congresspersons, violating the norms of the process, passed other amendments, approved by President Bush on October 28, 2000. On this occasion, Cuban-American congressman Lincoln Diaz-Balart stated: "It is the most important victory of the Helms-Burton Act. No "barter" trade, no credit granted, no imports from Cuba, no public or private financing. The denial of credits and tourism to Cuba is an important victory."[107] A new escalation occurred that same day, October 28, 2000, with

[105] United Nations General Assembly, forty fourth period of sessions: op.cit., paragraphs 20-24; fifty fifth period of sessions: op.ci., paragraph 18.

[106] United Nations General Assembly, fifty seventh period of sessions: op.cit., paragraph 127.

[107] Felipe Perez Roque: presentation of the resolution project A/55/L7 before the United Nations General Assembly, November 9, 2000. United Nations Web site http:www.un.org.

the approval of the law of protection for victims of traffic and violence that authorized the United States to appropriate Cuban funds in companies and banks frozen in U.S. banks to a value of 161 million dollars.[108]

A curious and recent fact, related to the legislature: the anticonstitutional nature of many of the economic measures against Cuba stemming from the 2004 and 2006 versions of the Bush Plan, referring to matters under the jurisdiction of the Congress, as per the legal framework derived from the Helms-Burton Act, met with but timid protest from a number of legislators. Once again, justice was defeated.

The civil liability suit brought against the United States government for economic damages caused to the people of Cuba

During the presentation of the draft resolution voted in the United Nations General Assembly on November 9, 1999, the President of the National Assembly of the People's Power, Ricardo Alarcon de Quesada, formally announced that Cuba would present a lawsuit for compensation of more than 100 billion dollars against the Government of the United States for the enormous damages caused to the Cuban people by the blockade.

The civil liability suit brought against the United States Government for economic damages caused to the Cuban people was presented by Cuban social and grassroots organizations to the People's Provincial Court of Havana and legally processed under Civil file number 1 of the year 2000 in the First Civilian and Administrative court of that Tribunal.[109]

In a detailed explanation of the different facets that compose the criminal structure of the economic war, experts and witnesses testified

---

[108] Idem.

[109] Suit brought by the Cuban people against the Government of the United States for economic damages caused to Cuba, presented to the People's Provincial Court of Havana on January 3, 2000. Publication Office of the Council of State, Havana, 2000.

during the period set aside for evidence, from February 28 to March 10 of that same year, providing powerful testimonies that proved the U.S. government's liability for acts of economic genocide against Cuba in the pursuit of a political end.[110]

Those who provided expert testimony are among the most qualified experts in the country in each of the spheres on which they were asked to report. The witnesses, at the same time, were selected through a search of citizens with different occupations, who have a direct experience of the impact of the blockade and, in general, of the subversive activities directed and organized by the Government of the United States in economic and social sectors in which they have moved.

The expert reports referred to general aspects of the blockade and U.S. economic aggression or their incidence on specific sectors.[111] Among the first was that of the well known jurist Olga Miranda, who explained the illegality of the economic blockade from the point of view of International Law and demonstrated Cuba's moral right to demand reparation for damages caused; that of the president of the Commission for Economic Affairs of the National Assembly of the People's Power, Osvaldo Martinez, who demonstrated that the blockade is, in fact, an act of genocide and rebuffed U.S. arguments that it imposes an "embargo" "on Cuba"; that of representative of the Ministry of the Interior Jose M. Perez Fernandez, who presented abundant evidence on the subversive actions carried out against the Cuban economy as part of the United States' policy of hostility towards Cuba; that of expert on migratory issues Jesus Arboleya Cervera, who referred to the counterrevolutionary function which the United States gave Cuban emigration; and that of the Minister of Science, Technology and the Environment Rosa Elena Simeon, who offered information about the high costs of the biological war against Cuba.

The experts who offered testimony on specific sectors did so in the sphere of foreign trade, food imports, Nickel sales, tobacco exports; the sugar industry, the monetary financial sphere; foreign investment;

[110] The national press published a summary of the session of proof. See articles by Maria Julia Mayoral, Alexis Schlachter, Sara Mas, Susana Lee: in Granma news paper, Havana, February 29 to March 11, 2000.

[111] The titles of the reports and executors is listed in the Bibliography. The date refers to when they were presented to the Tribunal.

international tourism; civil aviation; basic industry, the national education system; Higher Education; the spheres of culture; food industry, light industry, maritime and land transportation, communications, the fishing industry, about exotic harmful plagues affecting crops of economic importance; about the damages caused to the population of productive animals through the introduction of diseases in enemy actions; on the ulcer diseases of trout; the sugar agro-industry; agriculture, the national health system and the costs of national defense.

Numerous witnesses provided testimony on each of these spheres which contributed to broadening, deepening and clarifying the different aspects of the suit, including the blockade, sabotages, biological warfare efforts and other aggressions. Some witnesses offered exceptional testimonies, derived from their ties, as agents of Cuban State Security, to anti-Cuban terrorist organizations that abound in the United States and because of which they were able to learn of the preparation and execution of sabotages and other actions against the Cuban economy under the direction or with the complicity of United States authorities.

In the last day allotted the hearing of evidence, senior researcher and head of the foreign sector department of the National Institute for Economic Research Jose Alejandro Aguilar Trujillo presented a detailed expert report,[112] on an exceptionally important subject: the cost of the blockade and economic aggressions for the Cuban people. Hundreds of experts from all of the country's organizations and institutions participated in the preparation of this report, which evaluated the damages caused by the economic, commercial and financial blockade in different spheres of activities and acts of aggression against economic and social targets. According to the evaluation, the comparison with global estimates made to prevent the possible duplication of data, the expert reported that damages caused by the blockade at that time were of 67.093 2 billion dollars. According to 2007 reports, the total accumulated up to the year 2006 was 89.234 6 billion dollars broken down as follows: 40.990 3 for incomes not obtained through exports and services; 20.085 1 for losses

[112] José Alejandro Aguilar Trujillo: Expert report on damages to the Cuban nation by the economic, trade and financial blockade imposed by the United States of America and for actions of that country against economic, social and cultural objects of Cuba and against its nationals. March 2000.

arising from the geographic relocation of trade; 2.915 9 for damages to production and services; 8.593 5 in losses arising from the technological blockade; 1.565 3 for damages to services for the population; 8.805 for financial damages and 6.279 5 because of the encouragement to emigration and brain drain.[113]

A similar procedure was used to quantify acts of U.S. aggression, a task which saw the participation not only of State institutions but also the provincial Administrations of the People's Power. It was concluded that the costs associated to these damages, including the costs the country has had to assume to guarantee the safety and protection of the population and the nation's assets, were in the order of 54 billion dollars.

This sum, added to that of the blockade, gives us a total of 121 billion U.S. dollars, (143 billion in 2006). In answer to the lawyers' questions, the experts explained that the magnitude of these damages is 15 times higher the level of imports made by the country in 1989, the year with the highest volume of imports. At the very least, the blockade has set Cuba back fifteen years in terms of development. Had no economic war existed, though it impossible to calculate how much more the Cuban economy would have grown (between 1959 and 1989, it grew at an average of 4,6% yearly), what is certain is that the rhythm of growth would have been faster and more dynamic.

On May 5, 2000, the First Court of the Civil and Administrative People's Provincial Court handed down ruling number forty-seven, corresponding to Civil File number 1 of the year 2000.[114] The ruling was handed down after an in-depth doctrinal analysis and a review of the analysis conducted on the basis of the evidence presented and the results of the decisions of the acting experts. The court ruled to enforce the suit brought against the Government of the United States, sentencing it, for the illicit crimes committed, to compensate the Cuban people for 121 billion U.S. dollars, 6 405 in damages and 114.595 billion in compensation.

[113] United Nations General Assembly, sixty second period of sessions.

[114] Special supplement of Granma newspaper: Sentence of guilty. May 66, 2000. The President of the Court and deponent was the Master in Law, Rafael Enrique Dujarric Hart. Professional judges were the B. Sc.s Ana Maria Alejo Alayon and Ismary Castañeda Lima and the judges were Matilde Ramirez Richard and Altagracia Ramos Aguilera. The court secretary was Olivia Peña Figueredo.

What are the measures the Government of the United States must adopt to put an end to economic war against Cuba?

Upon referring to how the U.S. government authorized the sale to Cuban state companies of certain quantities of food, medicines and raw materials to produce these, in the exceptional circumstances following the passage of hurricane Michelle during the presentation of the draft resolution condemning the U.S. blockade against Cuba made before the United Nations General Assembly on November 27, 2001,[115] Cuban Foreign Affairs Minister Felipe Pérez Roque asked: "Does this imply the end to the blockade?" The Cuban minister rapidly answered: "No" He pointed out that it would be a mistake to understand this exception as a rule and explained, in depth, what measures the Government of the United States would need to adopt to lift the blockade and put an end to the economic war against Cuba. These are:

1. To repeal the Helms-Burton Act
2. To repeal the Torricelli Act
3. To eliminate the prohibition that any articles imported to the United States contain Cuban raw materials.
4. To put an end to the worldwide harassment, by U.S. embassies and agencies, of all Cuban negotiations and transactions.
5. To permit Cuba access to U.S. and international financial systems.
6. To allow Cuba to use U.S. dollars for its foreign transactions.
7. To authorize Cuba to purchase freely, like any other country, in the U.S. market.
8. To authorize Cuba to freely export to the U.S. market, like any other country.
9. To allow U.S. citizens to travel freely, as tourists, to Cuba.
10. To return Cuban assets frozen in U.S. banks, part of which have been arbitrarily stolen.
11. To authorize U.S. companies to invest in Cuba.

---

[115] Felipe Pérez Roque: presentation of resolution project A/56/L.9 in subject 34 of the fifty sixth program of the period of sessions of the United nations General Assembly, November 27, 2001. United Nations Web site http:www.un.org.

12. To establish regulations to protect Cuban labels and patents in the United States, in keeping with international legislation on intellectual property.
13. To eliminate discriminatory measures that prevent Cubans living in the United States to travel freely to Cuba and give economic aid to their families in the island.
14. To negotiate with Cuba a just and honorable agreement for the compensation of 6 thousand entities and U.S. citizens whose properties were nationalized during the first years of the Revolution in Cuba, taking into consideration, also, the serious economic and human damages inflicted on Cuba by the blockade.

To this, the Cuban Minister added that if it were to put an end to the policy of aggressions against Cuba, the following would be necessary:

1. Repeal of the Cuban Adjustment Act.
2. Cooperation with Cuba in the battle against drug trafficking.
3. Put an end to illegal television and radio transmissions to Cuba.
4. Put an end to the arbitrary inclusion of Cuba in the State Department list of States that support terrorism.
5. Put an end to subversive designs within Cuba, backed with handsome federal funding. Put an end to defamation campaigns and pressure against our country in international institutions. Put an end to the impunity of terrorists that have acted against Cuba from Miami.
6. To renounce to the continued occupation, against the sovereign will of the Cuban people, of the territory of the Guantanamo Naval Base.

With these words, Cubans recall the oath of Baragua, reaffirmed by millions of citizens in Mangos de Baragua, sacred site of the Homeland, on February 19, 2000.

References

I. OFFICIAL DOCUMENTS

Alarcón de Quesada, Ricardo. Closure of the Extraordinary Session of the V Legislature of the National Assembly of People's Power, February 16 1999. Granma daily, February 19 1999.

Constitution of the Republic of Cuba, Ministry of Justice, Havana, 1999.

Oath of Baraguá. Mangos of Baraguá, Santiago de Cuba, February 19 the 2000. Editora Politica, Havana, 2000.

Law 80, Law of Reaffirmation of Cuban Dignity and Sovereignty. December 24 1996.

Law 88, Law of Protection of the National Independence and the Economy of Cuba. February 16 1999.

Proclamation of the National Assembly of People's Power of the Republic of Cuba, September of 1999, 13 in Granma newspaper, Tuesday September, 1999, 14 third edition.

Resolutions of the United Nations General Assembly "Need to put an end to the economic, commercial blockade and financier imposed by the United States of America against Cuba": General Assembly of Nations: Resolution 47/19, November 24 1992; 48/16, November 3 1993; 49/9, October 26 1994; 50/10, November 2 1995; 51/17, November 12 1996; 52/10, November 5 1997; 53/4, October 14 1998; 54/21, November 9 1999; 55/20,

November 9 the 2000; 56/9, November 27 the 2001; 57/11, November 12 the 2002. I siege Web http:www.un.org.

Report of the General Secretary regarding resolutions demanding an end to the economic, trade and financial blockade imposed by the United States of America against Cuba": General Assembly of United Nations: Reports of the General Secretary, answer of the Government of Cuba (A/48/488), September 28 1993; A/49/398, September 20 1994; A/50/401, September 1st 1995; A/51/355, September 13 1996; A/52/342, September 15 1997; A/53/320, September 3 1998; A/54/259, August 18 1999; A/55/172, July 24 the 2000; A/56/276, 2001; A/57/150, July 26 the 2002. I siege Web http:www.un.org.

Presentation before the General Assembly of Nations Together of the Projects of Resolution "Need to put an end to the economic, commercial blockade and financier imposed by the United States of America against Cuba": Fernando Remírez de Estenoz Barciela, presentation of the Project of Resolution A/48/L. 14/ Rev.1, November 3 1993; Fernando Remírez de Estenoz Barciela, Resolution Project A/49/L.9, October 26 1994; Bruno Rodríguez Parrilla, Project of Resolution Polishes A/50/L.10, November 2 1995; Carlos Lage Dávila, Resolution Project A/51/L.15, November 12 1996; Roberto Robaina González, Resolution Project A/53/L.6, October 14 1998; Ricardo Alarcón de Quesada, Resolution Project A/54/L.11, November 9 1999; Felipe Pérez Roque, Project of Resolution A/55/L.7, November 9 the 2000; Felipe Pérez Roque, Resolution Project A/56/L.9, November 27 the 2001; Ricardo Alarcón de Quesada, Project of Resolution A/57/L.5, November 12 the 2002. I siege Web http:www.un.org.

Other documents presented by the Cuban government and circulated as official documents of the General Assembly of United Nations: "The illegal economic blockade of the United States against Cuba and the Cuban nationalizations: the historical truth." A/48/258 and annex, July 12 1993.

"The so-called Law of 1995 for Freedom in Cuba and Democratic Solidarity with Cuba. Legal and political analysis of the implications of the Law for Freedom and the Democratic Solidarity with Cuba." A/50/172, May 4 1995.

"The new attempts to strengthen the economic blockade of the United States against Cuba and the truth of the Cuban nationalizations." A/50/211, June 7 1995.
"Denunciation of new actions against Cuba in the Congress of the United States." A/52/162, May 30 1997.

II. LEGAL PROCESSES

Aguilar Trujillo, José Alejandro: Expert reports on the economic damages caused to the Cuban nation by the economic, commercial and financial blockade imposed by the United States of America and for the aggressions perpetrated by that country against economic, social and cultural objectives, of Cuba and its citizens. March, 2000.

Amador Pérez, Leonel C.: Expert report of evidence of the economic damages to the Ministry of the Light Industry. March, 2000.

Arboleya Cervera, Jesús: Verdict about the illegal use of migratory policy of the United States against Cuba. March, 2000.

Chao Trujillo, Eduardo; Gonzalo Fernández Rey and Orlando Jordán Martínez: Expert report of the Ministry of the Agriculture. March of the 2000.

Dotres Martínez, Carlos: Expert verdict of the economic consequences of the policy of the U.S. Government against the National System of Health. March, 2000.

Gómez Gutiérrez, Luis Ignacio; Francisco Fereira Báez and Jorge Hidalgo Prado: Verdict of damages caused to the National System of Education by the hostile policy of the U.S. Government. March, 2000.

González Febles, Gonzalo; Marino Murillo Jorge and Miguel A. Castillo Domínguez: Expert report about damages caused to the Food Industry by the blockade and United States Government aggressions against Cuba. March, 2000.

González Rodríguez, María del Pilar: Expert report regarding damages caused by the blockade in nickel trade. March, 2000.

Hernández Guillén, Orlando; María de la Luz B'Hamel Ramírez and Daniel Hung González: Expert report on the affectations caused by the economic, commercial and financial blockade of the United States Government against Cuba in the sphere of the foreign trade. March, 2000.

245

López, Ana: Declaration of damages caused by the United States economic blockade against Cuba in exports of tobacco. Expert report. March, 2000.

Lorenzo Piloto, Tomás: Expert report on the effects of the blockade imposed by the United States of America against Cuba in the monetary-financial sphere. March, 2000.

Martínez Albuerne, Carlos; Filiberto Au Kim and Onelio Alfonso Pérez: Actions that affected the branch of communications. March of the 2000.

Martínez Martínez, Osvaldo: The economic blockade imposed on Cuba by the U.S. Government. Expert report. March, 2000.

Martínez Samalea, Marta: Economic damages caused to the Ministry of the Fishing Industry. March, 2000.

Miranda Bravo, Olga: Legal Aspects of the blockade and aggressions. Expert report. March, 2000.

Nocedo de León, Iris; Lázaro Núñez Montero and Ofelia Perera Ibáñez: Expert report of damages caused by the blockade of EE. UU. against Cuba in sugar exports. March, 2000.

Office of Publications of the Council of State: *Demands of the Cuban people against the U.S. Government for the economic damages to Cuba*, presented to the Provincial Popular Tribunal of the City of Havana January 3, 2000,

Ojeda Vives, Argimiro; Nelson Viñas Valdés and Francisco José Corveas Ibarra: Expert report about damages caused by the economic blockade and aggressions to the civil aviation of Cuba (1960-1998). March, 2000.

Ovies, Jorge; Máximo Martínez and Luis Pérez: Expert report on the exotic plagues to crops of economic importance included in chapter 21 of the Demand of the Cuban People against the U.S. Government for the economic damages to Cuba. March, 2000.

Pérez Fernández, José: Expert report on forty years of aggressions against Cuba. March, 2000.

Portal León, Marcos; Vicente Llano Ross and Tomás Benítez Hernández: Expert report pf damages caused to the Ministry of the Basic Industry by the blockade imposed by the United States of America and the direct aggressions to their facilities. March, 2000.

Prieto Trujillo, Adela; Raquel Silveira Coffigny and María del Carmen Rodríguez: Informs expert referred to the illness ulcerativa of the trout. March of the 2000.

246

Rodríguez de la Vega, Eduardo: Informs expert about damages and damages to the sector of the international tourism in derived Cuba of the blockade imposed by the United States. March of the 2000.

Sarasola González, Andrés; Gerson Fernández Vega and Juan A. Godefoy García: Expert report of damages caused to sugar Agro industry by aggressions and the blockade of the United States of America. March, 2000.

Sentence N° 47 Civil File of 2000, First Civilian and Administrative Hall of the Provincial Popular Tribunal of City of Havana. May 5, 2000.

Serrano Ramírez, Emerio; Manuel Toledo Portela and Carlos Ortega: Expert report on the damages caused to the population of farm animals due to illnesses introduced by enemy actions in the period between the month of November of 1962 and April of 1996. March, 2000.

Simeón, Rosa Elena: Expert report on the biological aggressions against Cuba. March, 2000.

Sosa Brizuela, Jorge; Eduardo Santos Canalejo and Yamel Ruiz Barranco: Expert report presented by the Ministry for the Foreign Investment and the Economic Collaboration of damages caused to the Cuban economy, as a result of the blockade imposed by the Government of the United States and the application of the Helms-Burton Law in the sphere of the foreign investment. March, 2000.

Taboada González, Tatiana: Expert report evaluating the economic damages caused by the blockade in the sector of food imports. March, 2000.

Valle Álvarez, Rubén; Orlando Vistel Columbié and Benigno Iglesias Tovar: Expert report of the Ministry of Culture. March, 2000.

Valle Portilla, Amador: Verdict on the economic impact of the blockade imposed by the U.S. Government, including multiple aggressions by their agents against the Republic of Cuba in the sphere of the marine and terrestrial transportation. March, 2000.

Vecino Alegret, Fernando; Eduardo Cruz González and Obverto Santín Cáceres: Expert report on the effects of the aggressions of the economic blockade by the United States of America against Cuba that have affected the System of Higher Education. March, 2000.

III. ARTICLES AND DOCUMENTS IN THE DAILY PRESS

D'Stéfano Pisani, Miguel A.; Luis Sola Vila and Abel Sola López: "Protection of our independence and economy," in *Granma* newspaper, Havana, April 21 1999.

Information of the Ministry of the Interior, in *Granma* newspaper, Havana, October 29 1998.

Report of the special relator who visited Cuba from September 12 to 17, 1999, on mercenary actions to the United Nations Human Rights Commission; in a special supplement of *Granma* newspaper, April 8, 2000.

Molina, Gabriel: "The Ángel Mateo," in *Granma* newspaper, Havana, July 9, 1987, p. 3.

——————: "Our man in the CIA," in *Granma* newspaper, Havana, July 11 1987.

Pereira, Casilda: "Laying in wait," in magazine Moncada, Havana, 1987.

Rodríguez Calderón, Mirta: "I will Serve the same cause," chronicle on the penetration of the CIA by an agent of Cuban Security and Italian citizen, Mauro Casagrandi, in *Granma* newspaper, Havana, July 29, 1987, p.3.

Special tabloid N° 18 *Down with the blockade!*, contents of the seven instructive round tables carried out between July 5 and 13, 2000 (shorthand versions of the Council of State), published by the *Juventud Rebelde* newspaper, August, 2000.

IV. DOCUMENTS OF THE GOVERNMENT OF THE UNITED STATES

Act of the democracy for Cuba 1992 (Torricelli Act).

Central Intelligence Agency: Directorate of Intelligence: *The Cuban Economy*: A Statistical Review.

Presidential Decree N° 3447, February 6, 1962, 27 federal resolution N° 1085, embargo on trade with Cuba.

Department of State: Foreign Affairs of the United States, 1958-1960, Cuba, the United States government printing office, Washington, 1991, vol. VI (1991), X (1997), XI (1996).

Freedom and the Cuban Democratic Solidarity Law (Helms-Burton Law), 1996.

The Bay of Pigs: New Evidence from Documents and Testimony of the Kennedy Administration, the Anti-Castro Resistance, and Brigade 2506. Conference of Musgrove Plantation, St. Simons Island, Georgia, 31 May-June 1996.

National Security Act of 1947, Public Law 253, July 26, 1947.

V. GENERAL BIBLIOGRAPHY

Abdo Cuza, Michelle: "Impact of the Helms-Burton Law in international legal, financial and trade relations. Means to confront it." Master's thesis. Autonomous National university of Mexico, Law Faculty, Division of postgraduate Studies, January, 1997.

Agee, Philip: *Inside the Company: CIA Diary*. Penguin Books,1975. The Spanish version was also consulted: Diario de la CIA, Editorial Laia, Barcelona, 1978.

Agency of National Information (AIN): The War of the CIA against Cuba. Havana, 1988.

Alarcón de Quesada, Ricardo: "El embuste: arma inseparable de la agresión imperialista." Intervention in the II World Conference of Friendship and Solidarity with Cuba, November 10, 2000.

Alarcón de Quesada, Ricardo and Miguel Álvarez Sánchez: *Guerra económica de Estados Unidos contra Cuba*. Editora Politica, Havana, 2001.

Alzugaray, Carlos: *Crónica de un fracaso imperial*. Editorial de Ciencias Sociales, Havana, 2000.

Alvarado, Percy: *Confesiones de Fraile. Una historia real de terrorismo*. Editorial Capitán San Luis, Havana, 2002.

Arboleya, Jesús: *La contrarevolución cubana*. Editorial de Ciencias Sociales, Havana, 2000.

Barquín, Ramón C.: *Cuba: The Cybernetic era*. Cuban Studies/ Estudios Cubanos, vol. 5, nº 2, July, 1975.

Breckinridge, Scott E.: The CIA and the U.S. intelligence System. Westview Press/Boulder and London, 1986.

Castañeda, Rolando H. and George P. Montalbán: "Main Goals," *Cuba in Transition*, Association for the Study of the Cuban Economy, vol. 4, I August, 1994.

Diakov, V.; and S. Kovalov: *Historia de la antiguedad*. Roma. Cuban Book Institute, Havana, 1966.

Diez Acosta, Tomás: *La guerra encubierta*. Editorial Politica, Havana, 1997.

Documentos de poítica exterior de la USSR, 1917-1967. Editorial Progreso, Moscow.

Escalante Font, Fabián: *La guerra secreta*. Editorial de Ciencias Sociales, Havana, 2002.

Ferrera Herrera, Alberto: *Yo fui Regina para la CIA* Editorial Capitán San Luis, Havana, 1997.

Gaddis, John Lewis: *Estrategias de contención*. Grupo Editor Latinoamericano, Coleccion Estudios Internacionales, Buenos Aires, 1989.

Gordon, David L. and Royden Dangerfield: *The Covert Weapon. The Story of Economic Warfare*. Harper & Brothers Publishers, New York, 1947.

Kent, Sherman: *Inteligencia estratégica para la política mundial norteamericana*. Second edition. Princenton University Press, Political and Social Sciences, 1950.

Krinsky, Michael and David Golove: *United States Economic Measures Against Cuba. Proceedings in the United Nations and International Law Issues*. Aletheia Press, Northamptom, Massachusets, 1993.

León Cotayo, Nicanor: *El bloqueo a Cuba*. Editorial de Ciencias Sociales, Havana, 1983.

——————: *Sitiada la esperanza. Bloqueo económico de EE.UU. a Cuba*. Editorial Politica, Havana, 1992.

Martínez Parada, Alfonso: "Agresiones económicas del imperialismo yanqui contra Cuba," in Collectivo de Autores: *Agresiones de Estados Unidos a Cuba Revolucionaria*. International Law Association, Editorial de Ciencias Sociales, Havana, 1989.

Méndez Méndez, José Luis: *Salvar al mundo del terrorismo*. Editorial Politica, Havana, 2003.

Miranda Bravo, Olga: "La legislación norteamericana como instrumento de agresión imperialista contra Cuba," and "Cuba nacionalizaciones cubanas. Los tribunales norteamericanos y la enmienda Hickenlooper," in Colectivo de Autores: *Agresiones de Estados Unidos a Cuba Revolucionaria*. Cuban International Law Association, Editorial de Ciencias Sociales, Havana, 1989.

Pérez Fernández, José: *Historia para no olvidar. Cronología de agre-*

siones del gobierno de los Estados Unidos contra Cuba. (1959-
1999). Centro de investigaciones historicas de la Seguridad de
Estado; 2000.

Pichardo, Hortensia: *Documentos para la historia de Cuba*, volume
I. Cuban Book Institute, Editorial de Ciencias Sociales, Havana,
1971.

Puzo, Aida del: "Agresiones de Estados Unidos a la economía de
Cuba," in Colectivo de Autores: *Agresiones de Estados Unidos
a Cuba revolucionaria*. Cuban International Law Association;
Editorial de Ciencias Sociales, Havana, 1989.

Quintana, Dorys: "Respuesta jurídica cubana a la Ley Helms-
Burton." Report presented in the scientific event "40 years of
aggressions of the United States against Cuba," 17-5-2000.

Rodríguez García, José Luis: *Crítica a nuestros críticos*. Editorial de
Ciencias Sociales, Havana, 1988.

Rodríguez, Juan Carlos: La batalla inevitable. Editoral Capitán San
Luis, Havana, 1996.

Ronfeld, David. *Ciberspace and cyberology: political effect of the
information revolution*. Rand corporation, 1991.

Valdés-Dapena Vivanco, Jacinto: *La CIA contra Cuba. La actividad
subversiva de la CIA y la contrarrevolución, 1961-1968*. Editorial Capitán San Luis, Havana, 2002.

—————————: Operación Mangosta: preludio de la invación directa a Cuba. Editorial Capitán San Luis, Havana, 2002.

Yaklovev, Nikolai: La CIA contra la URSS. Editorial Progreso,
Moscow, 1983.

Zhukov, Gueorgui: *Memorias y reflexiones*. Editorial Progreso,
Moscow, 1990.